# CONTEM...
# ADOLE...

*A Social Psychol... ...pproach*

For Andrew, Cara, Matthew, and Philip —
at different stages of childhood and adolescence

# CONTEMPORARY ADOLESCENCE

## A Social Psychological Approach

### PATRICK C. L. HEAVEN

Charles Sturt University, Australia

First published 1994 by
MACMILLAN EDUCATION AUSTRALIA PTY LTD
107 Moray Street, South Melbourne 3205

Associated companies and representatives
throughout the world.

National Library of Australia
cataloguing in publication data

Heaven, Patrick C. L. (Patrick Charles Lionel).
    Contemporary adolescence: a social psychological
    approach.

    Bibliography.
    Includes index.
    ISBN 0 7329 2620 3.
    ISBN 0 7329 2619 X (pbk.)

    1. Adolescent psychology. 2. Youth — Psychology. I. Title.

155.5

Typeset in Plantin
by Superskill Graphics, Singapore

Printed in Hong Kong

Cover design by Maria Fontana

# Contents

# Preface

Although I initially trained as a social psychologist, I have, over the years, developed a strong interest in human development, particularly adolescent development. This is not a common interest for a social psychologist. Perhaps it resulted from my own experiences as an adolescent. On the other hand, it may have something to do with one of my earliest lecturing assignments: standing in for a colleague in human development. Perhaps having four quite different children is a factor. Whatever the reason, my interest in the psychology of adolescence has developed to the point where I consider this one of the more challenging fields of possible study.

Adolescence usually encompasses the second decade of life. Unlike other stages or periods of the life span, it has been referred to as a time of *transition*, as a time of *storm and stress*, and as a time of being *marginalised*. Teenagers are no longer children, yet are not quite adult. Physically, they are maturing rapidly. Emotionally and cognitively, however, their transition to adulthood appears somewhat slower. It is as though adolescents do not clearly fit into any life stage. That is what makes the adolescent years so different and why, for so many adolescents, this period of life is exciting and challenging, yet often filled with turmoil and confusion.

Hamburg (1990) has reminded us that being an adolescent in the late twentieth century is more difficult than ever before. There are several reasons for this. Firstly, adolescence is now much longer. The average age of menarche, for example, is lower than before. Moreover, many adolescents undergo post-school training, thus remaining financially dependent on their parents beyond their teenage years. Compare this to the late 1800s, when adolescents were a cheap source of labour in the rapidly expanding industries of Western Europe and the United States (Grinder 1990).

There are also other reasons. Hamburg (1990) notes the erosion of family and social support networks, as well as the easy access that adolescents now have to drugs, alcohol and other life-threatening substances such as weapons and vehicles. Thus, not only is adolescence a time of transition, but adolescents are also highly *vulnerable* to emotional maladjustment and a range of behaviours such as early sexual activity and associated health risks, depression, suicide, drug use, delinquency and dropping out of school (Hamburg 1990).

# Rationale of This Book

This book will expand Hamburg's (1990) ideas of vulnerability and examine the psychological principles associated with the *social* development of adolescents. This is not to suggest that the physical/ biological and cognitive aspects of adolescent development are not of prime importance: they are. This book, however, will concentrate on the social aspects of development, noting implications for adjustment.

A review of trends in adolescent research between 1976 and 1981 (Stefanko 1984) listed some of the most 'popular' research topics in adolescence. Included were problem behaviours like suicide; emotional problems (like depression); sexuality; parents and divorce; peers; issues connected with education; and work-related issues. This book will consider these and other issues.

It differs, I believe, from other similar volumes in a quite fundamental way. Unlike them, it attempts an in-depth review of psychological research findings, rather than the more descriptive review of results typical of books in this area. I have also attempted to incorporate findings from as many different cultures as possible. The book is therefore, directed at those students and professionals who are keen to read a little more deeply than usual.

# Overview

Chapter 1 introduces the reader to the field of study. It reviews some of the earliest and current images of youth. How have adolescents typically been portrayed? How does this differ from current stereotypes? It is noted that the teenage years, although regarded as 'intense' and rather 'exuberant', are not necessarily a time of storm and stress. A very important part of this chapter is the review of theoretical perspectives. The chapter does not consider all possible theories; only those regarded as the most influential have been included and evaluated. The importance of each to understanding adolescent development is considered. Theoretical points are referred to again at the end of each chapter.

In the second chapter, we consider identity formation and the search for self. Since adolescents are in the period of transition to adulthood, an important developmental task is the search for identity, personal, vocational and sexual. The chapter will consider various identity statuses and their implications for adolescent adjustment. The chapter concludes by considering the self-concept and the development of a sex-role identity.

Chapter 3 notes the importance of family processes in adolescent development. Important are factors such as differences in parenting styles, parent-child communication and the psychological health of parents. A significant section of the chapter is devoted to adolescent reactions to parental separation and divorce, and to how adolescents cope with living in new families. It is noted that it is not the family *structure* as such that is important when considering adolescent adjustment. Rather, it is the nature and quality of parenting in new families which helps determine adolescent emotional stability.

The influences of friendships and peer groups are dealt with in Chapter 4. They are an important source of emotional support and affiliation, and are therefore crucial to the adolescent striving for identity achievement. The chapter discusses the nature of friendships and peer groups as well as their specific functions and structure. The chapter also considers peer pressure and susceptibility to it, as well as the relative influence of parents versus peers. It concludes with reference to research on bullying at school.

The next chapter discusses the importance of the educational process on adolescent adjustment. There are many predictors of academic performance. The chapter discusses the importance of family life, the impact of family disruption, the role of personality factors and the role of causal attributions. It reviews high school drop-outs as well as the effect of type of school on academic attainment. Two factors are important, namely, gender and, private vs. public schools. Finally, brief consideration is given to the transition from high school to university.

Sexuality is discussed in Chapter 6. According to the available evidence, factors such as the family, peers and hormonal factors are complexly inter-related in determining whether adolescents are likely to engage in sexual behaviour at an early age. A major section of the chapter deals with factors related to condom use and the accompanying threat of AIDS. The chapter also briefly reviews the question of sexual preference, sex offenders and adolescent prostitution.

Chapter 7 discusses the unique problems of teenagers who are also parents. It begins by discussing pregnancy resolution and the options of abortion, adoption and keeping the baby. It notes the birthing outcomes associated with teenage mothers as well as the psychosocial adjustment of children born to teenage parents. Attention is also paid to research into teenage fathers, while brief mention is made of longitudinal research into adolescent mothers. This research notes the immense variability in long-term outcomes of adolescent mothers.

Work and money are discussed in Chapter 8. This notes the various developmental stages that children go through in acquiring beliefs about money, as well as a vocational identity. There are certain family and personality factors that must be considered in explaining work and money-related beliefs. In addition, cultural differences in these beliefs have also been noted. A major section of the chapter deals with adolescents in the workplace as well as the psychological effects of unemployment.

The next chapter discusses orientation to authority and delinquency. It notes the links that exist between attitudinal and behavioural components of orientation to authority, as well as the links with delinquency. There are several important theoretical perspectives on delinquency. The complex interaction between social factors and biological predispositions in explaining delinquency is noted.

Finally, Chapter 10 considers the important issue of suicide. It notes the theoretical and empirical links between hopelessness, depression and suicide. The chapter discusses developmental trends in depression and the importance of hormonal, genetic, cognitive and other influences. It also examines sex differences in depression as well as psychosocial factors related to teenage depression. With respect to suicide, incidence rates from numerous countries are recorded. The chapter concludes by noting the marked rise in suicide in rural areas and considers possible explanations for this phenomenon.

I have greatly enjoyed writing this book. To a large extent, this was made possible by my long-suffering family, who had to live with me through each of its phases and had to put up with the demands of writing. In particular, I am grateful to Leonora for her love and support.

I would also like to express thanks to a number of colleagues who either commented on earlier drafts of sections or made other useful suggestions. I would like to thank John Connors, Brian Hemmings and Sotirios Sarantakos. Naturally, I take full responsibility for the final product. Finally, I would like to thank Adrian Furnham who, although half a world away, demonstrated that social learning is alive and well, by serving as a formidable role model.

Patrick Heaven
Wagga Wagga, New South Wales

# Acknowledgements

The author and publishers would like to thank the following for permission to reproduce copyright material:
Table 1.1, p. 6 from B. Roscoe & T. Kruger (1990), *Adolescence* 25: 39–48 (Libra Publishers); Figure 1.3, p. 22 from J. Tanner & P. Davies (1985), *Journal of Pediatrics* 107: 317–29 (Mosby-Year Book, Inc.); Figure 3.1, p. 55 from P. Amato (1990), *Journal of Marriage and the Family* 52: 613–20 (National Council on Family Relations); Table 3.2, p. 61 from M. Payne & A. Furnham (1990), *Psychological Reports* 67: 611–18; Table 4.4, p. 92 from K. Rigby and P. Slee (1991), *Journal of Social Psychology* 131: 615–27 (Heldref Publications); Table 5.1, p. 99 from A. Furnham & B. Gunter (1989), *The Anatomy of Adolescence* (Routledge, London); Table 5.2, p. 102 from V. Masselam, R. Marcus & C. Stunkard (1990), *Adolescence* 25: 725–37 (Libra Publishers); Figure 5.1, p. 103 from L. Steinberg, J. Elmen & N. Mounts (1989), *Child Development* 60: 1424–36 (Society for Research in Child Development); Figure 5.3, p. 105 from B. Mednick, R. Baker, C. Reznick & D. Hocevar (1990), *Journal of Divorce* 13: 69–88; Figure 5.2, p. 111 from J. Ainley, J. Foreman & M. Sheret (1991), *Journal of Educational Research* 85: 69–80, reprinted with permission of the Helen Dwight Reid Educational Foundation, published by Heldref Publications, 1319 Eighteenth St., NW, Washington, DC 20036–1802; Tables 5.5 and 5.6, p. 116 from B. Graetz (1990), *Australian Journal of Education* 34: 174–91 (The Australian Council for Educational Research Ltd.); Table 6.1, p. 124 from S. Newcomer & J. Udry (1987), *Journal of Marriage and the Family* 49: 235–40 (National Council on Family Relations); Figure 6.1, p. 129 from J. Udry (1988), *American Sociological Review* 53: 709–22 (American Sociological Association); Table 6.6, p. 141 from L. Garnets & D. Kimmel (1991) in J. Goodchilds (Ed.), *Psychological Perspectives on Human Diversity in America: Master Lectures* (American Psychological Association); Figure 7.3, p. 158 and Figure 7.4, p. 159 from J. Correy, P. Kwok, N. Newman & J. Curran (1984), *Medical Journal of Australia* 141: 150–4 (Australian Medical Association); Figure 8.1, p. 176 from A. Furnham & B. Gunter (1989), *The Anatomy of Adolescence* (Routledge, London); Table 8.2, p. 178 from C. Bonnet &

A. Furnham (1991), *Journal of Economic Psychology* 12: 465–78 (Elsevier Science Publishers); Table 9.1, p. 195 from S. Reicher & N. Emler (1985), *British Journal of Social Psychology* 24: 161–8 (British Psychological Society); Table 9.2, p. 199 from P. Heaven & A. Furnham (1991), *Personality & Individual Differences* 12: 977–82 (Pergamon Press); Table 9.3, p. 200 from P. Heaven (1989), Australian *Psychologist* 24: 27–35 (Australian Psychological Society); Figure 9.2, p. 206 and Figure 9.3, p. 207 from P. Heaven (1993), *Personality & Individual Differences* 14: 67–76 (Pergamon Press); Table 10.1, p. 216 from A. Kazdin, N. French, A. Unis, K. Esveldt-Dawson & R. Sherick (1983), *Journal of Consulting & Clinical Psychology* 51: 504–10 (American Psychological Association); Table 10.3, p. 221 from J. Kashani, T. Rosenberg & J. Reid (1989), *American Journal of Psychiatry* 146: 871–5 (American Psychiatric Association); Figure 10.1, p. 223 from A. Petersen, P. Sarigiani & R. Kennedy (1991), *Journal of Youth & Adolescence*; Table 10.4, p. 230 from D. Lester (1988), *Adolescence* 23: 953–8 (Libra Publishers); Table 10.5, p. 234 from G. McLure (1986), *Journal of Adolescence* 9: 135–43 (Academic Press)

# 1  General Introduction

## Introduction

The scientific study of adolescence or the 'teenage years' is enjoying unprecedented attention not only from psychologists, but also other professionals. Whereas developmental psychologists previously tended to focus exclusively on the childhood years, there has more recently been a growing interest in the psychological study of the second decade of life. In the social sciences alone, this has resulted in an explosion of written material, the publication of new journals entirely devoted to the nature of adolescence, and the establishment of professional societies and conferences dealing with its theoretical and applied problems (Petersen 1988). Thus it would seem that the importance of sound enquiry and debate into the nature of adolescence has been established.

There are no doubt several reasons for this changing emphasis. As some writers have pointed out, one reason may well be the rising tide of unemployed youth in many countries (Coleman and Hendry 1990). Although typical of many Western democracies during times of economic contraction, relatively high levels of youth unemployment are now also of growing concern in many Central and East European countries, as they move towards market-driven economies. Whereas most youth were assured of some form of employment in the former Communist countries, this is no longer the case as unproductive factories and whole industries are either shut down or drastically restructured.

Rapid technological change has implications for those communities which have traditionally been reliant upon heavy industry or mining. Such change has had a major impact not only on the availability of jobs, but also on education policies, government training schemes, and so forth. It is not surprising, therefore, that many politicians, community leaders, and parents are mindful of the well-being and future of adolescents in the late twentieth century.

## Images of Youth

To a large extent, perceptions of and concerns about adolescents derive from our own experiences with teenagers, as well as the information available to us. In this regard, the print and electronic media are powerful and influential sources of information (and mis-information), which serve to shape our perceptions, expectations, and stereotypes of youth.

A popular conception of adolescence is that it is a time of 'storm and stress', although some are doubtful about the amount of empirical evidence supporting this view (Petersen 1988, Violato and Wiley 1990). Nonetheless, such a view of the teenage years has remained quite stable, over several hundred years. On the basis of a review of images of adolescence as reflected in English literature since the works of Chaucer, it was found that the adolescent years have usually been portrayed as turbulent, excessive, and filled with passion (Violato and Wiley 1990). The authors remind us that Chaucer (1340–1400) described youth as frivolous, and as being devoted to love and silly pleasures. Shakespeare (1564–1616) saw adolescence as a time of exuberance, excess, passion, and sensuality, while Lewis Bayly (1565–1631) saw teenagers as individuals, without much character and rather coarse. As Bayly (cited in Violato and Wiley 1990: 257) explained:

> What is youth but an untamed beast all whose actions are rash and rude, not capable of good council when it is given and ape like delighting in nothing but toys like babies.

In the writings of Charles Dickens (1812–1870), one theme that is developed is that of impetuosity. For instance, in *David Copperfield*, David falls on hard times, but later shows adolescent impetuosity and passion. Thus one might conclude (with Violato and Wiley 1990: 262):

> Dickens uses David to depict the 'storm and stress' of adolescence and the transcendent nature of the 'goodness' of youth. For both David Copperfield and Oliver Twist, life was full of turbulence, excess, and passion.

**Twentieth Century Views**

In 1904, the psychologist Hall first alerted the scientific community to the importance of adolescence as a life stage deserving formal and sound enquiry. In his attempts to lead the way, he borrowed heavily from the past, picking up on the idea of adolescence as a period of 'storm and stress' (Dusek 1991, Petersen 1988, Violato and Wiley 1990). This point was also taken further by psychoanalytic writers, who saw teenagers as suffering from emotional turmoil (Susman 1991). Perhaps as a consequence of such views, which tended to prevail until the 1960s and 7‒‒, problems and difficulties were thought to be quite typical of adolescence, and hence were not investigated (Petersen 1988).

Although later writers may not have thought of adolescence as a particularly stressful period, the media continued to stereotype this life stage as, if not stressful, certainly turbulent. For instance, by the mid-1960s Adelson (1964) reported the media describing teenagers as 'moody' and suffering from 'wild enthusiasms' (p. 1). Later, the typical youth was described as a 'symbol of renewal' and seen as a voice against injustice (Ewen, cited in Violato and Wiley 1990).

More recently, writers have questioned the notion of 'storm and stress'. In one review (Petersen 1988), it was argued that there is little support for the idea that parents and adolescents suffer from the much-heralded 'generation gap' or that adolescent development is 'stormy'. Susman (1991) noted that, although some data suggest that adolescence may be a stressful stage of life, many findings are inconsistent. Indeed, it would appear that only a small proportion of adolescents in any group ever report feeling stressed. Although some teenagers may be maladjusted and at risk, most successfully meet the challenges of the adolescent years (Masten 1991).

These views have been supported by a review of several research studies (Gecas and Seff 1990). The authors cite a cross-cultural study conducted in ten countries which found that most of the adolescents surveyed had good relations with their families, and had a favourable attitude towards themselves. They were also relatively interested in work-related matters. In one of the studies, less than 10 per cent of the adolescents noted a deterioration in family relationships in the teenage years. These findings suggest that most adolescents get on quite well with their school work, maintain satisfactory relationships with their parents, and at the same time prepare themselves for lives as adults.

Conger and Petersen (1984: 26–27) conclude:

> While many adolescents face occasional periods of uncertainty and self-doubt, of loneliness and sadness, of anxiety and concern for the future, they are also likely to experience joy, excitement, curiosity, a sense of adventure, and a feeling of competence in mastering new challenges.

How do we view adolescents in the late twentieth century? Have our perceptions of teenagers remained relatively constant? Stereotypes that could be used today include 'rebellious', 'drug users' and 'promiscuous' (Santrock 1990). On the other hand, one also notes that many adolescents today are 'competitive', and that they 'find it difficult to get a job'. They are under a lot of 'pressure to succeed'. In one recent survey of university undergraduates in the United States, respondents were asked to think how today's adolescents differ from those of ten or twenty years ago. Respondents noted several differences. Here are just a few (Santrock 1990: 22):

Today's adolescents are:

• More achievement- money- and college-oriented
• Growing up earlier, experiencing things earlier, being pushed into life-stages sooner
• More likely to be working at a job
• More financially dependent on parents for a longer period of time
• Using alcohol more (especially females).

## Developmental Tasks

The developmental tasks of a particular life stage are those skills, knowledge and functions that a person must acquire or master in order successfully to move on to the following stage. Each stage of the life span has its own developmental tasks which involve motor, physical, social or emotional aspects of behaviour, and each task is normally mastered at the appropriate time. Being a unique stage in life, adolescence has its own associated problems, difficulties and developmental tasks (Ausubel, Montemayor and Svajian 1977). Children who do not successfully complete the developmental tasks of childhood will be at a disadvantage as they enter the teenage years. The same applies to adolescents moving into adulthood.

Havighurst (1972) proposed developmental tasks for various life stages and noted the following for adolescents:

• Developing new relationships with peers of both sexes
• Acquiring a masculine or feminine social role
• Accepting one's physique and using the body effectively
• Becoming emotionally independent of parents and other adults
• Preparing for marriage and a family life
• Selecting and preparing for an economic career
• Acquiring values and an ethical system as a guide to behaviour
• Desiring and achieving socially responsible behaviour.

Newman and Newman (1987) have proposed a different set of tasks, and focus on those areas that are critical to the individual's social and psychological growth. Specifically, they concentrate on tasks they believe are relevant for modern Western society and suggest the following for those aged 12–18 years (pp. 320–51):

| | |
|---|---|
| • Physical maturation | Adjust to changing body image |
| • Formal operations | Ability to reason and think abstractly |
| • Emotional development | Accept volatile emotions and mood swings |
| • Join peer groups | Important for psychological development |
| • Heterosexual relations | Opposite sex friendships become more important (also important for sexual identity). |

They proposed the following tasks for those aged 18–22 years (pp. 373–92):

| | |
|---|---|
| • Autonomy from parents | Regarded as a symbol of independence |
| • Sex role identity | Adopt sex-role congruent with self-concept and body image. |
| • Internalised morality | Need to learn to exercise moral judgements and accept principles of justice. |
| • Career choice | Congruent with self-concept, attitudes, values, and ability. |

There are some similarities between the tasks noted by both Havighurst and the Newmans. Some of these are:

- relationships with peers
- emotional independence
- preparation for career
- sense of morality (or ethical system)
- development of a sex-role identity.

There are also some noticeable differences, concerning marriage and the development of formal operational thinking. The latter task is no doubt more necessary for those living in a technological society. With respect to marriage, one can question the validity of this developmental task. There is an increasing number of households in which the partners are not married. It would therefore be reasonable to assume that developmental tasks (at least for the post-childhood stages) are not fixed, but to some extent reflect the culture within which the adolescent lives (Hooker 1991), as well as the social context of the writer.

To what extent are older adolescents *actually engaged* in developmental tasks? Are they fully preoccupied with the tasks of adolescence, or do they work on some tasks of childhood and early adulthood? This was the focus of a study of over 400 university undergraduates in the United States (Roscoe and Peterson 1984). Most of the respondents were in their first year of study, with those who were married or parents not included in the analyses.

The students were presented with a selection of developmental tasks for middle childhood, adolescence, early adulthood and later adulthood. Although most (93 per cent) of the respondents indicated that they regarded themselves as being in early adulthood, the results showed that they were working primarily on the developmental tasks of adolescence, with some attention being paid to the tasks of childhood and early adulthood. In Table 1.1 are presented the main findings with respect to the developmental tasks of adolescence.

It shows that nearly all the respondents were engaged in achieving mature relations with age mates, or in achieving emotional independence from their parents. Many were concerned with achieving socially acceptable behaviour. Very few (33 per cent) were preparing for marriage and family life.

## Theoretical Perspectives on Adolescence

There are several major theoretical perspectives which are useful when thinking about the social development of adolescents. Such perspectives or theories are quite handy, since they organise a body of knowledge so that one may make predictions about future behaviour and make sense of otherwise chaotic data or phenomena.

**Table 1.1** *Responses of Students to a Selection of Developmental Tasks of Adolescence*

| Developmental task | Respondents reporting engagement (%) | Respondents reporting non-engagement (%) |
|---|---|---|
| Achieving mature relations with age mates | 94 | 6 |
| Achieving emotional independence from parents | 84 | 16 |
| Achieving socially responsible behaviour | 80 | 20 |
| Acquiring a set of values | 73 | 27 |
| Achieving appropriate social roles | 58 | 42 |
| Preparing for marriage and family life | 33 | 67 |

*Source:*    Roscoe and Peterson 1984

Theories, therefore, serve a very useful function. As Hollander (1967: 55) explained:

> Basically, a theory consists of one or more functional statements or propositions that treat the relationship of variables so as to account for a phenomenon or set of phenomena.

In psychology, theories of social behaviour are normally quite elaborate explanations of the causes and principles underlying that behaviour. In other words, they explain how the behaviour works. Theories break down the behaviour into parts that can be separately analysed. A useful theory sets out to explain how the different components are interrelated in determining behaviour (Williamson *et al.* 1982).

A detailed exposition of all of the theories of adolescence is clearly beyond the scope of this chapter. Instead, some of the main theoretical approaches to understanding adolescence will be briefly described. Readers seeking more detailed accounts should consult other sources such as Muuss (1988), Crain (1985) and Miller (1989).

## From the Middle Ages to the Enlightenment

Although early Greek writers such as Plato and Aristotle formulated their philosophical ideas about the nature of the human soul many hundreds of years before the Middle Ages, these were lost to European culture during the Dark Ages after the fall of the Roman Empire. The Middle Ages represented a neglect of the study of human development. Most people were preoccupied with survival, not only contending with wars and feudal conflicts, but also with disease. The population was generally poorly educated and the intellectuals of the time had little inclination, it seems, to consider the intricacies of human development (Hughes and Noppe 1985).

The prevailing view was that a miniature adult (called a *homunculus*) was found within the sperm. It was thought that, once conception occurred, the small adult simply grew in size within the mother. According to this view, humans were 'preformed', giving rise to the concept of *preformation*. This doctrine dominated scientific thinking during the Middle Ages and held sway until the eighteenth century, when more scientific investigations contradicted accepted views (Crain 1985). Writers such as Crain have suggested that, among religious leaders and moralists, preformation ideas receded as early as the sixteenth century, when the unique virtues of children began to be understood.

Preformationist views had a dominant influence on how children were viewed by adults, and depicted in art. They were treated as 'young adults' and expected to be obedient and well-behaved. In paintings, they were simply portrayed as small adults. No attention was given to the special needs or circumstances of children or adolescents. This reflected another view at the time, namely that the purpose of education was to counteract innate sin and so reveal God's laws (Hughes and Noppe 1985).

The Renaissance heralded a re-evaluation of social thought and the value of education. The works of Plato and Aristotle were re-discovered and writers such as Descartes stimulated interest in human nature. An important thinker of the time was John Locke (1632–1704). He proposed that the mind of a child is like a blank slate, or *tabula rasa*, and that children learn behaviour according to their own unique experiences. Thus Locke laid the foundation work for later behaviourists such as Pavlov and Skinner (Crain 1985).

According to Locke, nature forms the mind of the child. This occurs through *association, repetition, imitation, rewards* and *punishment*, concepts well-known to learning theorists (Crain 1985). For instance, a child associates a behaviour with punishment and quickly learns not to repeat it. For this, the child is rewarded. We also learn through repetition (or practice) and imitation (or modelling). Locke's views about the acquisition of behaviour, although seminal, were to lie dormant until the early part of the twentieth century.

The writings of Jean-Jacques Rousseau (1712–78) best reflect the mood of the Enlightenment. He strongly influenced the later work of Gesell, Montessori and Piaget (Crain 1985). Rousseau was not an environmentalist. Unlike Locke, therefore, he did not view the mind as a blank slate waiting to be written upon. Rather, he suggested that children have their own capacities and modes of thinking, and that they should be allowed to grow and develop at their own pace, and in their own way.

Rousseau proposed the following stage theory of development (Crain 1985):

- Infancy             Birth to 2 years: children learn through their senses, are inquisitive and learn quickly
- Childhood           2–12 years: they can reason but not abstractly, and their actions represent their cognitive ability
- Late childhood      12–15 years: not interested in social relationships, they gain physically and cognitively, but cannot think theoretically

- Adolescence  15 years: marks the beginning of puberty, with dramatic physical, emotional, and cognitive changes.

## Evaluation

The proposals of Locke and Rousseau are invaluable to contemporary views about adolescent development (see Figure 1.1). Both were ahead of their time and laid the foundation for the current debate regarding the relative influences of nature and nurture. Whereas Locke emphasised external processes in the way behaviours are learned, Rousseau suggested that development is an innate process following a biological timetable. Both sets of ideas will be elaborated later.

**Figure** 1.1 *Influence of Some Early Thinkers on Current Theories of Development*

**MIDDLE AGES**

Innate sin

Homunculus

Preformation

**RENAISSANCE**

Descartes

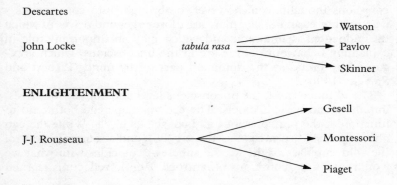

John Locke                    *tabula rasa*                    Watson
                                                               Pavlov
                                                               Skinner

**ENLIGHTENMENT**

J-J. Rousseau                                                  Gesell
                                                               Montessori
                                                               Piaget

**Psychoanalytic Theory**

Originally formulated by Freud, this perspective has undergone reformulation by others such as Anna Freud, Erikson, and Blos (Muuss 1988). Erikson's approach will be dealt with in some detail in Chapter 2, in connection with identity formation.

Freud developed his theory of personality on the basis of his work with individuals suffering from mental and emotional problems (Santrock 1990). He was opposed to the structuralist tradition which emphasised the experimental approach to understanding behaviour. Rather, Freud emphasised the unconscious motives of behaviour and considered mental processes, urges, drives, passions, and repressed ideas and emotions as important (Hall and Lindzey 1978). He made only passing reference to the adolescent years, believing that the first five years of life determine later development (Talwar and Lerner 1991).

Freud suggested that human behaviour can be explained in terms of drives. He noted two types, namely, *self-preservative* and *sexual* drives. The latter refer to all pleasurable activities, Freud believing that behaviour is motivated by the urge to attain pleasure. Freud later added the *aggressive* drive to explain destructive behaviour (Liebert and Spiegler 1990). He also proposed a basic structure of personality, which was then incorporated into his psycho-sexual stages of development. Freud proposed two distinct but related structures of the mind (Muuss 1988). These are:

- Unconscious
- Preconscious
- Conscious
- Id
- Ego
- Superego

The conscious refers to our awareness. Only a small proportion of one's thoughts and feelings are actually *in* consciousness. Preconscious thoughts can, however, be brought into consciousness with relative ease. Finally, there are those urges and drives of which the individual is unaware, and which play an important role in explaining behaviour. These are in the unconscious, which is regarded by Freud as the dominant part of the mind (Liebert and Spiegler 1990).

The id functions at the unconscious level and consists of drives, impulses, and basic instincts. The ego and superego both tend to function at the pre-conscious and conscious levels. While the ego obeys the 'reality principle' (Muuss 1988), and attempts to control the wild impulses of the id, the superego coincides with what we would call our 'conscious' (Santrock 1990), reflecting learned values and morals. In a sense, the superego represents social norms, values and expectations.

The psycho-sexual stages of development begin in infancy and progress through adolescence. They are listed in Table 1.2. During the adolescent years, the individual reaches sexual maturity, with sexual instincts being directed towards heterosexual relationships.

Three main themes pervade psychoanalytic theory (Coleman 1992). In the first place, drives, instincts, and motives play an important part in personality development. Such drives and instincts are particularly problematic during puberty and adolescence, when a developing sexuality needs to be incorporated into the overall structure of personality. As Muuss (1988) notes, this basic drive is exacerbated by current social, moral, and religious convention, such that the id comes into conflict with the ego and superego. According to this view, the superego finds the basic instincts of the id unacceptable, while the ego seems to have little control over the id. As a consequence, the adolescent experiences turmoil and conflict. When externalised, such turmoil may be manifest in a number of ways, including conflict between parents and teenagers.

The second theme refers to defence mechanisms (Coleman 1992). These are strategies one develops and learns in order to resolve conflict or anguish, or to help defend oneself against the id. Such

**Table 1.2** *Freud's Psychosexual Stages of Human Development*

| Stage | Main features |
|---|---|
| Oral | From birth until child is weaned; mouth, lips, and tongue associated with pleasure<br>From 8–18 months referred to as oral-biting stage |
| Anal | 6 months–4 years: chief pleasure is excreting faeces and urine. Toilet training important, since restricts child's behaviour |
| Phallic | 4–7 or 8 years: genitals are object of erogenous interest.<br>Boys suffer from Oedipus complex (see father as competitor for mother's affection)<br>Girls suffer from Electra complex and penis envy (they blame mother for their 'castration') |
| Latency | 6 or 8 years–12 or 13 years: sexual drive does not continue. Oedipus/Electra complexes should be resolved |
| Genital | Begins with puberty: individuals are sexually mature and directed toward heterosexual pleasure. |

*Source:* Phares 1991

mechanisms include repression, sublimation, reaction formation, regression, displacement, rationalisation, identification and projection (Muuss 1988, Santrock 1990). These are further explained in Table 1.3.

The third theme concerns the process of disengagement (Coleman 1992). Adolescents, having successfully resolved the Oedipus or Electra complex (see Table 1.2), begin to form closer relationships first with the same-sex peer group, and then with members of the opposite sex (see Chapter 4). By this process, a gradual disengagement from the family, or a loosening of ties, begins to occur. Establishing oneself as independent from one's parents is essential, particularly in later adolescence, since this has implications for future mature emotional and sexual relationships.

Freud's daughter Anna developed her father's ideas on adolescence. She stressed the importance of Oedipal feelings within the adolescent, and suggested that many teenagers feel anxious in the presence of their parents. Thus they may resort to solitary behaviour, such as spending long periods alone in their rooms, or to running away from home (Crain 1985). She also suggested that adolescents often become contemptuous of their parents, adopting a belligerent attitude. According to Anna Freud, many teenagers adopt many defence mechanisms against a variety of feelings and impulses. Crain mentions two: asceticism, denial of pleasure, as for

**Table 1.3** *Defense Mechanisms to Help Defend Oneself Against the Id*

| Mechanism | Description |
| --- | --- |
| Repression | Unacceptable thoughts are deliberately kept in the subconscious |
| Sublimation/displacement | Drives or urges are directed towards another goal more valued by one's peers or by society |
| Reaction formation | One attempts to reverse an unacceptable urge or behaviour by turning it into its opposite |
| Regression | One reverts to satisfying behaviours characteristic of an earlier phase in the life span |
| Rationalisation | A form of reasoning to convince us of the merits of our action |
| Identification | An attempt to be just like someone else |
| Projection | One's desires or behaviours are believed to be characteristic of someone else. |

instance, in the following of strict diets. The second is intellectualisation, that is, the construction of elaborate theories about social and moral issues, such as love and war.

## Evaluation

Freud's ideas about development and the nature of personality have made an enormous impact on psychology and psychiatry. He has, however, drawn criticism from a number of sources. Feminists have suggested that his ideas are culture-bound and sexist, and that his views of women are outdated. Others, such as Liebert and Spiegler (1990) suggest that Freud viewed the male personality as the 'prototype' on which he tried to base the female personality. Still more have questioned his views on 'penis envy'. Crain (1985: 158) echoed this argument as follows:

> Freud assumed that penis envy is based on a real biological inferiority – a view that fit well with his society's prejudice. Actually . . . penis envy is much more of a culture problem; girls feel inferior to boys because girls lack the same privileges in a male dominated society . . . Freud ignored women's legitimate desire for social equality.

Other writers have evaluated psychoanalytic theory in terms of its scientific contribution, and found it wanting. Eysenck (1985), for instance, notes Freud's own relationship with his mother (he was her 'undisputed darling'), as well as his addiction to cocaine, suggesting that both shaped and biased his views on personality. In addition, Eysenck (1985) and others like Liebert and Spiegler (1990) have criticised the untestable nature of many of Freud's ideas, noting also that many of his concepts are poorly defined. Thus, according to Eysenck (1985: 20):

> Psychoanalysis as an art form may be acceptable; psychoanalysis as a science has always evoked protests from scientists and philosophers of science.

## Behavioural Theory

Like the psychoanalytic approach, learning theory, in its classic behavioural and social learning perspectives, has had a fundamental influence on conceptions of human development and behaviour. Learning theory derives from the ideas of Locke.

The classic behaviourist approach was first formulated by writers such as Pavlov, Hull, and Skinner (Muuss 1988). It was

Pavlov, for instance, who noticed that dogs salivate in anticipation of being fed. This led him to conduct a range of different experiments on the so-called *conditioning response*. He demonstrated, for example, that food could be associated with another stimulus, such as a tone, and that dogs would salivate when they heard that. Thus were born the concepts unconditioned stimulus (the food), conditioned stimulus (the tone), unconditioned reflex (salivation to the food) and conditioned reflex (salivation to the tone) (Crain 1985).

The basic principles of classical conditioning are shown in Figure 1.2. Once conditioning has occurred, it is possible to pair the conditioned stimulus (the tone) with a new stimulus (such as a light) until it elicits the desired response (salivation). This is referred to as higher order conditioning.

Further laboratory experiments demonstrated just how short-lived conditioned stimuli are, and that it is possible for such stimuli to lose their effect (so-called extinction). Elimination of the reward

**Figure 1.2** *The Classical Conditioning Process*

## CLASSICAL CONDITIONING

Food ⟶ Salivation

After food is associated with tone:

Tone ⟶ Salivation

## HIGHER ORDER CONDITIONING

Tone is paired with light so that:

Light ⟶ Salivation

reduces the likelihood that salivation will follow the tone. Moreover, it was also shown how previously extinguished stimuli can recover their effect: that is, we can re-learn behaviours that have been extinguished. Finally, Pavlov also showed experimentally that it is possible to distinguish between different stimuli. At the same time, it is also possible that similar stimuli, such as two tones, elicit the same response.

In an extension of these ideas, Skinner maintained that the consequences of our actions actually determine our behaviour. In other words, rewards will enhance behaviour. As Skinner explained, it is therefore possible to *shape* behaviour (Phares 1991). Using this operant conditioning method, he was able to demonstrate that we do not learn behaviours in an all-or-nothing fashion, but that one moves *towards* the correct response. He showed, for instance, how one can teach a pigeon to peck at a button: the pigeon is first rewarded for facing the button. Food (the reward) is then witheld, until the bird moves towards the button. Next it is rewarded for pecking closer and closer to the button. Finally, it is rewarded for executing the desired action or behaviour (Crain 1985).

Central to all forms of learning theory is reinforcement. Classical theorists demonstrated the link between removal of reward and extinction of responses. Skinner distinguished between positive and negative reinforcement and punishment. Whereas in the former a stimulus is presented after the correct behaviour, in negative reinforcement a stimulus is removed following correct behaviour. For example, the threat of punishment is withdrawn once a child performs acceptable behaviour. Both positive and negative reinforcement increase the likelihood of acceptable behaviour occurring. Punishment, on the other hand, reduces the likelihood of unacceptable behaviour (see Figure 1.3 for a summary).

**Figure 1.3** *Principles of Operant Conditioning*

---

**Positive reinforcement**
*Example: Praise*
Presented after the desired behaviour; increases its rate

**Negative reinforcement**
*Example: Scolding*
Removed after correct behaviour; increases the rate of behaviour

**Punishment**
*Example: Cancellation of pocket money*
Presented after incorrect behaviour; suppresses behaviour.

---

Fundamental to learning or behavioural theory, therefore, is the fact that one is rewarded for acceptable behaviour. Thus, individuals (including adolescents) are much more likely to execute certain behaviours if they gain from doing so. If, in order to gain acceptance by the peer group (highly rewarding), a teenager needs to behave in a certain way, or dress in a certain style, then it is highly likely that he or she will do so. If certain ways of behaviour need to be avoided to gain approval by the group, then again it is highly likely this will occur. Thus a reward for correct behaviour fixes in the mind of the individual the close association between a stimulus and a particular response. Likewise, punishment indicates that certain behaviours or attitudes are inappropriate.

## Evaluation

Behaviourists such as Pavlov and Skinner do not discuss internal states. Rather, they focus on external events such as stimulus and response. For the classic behaviourist, personality is simply the sum of all previously learned responses, while cognitive input is not given much credence. For some developmentalists, an adolescent's feelings and thoughts, likes and dislikes, are intimately tied up with behaviour. Skinnerians would argue, however, that behaviour is constantly shaped and determined by the environment (Crain 1985).

Other writers (e.g. Liebert and Spiegler 1990) have suggested that the radical behaviourist approach is dehumanising, as well as being rather simplistic. Such writers argue that human behaviour and development is much more complex than what is reflected in learning theory, and that behaviour cannot be reduced to simple stimulus and response categories. By so doing, behaviourists ignore the complexity of behaviour as well as individual differences, cultural influences and free will.

## Social Cognitive Theory

Dollard and Miller were the first to use the term social learning theory (Liebert and Spiegler 1990). They elaborated some of the principles of behavioural theory, suggesting that human behaviour is also determined by factors such as drives and cues (Phares 1991). Thus, there are internal stimuli (or drives) such as hunger that cause us to look for food (a response). Just where or when we eat, however, is dependent upon certain cues (e.g. 'I'll eat when I see the pizza sign' or 'I'll eat when I have completed this task'). In this way, correct (or acceptable) behaviour is appropriately rewarded. According to Dollard and Miller, human behaviour is learned through drive reduction, attaching responses to new stimuli, reinforcing or rewarding new responses, and creating secondary motives (Phares 1991).

Dollard and Miller acknowledged the importance of *social models*, or modelling cues. Unlike more recent social learning theorists, Dollard and Miller overlooked the possibility that one can learn simply by observation rather than through direct experience.

These ideas were later expanded by Rotter and Bandura, yet it is Bandura who is synonymous with social learning or social cognitive theory. Although he acknowledged the importance of classical and operant conditioning, he also emphasised the importance of observational learning, modelling, imitation, and identification in human development. Together with his colleagues, Bandura demonstrated empirically that young children can learn aggressive behaviour, for example, simply by watching violent films, and that such observational learning is not merely confined to young children.

Bandura was of the opinion that adolescents and adults also learn a variety of behaviours by observing the actions of others. Teenagers will emulate the behaviour or dress of their idols through observation and imitation. In addition, identification with their idol facilitates learning. Likewise, the role of the peer group should not be underestimated. Adolescents are highly likely to smoke or engage in early sexual intercourse, for example, if some of their closest friends are already doing so (Kandel 1990, Muuss 1988). As will be noted in Chapter 4, the peer group sets the cultural norms or 'rituals' for acceptable behaviour.

Because it is possible to learn behaviour simply by observing the actions of others, Bandura pointed out that social learning also involves a cognitive element (Crain 1985). We have inner representations of behaviour which allow the observer to perform a new behaviour. Moreover, Bandura stresses the importance of *vicarious reinforcement*. This refers to expectations about reinforcement or reward without actually performing the behaviour. In other words, we have the capacity to think about the likely consequences of our actions before performing them. If we *expect* to be rewarded, then we are likely to perform an action. An expectation of very little reward reduces the likelihood of action.

There are four fundamental components of observational learning (Crain 1985, Huston 1983). They are:

- Attentional processes
- Retention processes

- Motor reproduction processes
- Reinforcement and motivational processes.

In order to perform a behaviour we first need to pay attention to the model performing the action. Thus, we watch a television character or pay attention to the behaviour of others in our environment. Implicit is an understanding of the observed behaviour, itself a cognitive process. Having observed and understood behaviour, we also need to remember what we have seen so that we can later recall and reproduce the actions. We also need to be physically mature enough to execute what is required. A young child is incapable of learning to ride a bicycle unless physically and cognitively mature enough to do so. Finally, behaviours are strengthened through rewards and reinforcement.

Social cognitive learning is a three-stage process. The first two stages, namely, exposure and acquisition, have been discussed. The third stage is referred to as acceptance. It has been defined as follows (Liebert and Spiegler 1990: 452):

> Acceptance refers to whether or not the observer uses (accepts) the modelling cues as a guide for her or his own actions.

There are no doubt many factors which determine whether the observer finds others' behaviour acceptable. They may include the status of the person being observed, the personality of the observer, the observer's own values and attitudes, the desirability of the observed behaviour, and so forth.

## Evaluation

Some (e.g. Crain 1985) are of the view that theorists such as Bandura have greatly enhanced our understanding of social learning. Although the theoretical principles are well-founded in laboratory experiments, it is not clear whether *all* human behaviour can be explained as a function of observation and imitation. Indeed, some have argued that this approach is far too dependent on laboratory experimentation (Liebert and Spiegler 1990).

Secondly, some would argue that social learning theorists overemphasise the importance of the environment on the acquisition of new behaviour. At the same time, social learning theorists appear to under-value the role of internal processes such as human values and beliefs, and a range of personality factors.

## Cognitive-developmental Theory

One cannot consider the impact of cognitive change on human development without considering the work of Jean Piaget. Piaget was a gifted thinker, writing his first scientific paper while still a teenager, and earning his doctorate at the age of twenty-one. Working first on intelligence tests for children, he later became interested in childrens' patterns of reasoning (Crain 1985).

Piaget proposed a stage theory of intellectual development. Although he did not see a formal link between stage and age of the child, he firmly believed that each of us progresses through the stages in the same order. Each stage represents a more complex way of thinking, as explained in Table 1.5.

It is clear that the adolescent years coincide with the advent of formal operations. This means that teenagers are not constrained by having to function only at the non-abstract level, but are increasingly able to think about imaginary and hypothetical events: that is, they are able to reason abstractly. Adolescents are not only able to understand relationships between actual events, but also understand relationships between actual and possible events. This appears to be much more marked in the physical field (for instance, dealing with chemical relationships) than in the social field (Boyle

**Table 1.5** *Piaget's Stages of Cognitive Development*

| Stage | Main features |
| --- | --- |
| Sensori-motor intelligence | Birth to 2 years: knows environment through senses and motor activity. Constructs schemes. Later responds to interesting events outside body. Will later look for objects that have disappeared. Also develops object permanence and recognises self |
| Pre-operational stage | 2 years to 7 years: toddlers capable of mental representations. Are able to imitate behaviour |
| Concrete operations | 7 years to 11 years: can reason about concrete events. Can deal with concepts of classes, relations, and quantity. Has developed conservation of number, quantity, mass, volume, etc. Capable of cognitive conceit |
| Formal operations | 12 years to adulthood: begins to reason abstractly. Develops hypothetico-deductive reasoning, combinatorial analysis, contrary-to-fact reasoning. |

*Source:*   Crain 1985, Hughes and Noppe 1985

1969). Typically, adolescents tend to be egocentric, and, in terms of emotional and interpersonal relationships, far less able to distinguish the possible from the actual. They attain formal operational thought, therefore, in some areas before doing so in others.

Egocentrism during adolescence can be manifest in a number of different ways. It is well known, for example, that many teenagers are overly concerned with their appearance, and spend long periods in front of the mirror, grooming themselves. They appear to be convinced that they are invariably the centre of attention. Consequently, they play to what Elkind (1967) referred to as an 'imaginary audience'. Adolescents construct a 'personal fable' (Elkind 1967) thinking of themselves as quite special people who experience events in a very intense way. They believe that no-one else can feel as passionately about something as they do.

The teenage years mark a significant qualitative change in reasoning ability. With formal operational thinking comes the ability to begin to deal with a range of complex issues. Of course, not every dilemma they face will be successfully resolved. However, given that they are now able to combine the possible with the actual, their capacity to deal with the many challenges (biological, social, emotional, and educational) they will confront increases enormously.

Although many adolescents may attain the stage of formal operational thought, they are still *en route* to becoming adults. Very often, they are unable to view a problem or dilemma from the more experienced viewpoint of their elders. Only with increasing maturity are they able to think more realistically.

One may ask how an individual progresses through the various Piagetian stages. According to Piaget, one acquires new knowledge through the processes of assimilation, accommodation and organisation. Assimilation refers to the ability to absorb or take in new information. Once such information has been assimilated, it needs to be accommodated in pre-existing or newly constructed mental categories. An adolescent, for example, could accommodate negative information about a good friend in a variety of ways, such as changing her views about the friend or questioning the motives of the person providing the information. This process restores equilibrium. Thirdly, teenagers must organise their information into coherent theories or views about phenomena.

**Evaluation**

Piaget made a profound contribution to our understanding of

cognitive development – and not just during the adolescent years. Indeed, no discussion of such development is complete without reference to his work. According to Crain (1985), an enormous amount of research has been generated by Piaget's ideas, most of it supporting the stage sequence.

According to some critics, it is doubtful whether all teenagers and adults employ formal operational thought. It has even been suggested that most adults in their everyday lives function at the concrete operational level. Only periodically is it necessary to function at the highest level of reasoning.

## Biological Theory

An early exponent of this approach was Gesell. Although he believed the environment plays some role in the development of young children, internal biological and genetic processes were thought to be the primary factors accounting for human development (Crain 1985). Gesell is well known for the construction of his behaviour norms, although it is to physical development that he devoted most of his attention.

Gesell argued that much of human development is biologically predetermined. A child crawls before it can walk, and walks before it can run. Likewise, development of the foetus and embryo follow specific patterns. For example, the development of the brain begins before that of the arms and legs (Crain 1985). Thus there appears to be a genetic principle or schedule governing one's development. Although we may not all begin to walk at the same age, we all follow the same sequence of development. Like Rousseau, Gesell firmly believed that children perform certain actions (e.g. walking) when they are biologically ready, and that parents should refrain from attempts to train them. We are all governed by 'intrinsic maturational forces', he argued (Crain 1985).

The physical and biological changes occurring during puberty and adolescence have been well documented. Nearly all adolescents are subject to what has been described as the 'growth spurt'. Boys seem to have a greater growth spurt than girls. In one report (Tanner and Davies 1985), the average boy is said to grow about 10 cm per year in the fastest year of the growth spurt, about twice as fast as the previous year. These trends are illustrated in Figure 1.4.

More recently, Tanner (1991) has documented the composition of some aspects of the growth spurt. He noted that all skeletal and muscle parts undergo change, while the peak weight spurt occurs about six to nine months after the height peak. Importantly, in

**Figure 1.4** *Differences in Growth Spurt for Boys and Girls*

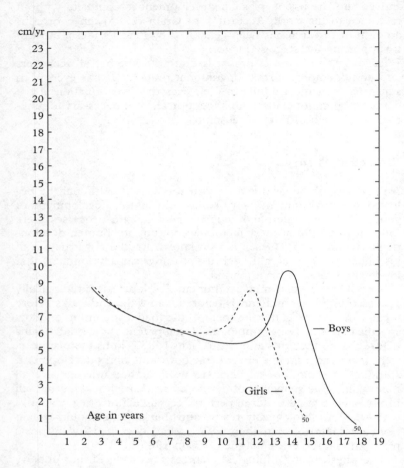

*Source:*   Tanner and Davies 1985

Gesell's terms, is the fact that growth peaks follow a particular sequence. Tanner (1991: 422) explains this as follows:

> There is a regular order to the peaks; leg length as a rule reaches its peak . . . first, with trunk length . . . about a year later. In between occur the peaks of shoulder and hip breadths. The muscles' peak coincides with that of trunk length, and so follows after the height peak.

The development of secondary sex characteristics also follows a specific pattern. In girls, breast budding is followed by the appearance of pubic hair, followed by menarche. In boys, testicular growth occurs before spermarche, which can occur together with early pubic hair growth (Paikoff and Brooks-Gunn 1991).

An integral part of biological and physical change during adolescence is the changing nature of the endocrine system. During this time, it changes into its adult form, resulting in a significant increase in hormonal levels. This is noteworthy, since hormonal increases have been linked to behavioural change (Offer and Church 1991, Susman and Dorn 1991). The actual mechanisms explaining the effect of hormones on behaviour are, however, not clear (Susman and Dorn 1991).

During late childhood and early adolescence, the levels of three types of hormones rapidly increase (Susman and Dorn 1991). These hormones are:

- **Gonadotropins:**    **Luteinising hormone (LH)**
  **Follicle stimulating hormone (FSH)**

These have a stimulating effect on the testes and ovaries

- **Gonadal steroids:**    **Testosterone (T)**
  **Oestrogen (E)**

These steroid hormones initiate and maintain masculine body changes in males and females; produced by the testis and ovary (Rabin and Chrousos 1991a)

- **Adrenal androgens:**    **Dehydroepiandosterone (DHEA)**
  **Dehydroepiandosterone sulphate (DHEAS)**

These are secreted by the adrenal cortex and cause masculine-like changes in the male or female body. Excess production of this hormone may result in ambiguous development of the sex organs in the female foetus as well as heightened sexual activity in adolescents (Rabin and Chousos 1991b).

It is beyond the scope of this chapter to explain in any detail the functions of these hormones and their relationship with observable behaviour. Suffice to say that the link between some hormones and behaviour has been well recorded. Research findings have demonstrated a relationship between certain hormones and aggressive and 'acting out' behaviour among boys, but not girls (Susman and Dorn 1991). A link has also been demonstrated between hormone levels and sexual motivation, although the effects appear to be different for boys than girls. (This point will be taken up again in Chapter 6.)

Some evidence suggests a link between hormonal changes and depressive affect, particularly among girls (Paikoff and Brooks-Gunn 1990; see also Chapter 10). Findings, however, appear less clear with respect to hormones and mood lability. Hormonal changes have also been implicated in changes in the parent-child relationship (Paikoff and Brooks-Gunn 1991), through their effect on secondary sex characteristics. Teenagers react differently to these changes, which have an impact upon social and familial relationships and child-parent communication (see also Chapter 3).

## Evaluation

Since the early work of Gesell, modern technology has enabled us to make great strides in our ability to detect hormonal levels (some quite small) and to link these with changes in adolescent behaviour. This link remains correlational, and more sophisticated research is required in order to detect any cause-effect relationships.

## The Nature-Nurture Debate

This review of theories of adolescence has uncovered an age-long debate, namely, the relative effects on behaviour of heredity versus the environment. Unfortunately, this debate has at times taken on ideological overtones. Objective analysis, however, would reveal that human development, rather than being influenced by only one determinant, reflects the interaction between the forces of heredity and genetic endowment on the one hand, and the influences of the environment on the other. Thus, this viewpoint recognises that behaviour is multi-dimensional and is influenced by a range of different factors.

Each of the theories presented in this chapter emphasises different sides of the nature-nurture debate. Freud, for example, emphasised inner sexual urges and drives, at the same time recognising the importance of parent-child relationships by referring to such issues as identification with the parent. Most psychologists today would argue that both heredity and environment determine behaviour. As Miller (1989: 25) notes:

> The way that heredity is expressed depends on the specific environment in which this expression occurs. In other words, a given hereditary influence can have different behavioral effects in different environments.

## Summary

The importance of the adolescent period as worthy of academic study is firmly established in psychology. This chapter has noted traditional images of youth as well as recognised developmental tasks. It was suggested that, with regard to images of youth, an enduring stereotype is one of turbulence, exuberance and passion. Certainly, adolescents tend to live life 'intensely' as they play to imaginary audiences and create personal fables (Elkind 1967). However, the view that this period is one of 'storm and stress' is increasingly being questioned (Gecas and Seff 1990). With respect to noted developmental tasks, some of these (e.g. preparation for marriage) can be questioned in the light of changing cultural norms and expectations.

This chapter briefly reviewed several important theories of adolescent development. Theories serve an important function since they direct our thinking and help us to understand our observations of adolescent behaviour and interpretations of research data. What is quite clear is that each theory highlights unique or selected aspects of development. Some are based on extensive laboratory research, while others are grounded in observation and subjective interpretation. No theory, however, is absolutely comprehensive, nor is it able fully to explain adolescent development in all its richness and diversity. It is suggested that each contains elements that aid us in understanding adolescence.

In the following chapters we shall consider some important aspects of adolescents' social development. The necessity for considering each topic will be highlighted, followed by a careful consideration of available research evidence. Each chapter will conclude by considering the fit between theory and available research data. We begin by considering adolescents' attempts to understand the self and achieve a personal identity.

## Additional Reading

Crain, W. (1985) *Theories of Development: Concepts and Applications*. Englewood Cliffs, N.J.: Prentice-Hall

Miller, P. (1989) *Theories of Developmental Psychology* (2nd edn). New York: W.H. Freeman and Co.

Muuss, R. (1988) *Theories of Adolescence* (5th edn) New York: Random House

Petersen, A. (1988) 'Adolescent Development,' *Annual Review of Psychology* 39: 583–607

## Exercises

1. Which theory do you find most helpful when thinking about adolescent development? Explain why you find this particular theory appealing. What are its strengths/weaknesses compared with others?
2. List *your* developmental tasks of adolescence. How do they differ from those of the Newmans, for instance?

# 2 Identity and the Self

## Introduction

As the individual progresses from infancy and childhood into adolescence, an important developmental task is the awareness and acceptance of self: that is, the teenager must develop a sense of identity and discover just *who* he or she is. This means that as teenagers mature, they come to the realisation that they differ from others in the social environment in important and fundamental ways. It is desirable to come to terms with one's self as a unique individual and reach acceptance of what one is: someone of value and worth. A crucial aspect of development during these years is attaining a sense of psychological well-being, a sense of knowing where one is going (Erikson 1968: 165).

Fundamental to identity formation is the merging of one's past with future aspirations, while at the same time recognising one's present talents, limitations and characteristics (Newman and Newman 1988). Not only is this an important aspect of identity formation, it is also a relatively difficult task and requires of the adolescent a fine sense of judgement and level-headedness. Once the task is complete, the person can expect to experience increased awareness of self-worth and importance, as well as a sense of self-assurance.

The processes of identity formation and self-conceptualisation have their roots in infancy. This is characterised by the emergence of self-recognition. We know that at a very young age (by about 12–18 months), the child is aware of others as quite separate and distinct from the self. Identity formation and the development of self-awareness continue throughout adolescence and beyond. Of importance during adolescence is the coincidence of developing identity and self-concept with physical and sexual maturation. Thus, the teenager has the challenging task of integrating his or her physical, sexual, and psychological identities.

In this chapter, we shall examine the nature and development of adolescent identity. We shall also examine the concept of self and the formation of sex-role identity. We begin with identity formation.

## Identity Formation

Identity formation and development are synonymous with the work of Erik Erikson (1968). Although he never trained as a psychologist (indeed, he holds no formal academic qualification), he has been recognised by the American Psychological Association for his theoretical contributions to psychology. In 1955 he was elected a Fellow of the Division of Developmental Psychology. Many of his ideas were adopted by the White House Conference on Children, and in 1960 he was offered a professorship at Harvard University (Crain 1985, Sprinthall and Collins 1988).

Strongly influenced by the work of Sigmund and Anna Freud, Erikson proposed psychosocial stages of development. Seen as an expansion of Freud's psychosexual stages of development (see Chapter 1), Erikson's proposals emphasise the importance of the social context and social forces in the life of the individual.

Unlike Freud, Erikson's stage theory encompasses the whole of the life span. It does not concentrate on sexual drives and instincts, but rather focuses on social drives and the impact of social experience (Gray 1991). A further essential feature is that each stage is characterised by two opposing poles, reflecting what has been referred to as a 'social crisis' (Muuss 1988). Many such crises are faced throughout life. One pole or possible response option ensures positive emotional development, while the other hinders such growth. Throughout development, therefore, the individual faces many choices, the outcome of which often determines future behaviour. Although a certain amount of tension may exist between any two given poles, one should not assume that all teenagers will experience turmoil (Douvan and Adelson 1966, Noller and Patton 1990). Generally, successful resolution of one stage facilitates the successful resolution of the following one (Erikson 1968).

According to Erikson there are eight stages across the life span. They are:

| | |
|---|---|
| • Trust vs. mistrust | birth to 1 year |
| • Autonomy vs. shame and doubt | 1 to 3 years |
| • Initiative vs. guilt | 3 to 5 years |
| • Industry vs. inferiority | 5 to 12 years |
| • Indentity vs. identity confusion | adolescence |
| • Intimacy vs. isolation | young adulthood |
| • Generativity vs. stagnation | middle adulthood |
| • Integrity vs. despair | late adulthood to death. |

A healthy or *vital* personality weathers each of these psychosocial stages to emerge with an enhanced sense of what Erikson calls inner unity (Erikson 1968). Progressing through each stage, the individual faces a potential crisis or turning point. Erikson sees each phase as a crucial period during which the individual is susceptible to maladjustment, although successful resolution often facilitates positive emotional and social adjustment. It is not possible here to discuss each of Erikson's life stages. Rather, attention will be devoted to identity vs. identity confusion, which is salient during the adolescent years.

## Adolescent Identity

Adolescents find themselves caught between childhood and adulthood. They must deal with physiological maturity and the impending demands and roles of an adult life. It is not surprising, suggests Erikson, that teenagers, living in a 'no-man's-land' become preoccupied with their own subculture and initial identity formation. In this regard, the influence of the peer group assumes a growing importance (see also Chapter 4). As the adolescent explores an awakening socio-emotional, sexual and physical identity, the peer group will play a prominent role in providing acceptable role models, and will set the boundaries for behaviour. The growing importance of this group will totally engage the teenager. It is possible to explain this process in the following terms (Muuss 1988: 61):

> Conforming to the expectations of peers helps adolescents find out how certain roles fit them. The peer group, the clique . . . aid the individual in the search for a personal identity, since they provide both a role model and a specific social feedback.

A fundamental task for the adolescent is the integration of biological and cognitive change, own free choice, and the pressures of parents and peers. Very often, adolescents feel impelled by their friends to engage in new behaviour. At the same time, teenagers must confront the expectations of their parents, whose values often contradict those of the peer group. Thus the adolescent walks a fine line in balancing others' demands and personal needs. To save face and avoid embarrassment, it is important that decisions reached are seen to be those of the teenager.

Implicit in identity formation is role experimentation (Newman and Newman 1988). Whereas younger children are more narrowly socialised into what is acceptable behaviour, teenagers are aware of a variety of behaviours, roles, values and life styles. In this respect, social modelling is important, with adolescents learning from external agents such as friends, magazines, and television. Within the limitations set by the family, and with encouragement from friends, adolescents are likely to experiment with a range of behaviours and roles as they set out to achieve their identity. In experimenting with different modes of conduct, they may challenge family norms; this often results in parent-adolescent misunderstanding and conflict.

Heterosexual relations during the adolescent years form an integral part of self exploration and identity formation. These friendships, as well as the more serious instances of 'being in love,' are also a form of role experimentation and assist teenagers in uncovering their underlying socio-emotional and sexual identities. Moreover, such close and more intimate friendships act as a sounding board (see Chapter 4) and reflect one's own values, attitudes and emotions. As such, they are an invaluable part of self-growth and identity formation. As Erikson (1968: 132) puts it:

> To a considerable extent adolescent love is an attempt to arrive at a definition of one's identity by projecting one's diffused self-image on another and by seeing it thus reflected and gradually clarified.

In this wider search for meaning, it is important that adolescents avoid *identity confusion*. Unless they successfully resolve their identity and move beyond their childhood identifications, then the adolescent process will remain incomplete (Erikson 1968). As we have been reminded (Muuss 1988), personal identity does not necessarily come with age, as does physical maturity. Teenagers need actively to seek out and uncover their identity and come to terms with their own shortcomings and inadequacies. In some individuals, this process is still underway during early adulthood.

Since it is natural for adolescents to experiment with a wide variety of behaviours, roles and friendships, it follows that adolescents are particularly susceptible to *role diffusion*. Most of these activities and behaviours, argues Erikson, are simply experimentation in 'fantasy and introspection' (p. 164) and serve, ultimately, to clarify personal identity.

Closely linked with the development of a personal identity are vocational identity and a personal philosophy (Muuss 1988). The development of the former is but one way by which the adolescent loosens what are normally close parental ties. Acquiring paid employment or embarking on post-school training signals a new-found identity and independence from the family. By developing a vocational identity, the individual lets it be known that he or she has skills and qualities others do not have. Thus, vocational identity reinforces personal identity.

The inability of some teenagers to develop a vocational identity or to acquire paid employment, has detrimental effects on identity formation and self-esteem. This view is shared by many authors. In one study, for example, the researchers (Winefield and Winefield 1992) conducted a longitudinal study of Australian youth. They were interested in the effects of employment, post-school education at university and unemployment on the mental health of school leavers. The respondents' psychological health was assessed in various ways: self-esteem, locus of control, depressive effect and negative mood. The results showed that the employed group as well as the students had greater psychological well-being on all measures than the unemployed group. Thus a vocational identity, or just being employed, reinforces, for the young teenager, a sense of identity, leading to overall psychological health.

Not all adolescents accomplish identity formation adequately. Many difficulties and challenges remain unresolved beyond the teenage years and may only be accomplished in early adulthood, or later. The death of a loved one or the breaking off of a close relationship can plunge the adolescent into a new crisis which can take some time to resolve. Identity, therefore, is established at different times for different people, although it is desirable that the adolescent makes some progress toward identity formation. Perhaps the best one dares hope for is that, upon leaving adolescence, teenagers will have grown in maturity, independence and have acquired some sense of psychological well-being and personal accomplishment.

## Identity Statuses

Marcia (1966; 1980) has elaborated Erikson's (1968) model by suggesting that adolescents can resolve their identities in one of several ways. Central to identity formation are *crisis* (or exploration) and *commitment*. Crisis refers to teenagers selecting various behavioural and attitudinal options or alternatives. Commitment refers to the extent to which teenagers make a personal investment in attitudes and behaviours. As some authors (e.g. Newman and Newman 1988: 552) see it:

> Essential to identity achievement is that commitments be made following a period of experimentation or crisis and that these commitments are perceived as an expression of personal choice.

Crisis and commitment vary from individual to individual, giving rise to the following four *identity statuses*:

- Identity diffusion
- Identity foreclosure
- Identity moratorium
- Identity achievement

### Identity diffusion

These teenagers have not yet made a personal commitment to a set of beliefs or an occupation. They have not yet felt compelled to make choices from a range of available options. In other words, they have not yet experienced an identity crisis (Muuss 1988).

Of course, it is quite natural that teenagers in early adolescence may have diffused identities. They may not yet have faced crises regarding attitudes, values or behaviour and are therefore unlikely to have made a personal commitment. Should identity diffusion persist into late adolescence or adulthood, however, this would be cause for some concern.

Identity diffused adolescents appear to have lower self-esteem scores than those in other status groups. They also appear more willing than other groups of teenagers to accept incorrect personality descriptions about themselves, and are prone to change their own opinion (Muuss 1988). These findings therefore underscore just how little these individuals know about their true identities.

### Identity foreclosure

These adolescents have made a personal commitment to certain values, beliefs, acceptable behaviours and an occupation or course of study. They have not, however, experienced a crisis, nor have they had to struggle and consider different alternatives. Most often, these teenagers simply adopt the beliefs and wishes of their parents.

Foreclosure teenagers have been strongly socialised by their parents or peer group. Muuss (1988) notes that they have not been sufficiently challenged to make their own decisions and have adopted a set of 'preprogrammed' (p. 70) values and beliefs.

### Identity moratorium

Adolescents in this phase may be experiencing a crisis, but have not yet made choices or a personal commitment. In some instances (e.g. 'What should I do once I have left school?'), it may take some time to resolve this crisis, and require professional guidance. During this stage, adolescents are engaged in a personal struggle and are busily evaluating alternatives.

It is quite likely during this phase for teenagers to experiment with different roles and behaviours. They may follow peer group pressure one moment and then abandon that for something else. Contact may be lost with friends, while new friendships are made. Although parents may find this rather tedious, the adolescent is fully engaged in identity formation. Moratorium, therefore, is essential for identity achievement (Marcia 1980).

*Identity achievement*
This stage is synonymous with maturity and, ultimately, identity formation. It marks the completion of adolescence, and signals that identity crises have been successfully resolved. Having experienced a crisis (or crises), the individual has now made a commitment. This is an important accomplishment. It has been suggested, therefore, that an achievement of identity helps link in the mind of the adolescent future aspirations with the past, thus creating a sense of personal continuity (Muuss 1988).

# Identity Statuses: Research Evidence

## Development of Identity

Not all teenagers who move into early adulthood will have accomplished complete identity achievement. According to some writers (e.g. Waterman 1982), one would expect developmental shifts to occur throughout adolescence. Such shifts or changes can take several forms. For example, it is possible for someone to be in the moratorium phase for most of adolescence before seriously contemplating making firm commitments.

Research evidence has shown that younger teenagers are more likely to be in the identity diffusion and foreclosure stages. One may therefore expect *progressive identity formation* (Waterman 1982) as adolescents move through the teenage years. This is manifest in a number of ways, such as stability of attitudes, values and personality traits.

It could be argued that the greatest advances in identity formation and achievement usually occur at university, due to a diversity of social and intellectual stimuli. A university education certainly appears to facilitate the development of vocational identity, although it has a negative effect upon the development of religious beliefs (Waterman 1982).

## Family relations and identity

Several research studies have examined family functioning and identity status among adolescents. The expectation is that adolescent competence and adjustment are related to the quality of family relations (Papini, Sebby and Clark 1989, Waterman 1982). Specifically, it is suggested that supportive and communicative families are likely to create a climate within which the adolescent is able to resolve crises and progress toward identity achievement. Parental rejection, on the other hand, has been found to be associated with a lack of identity crises (Papini *et al.* 1989). Table 2.1 summarises some of the family antecedents of identity statuses.

Of particular interest is the finding that identity exploration among adolescents can still occur, notwithstanding disagreements between parents and adolescents. This is just the opposite of what happens among foreclosure adolescents, who adopt (without dissension, it seems) parental belief systems. It has been noted that greater emotional distance between an adolescent and parents tends to be associated with an increased exploration of the self among teenagers, a prerequisite for identity achievement (Papini *et al.* 1989). It is suggested, nonetheless, that communicative families have the necessary skills to facilitate the resolution of crises, thus enhancing adolescent identity formation.

Other writers (e.g. Campbell, Adams and Dobson 1984) have also recognised the role of the family in facilitating identity achieve-

**Table 2.1** *Family Antecedents of Identity Statuses*

| Identity Diffusion | Adolescents report distance from their families<br>Parents are indifferent, inactive, detached, not understanding and rejecting<br>College males likely to come from broken homes |
| --- | --- |
| Identity Foreclosure | Adolescents view family as being child-centred<br>Fathers possessive and intrusive to sons<br>Fathers supportive and encouraging of daughters<br>Adolescents involve the family in important decisions |
| Identity Moratorium | Adolescents likely to be in conflict with parents<br>Sons tend to make decisions on their own |
| Identity Achievement | Adolescents likely to be in conflict with parents<br>Sons tend to make decisions on their own<br>Two-thirds of females in one study from broken homes, or had experienced death of one parent. |

*Source:*  Waterman 1982

ment. They argue that adolescents need to develop independence from their family, yet at the same time maintain a degree of connectedness, thereby enhancing identity formation. On the other hand, poor communication, weak affectionate bonding with parents, and psychological withdrawal, often lead to feelings of insecurity and inadequate identity formation among youth.

A principal ingredient therefore, appears to be the degree of separation or independence from parents, while also maintaining emotional warmth. Diffused youth, it would seem, lack a secure family base from which to engage in identity-seeking behaviour. Foreclosed youth, while having a strong emotional attachment to their parents, lack independence. This leads one to the conclusion (Campbell *et al.* 1984: 512) that

> a moderate degree of connectedness, reflected through shared affection and an acceptance of individuality, provides the psychological foundation and security to begin the searching process for self-defined commitments.

It has also been argued by some writers that a key factor in understanding family relationships and identity is pubertal change. These dramatic physical changes signal that the adolescent is about to leave childhood and assume new roles. It is not surprising, therefore, that the quality of family relations change (see also Chapter 3). This combination of physical maturation and a change in family relations is an important impetus for identity achievement (Papini *et al.* 1989).

## Personality Traits

Identity status has been found to be related to certain personality traits. In one study (Adams, Abraham and Markstrom 1987), it was found that identity achieved teenagers were more self-assured and tended not to be self-conscious. By engaging in identity exploration, it would seem that teenagers develop a satisfying self. They are also unlikely to be anxious or embarrassed should they be the focus of attention.

Other personality traits have also been found to be related to identity status and are reviewed by Muuss (1988). Briefly, he notes that foreclosures tend to be conventional and more authoritarian than others. Moratorium teenagers are more questioning of authority and more anxious than other statuses, which may be due to the fact that they are experiencing a crisis and are insecure. Identity achieved and moratorium teenagers seem to have the highest self-esteem. One study, however, noted that foreclosure women also have high self-esteem scores.

## Sex Differences

It is quite clear from the above finding that sex differences may exist with respect to identity status and personality variables. Indeed, one review of research findings in this area leads to the conclusion that the developmental paths towards identity achievement may differ for the two sexes (Muuss 1988). Among males, identity achievers and moratorium respondents tend to be closely grouped. They are usually internally controlled and more resistant to manipulation of self-esteem. They also tend to score higher on tasks such as concept attainment.

Among females, identity achievement and foreclosure statuses are normally close together. These teenagers have high self-esteem, are more resistant to peer group pressure, less anxious and more independent. Some authors, therefore, have suggested that the achievement and moratorium statuses are stable for men, while the achievement and foreclosure statuses are stable for women.

## Identity Formation: An Evaluation

It has been suggested that identity achievement as originally formulated is male oriented in that it espouses the values associated with white middle class males, while under-valuing female virtues, such as warmth and understanding (McKinney and Vogel 1987, Wearing 1984).

It is also doubtful whether Erikson's (1968) view's on identity achievement can be applied to working class youth. It has been noted (Wearing 1984: 18) that:

> Research which has applied Erikson's identity statuses to employed working class youth . . . indicates that for these youth the route to identity is more concrete and direct than for their middle-class counterparts. They do not have the luxury of the extended moratorium associated with tertiary education.

It would appear from these arguments that middle class youth (particularly those at university or college) have a distinct advantage over their working class counterparts. Middle class youth have an opportunity while at university to engage in leisurely identity exploration, particularly of a vocational nature.

As far as Marcia's (1980) elaboration of Erikson's stages is concerned, some authors have questioned whether statuses can be referred to as stages or not. Some have also noted that the developmental sequence of the identity statuses remains unclear (McKinney and Vogel 1987).

In conclusion, it has been argued that, rather than adolescents having to acquire *stable* identities, it might be more desirable that they acquire *flexible* ones (Wearing 1984). Societal values and norms are in a state of constant flux. For example, adolescents in Central and Eastern Europe are living amid radical social and political change. This may require that adolescents re-evaluate any commitments they may already have made, particularly of an ideological nature. In many Western nations, teenagers have to cope with relatively high levels of youth unemployment, and changing views about such matters as abortion, drugs and gender. It is therefore increasingly unrealistic to expect a teenager to adopt belief systems believing that these will remain largely unchanged throughout life.

# The Developing Self-system

As identity formation and achievement imply a discovery of the self, it follows that they cannot easily be divorced from such concepts as self-understanding, self-concept, and self-esteem.

Early writers, such as William James (1892), suggested that there are two crucial or fundamental aspects of the self (Harter 1983). These are the self as actor (the 'I') and the self as the object of evaluation (the 'Me'). The I observes the Me; the Me characterises the individual as a unique being, while the I interprets experience (Damon and Hart 1982).

## Self-concept: The Development of I and Me

As noted earlier, the journey of self-discovery begins in infancy. Young children of about eighteen months of age are aware of others as distinct from the self. It is around this age that children recognise their reflected image. When viewing themselves in a mirror, they may smile, chatter to themselves or even reach out to their reflection (Brooks-Gunn and Lewis 1984).

During childhood, the young individual is busily formulating a 'personal theory' or *self-concept* (Berk 1989). As the child matures, this takes on different forms, first being rather rudimentary and ill-defined. The young child is aware of being 'a boy' or 'a girl'. This is referred to as the *categorical self* (Berk 1989).

As the child develops cognitively, the view of the self undergoes some change. The pre-schooler becomes aware of an *inner self*, that is, thoughts that no-one else has access to. Later, a *psychological self* emerges which continuously changes in nature, throughout adolescence (Harter 1990). One study (Montemayor and Eisen 1977) demonstrated that, as children grow, their self-concept becomes more abstract. This move towards more abstract and subjective descriptions is illustrated in Figure 2.1, which sets out the self-descriptions of a seventeen-year-old adolescent and two younger children.

The self-descriptions of older adolescents are more tortuous and evaluative. Whereas the descriptions of children can be described as 'unreflective self-acceptance', those of the adolescent are more searching (Harter 1983). Thus, it is clear that the self-concept changes as the individual matures cognitively. Research evidence and theory indicate that, as identity achievement is reached, the searching process subsides to some extent (but see Wearing 1984).

Based on a review of the literature, Damon and Hart (1982)

**Figure 2.1** *Self-descriptions of Three Individuals*

---

**9-year-old boy**
My name is Bruce C. I have brown eyes. I have brown hair. I have brown eyebrows. I'm nine years old. I LOVE! Sports. I have seven people in my family. I have great! eye site. I have lots! of friends. I live on 1923 Pinecrest Dr. I'm going on 10 in September. I'm a boy. I have a uncle that is almost 7 feet tall. My school is Pinecrest. My teacher is Mrs V. I play Hockey! I am almost the smartest boy in the class. I LOVE! food. I love fresh air. I LOVE School.

**11¹/₂-year-old girl**
My name is A. I'm a human being. I'm a girl. I'm a truthful person. I'm not pretty. I do so-so in my studies. I'm a very good cellist. I'm a very good pianist. I'm a little bit tall for my age. I like several boys. I like several girls. I'm old-fashioned. I play tennis. I am a *very* good swimmer. I try to be helpful. I'm always ready to be friends with anybody. Mostly I'm good, but I lose my temper. I'm not well-liked by some girls and boys. I don't know if I'm liked by boys or not.

**17-year-old girl**
I am a human being. I am a girl. I am an individual. I don't know who I am. I am a Pisces. I am a moody person. I am an indecisive person. I am an ambitious person. I am a very curious person. I am not an individual. I am a loner. I am an American (God help me). I am a Democrat. I am a liberal person. I am a radical. I am a conservative. I am a pseudoliberal. I am an atheist. I am not a classifiable person (i.e. I don't want to be).

---

*Source:*    Montemayor and Eisen 1977

have suggested that the development of an understanding of Me proceeds through four phases. These are:

- The physical self
- The active self
- The social self
- The psychological self.

The social self becomes important in early adolescence, and by late adolescence, there is the realisation that personality traits form the basis of many actions of the self. The psychological self is fully developed by late adolescence, when belief systems characterise the active self. This congruency between belief systems and true self is one of the hallmarks of identity achievement.

Burns (1979) has remarked that Me is indistinguishable from self-concept or one's judgement of self. This includes what one believes to be the perceptions of others as well as one's ideal self. These perceptions are the result of everyday experiences and inter-actions with others.

As the understanding of Me evolves, so too is there a gradual emerging of the I. The following aspects are involved (Damon and Hart 1982):

- Continuity:          An unchanging physical self
- Distinctiveness:     No one experiences things as I do; I am a unique individual
- Volition:            Mind can deceive others; can manipulate self's experience. I can make decisions
- Self-recognition:    Recognition of conscious and unconscious processes.

## Self-evaluation

It has been suggested that a constituent part of the self-concept is self-evaluation (Burns 1979: 55). In evaluating the self, one is making:

> . . . a conscious judgement regarding the significance, and importance of oneself or of facts of oneself.

One therefore makes a judgement about one's behaviour and abilities, personality and physical attributes. Self-evaluation comprises three important facets (Burns 1979). In the first instance, one has an ideal self, that is, a view of how one would like to be. One sets out to attain the ideal and to achieve self-actualisation.

This means that we strive to be self-sufficient and autonomous individuals. Self-actualisation fosters personal growth (Liebert and Spiegler 1990). Problems of adjustment arise when large discrepancies exist between the ideal self and the real or actual one. If the ideal self appears out of reach or unattainable, low self-esteem could result.

The second important facet relates to our beliefs about how others view us. Well-known authors such as Cooley and Mead (cited in Berk 1989) have argued that an important process of developing a psychological self is the ability to accurately perceive what others think of us. Such an ability is more evident with older and more cognitively mature adolescents. Should one consistently perceive others' evaluations of us as negative, this is likely to lower individuals' self-concept. Naturally, this process also works in reverse. One may deliberately misinterpret a negative experience in order to maintain positive self-esteem. This is referred to as *perceptual distortion* (Liebert and Spiegler 1990).

It is therefore not surprising that significant others (such as parents, teachers and friends) play an important role in how adolescents evaluate themselves. Some authors have examined the extent to which these effects are age-related. Not surprisingly, researchers have found that younger children and adolescents tend to be more influenced by the beliefs of parents and teachers, whereas older adolescents are more likely to be sensitive to the opinions of peers (but see Lackovic-Grgin and Dekovic 1990).

## Multidimensionality of the Self-concept

In addition to making an overall evaluation about oneself (e.g. 'I am liked by most people'), it is also possible to evaluate various aspects of the self (e.g. 'Most people are better than me at mathematics, although I am quite good at marathon running'). The self-concept is therefore a multidimensional or many-sided construct and evaluations may include academic and physical ability as well as one's relationships with significant others (see also Harter 1990). Young people are well aware of their strong and weak points.

Shavelson and colleagues (1976) have also proposed that the self-concept is hierarchically ordered. Individual experiences of a particular nature (e.g. not getting on with one's mathematics teacher and consequently not doing as well as one could), have implications for academic self-evaluations ('Perhaps I am not good at mathematics after all' or 'I am not good at schoolwork'). Such evaluations may, ultimately, have consequences for one's general

**Figure 2.2** *The Structure of Self-concept*

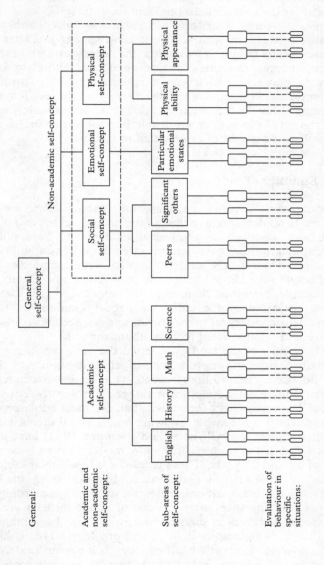

*Source:* Shavelson *et al.* 1976

self-concept. In this sense, then, self-concept has a hierarchical structure. This is illustrated in Figure 2.2.

One empirical study (Marsh, Relich and Smith 1983) found support for the multidimensional nature of the self-concept among young adolescents. The various facets of self-concept showed predictable correlations with academic achievement and attributions for success and failure. It was noted that adolescents who explained personal success in terms of their *own* effort and ability were most likely to have elevated levels of self-concept. Not surprisingly, academic performance was closely related to academic self-concept. Other factors such as achievement motivation and the expectation of succeeding, are also important factors in this regard, and will be discussed in more detail in Chapter 5.

## The Stability of Self-concept

Although early theorists such as Hall (cited in Petersen 1988) referred to adolescence as a time of 'storm and stress', that view has since been openly challenged (see also Chapter 1). Several important empirical studies have demonstrated the relative stability of the self-concept during the adolescent years. One longitudinal study conducted in the United States (Savin-Williams and Demo 1984), for example, examined changes to the experienced self (that is, the self as evaluated by the individual), the presented self (that is, the self which we reveal to the world) and self-feelings (those more diverse and differentiated feelings about the self).

The results of the study supported the view that there are no dramatic changes in various aspects of self-evaluation. Any changes that do occur, the authors argued, tend to be associated with normal adolescent development rather than a turbulent adolescence. The researchers concluded that, for most adolescents, the self-concept is quite stable, showing only gradual increase.

Other studies (e.g. O'Malley and Bachman 1983) have demonstrated that self-concept scores show moderate rises between the ages of 13 and 23 years. These researchers based their conclusion on the results of a large longitudinal study conducted in the United States. Such a rise in self-concept is not surprising, according to the authors. For instance, after the age of about thirteen years, the adolescent increases in physical size, while also beginning to assume adult roles, responsibilities and privileges. This is likely to have a positive effect on the self-concept. It is also around this time that most adolescents make the transition to high school. For some, this is a stressful period, resulting in lower self-concept. This is only a temporary phenomenon, of course, whereafter self-concept levels can be expected to increase.

Other writers (e.g. Harter 1990) have also suggested that, with increasing age, teenagers experience more autonomy and are also more likely to associate with support groups, peers and friends who enhance self-evaluation. Once the teenager leaves school, academic achievement becomes less salient. The adolescent is therefore more likely to judge him or herself in terms of personal happiness and life satisfaction.

## Sex Differences in Self-concept

The question as to whether there are sex differences in regard to various psychological traits is an important issue in contemporary psychology, generating much research and debate. Much has been written on this topic, including the now classic volume by Maccoby and Jacklin (1974). They reviewed the literature concerning sex differences in self-concept, their review of adolescent studies yielding equivocal findings. Only a small number of studies showed that males have higher general self-concept than females. In fact, many of the studies reviewed found no significant sex differences at all.

A different picture emerges when considering various *facets* of self-concept, however (Marsh *et al.* 1983, Maccoby and Jacklin 1974). For example, it has been observed that girls are much more likely to underestimate their chances of success at a task than are boys. The following explanations are feasible (Maccoby and Jacklin 1974): firstly, observed sex differences may reflect the *nature* of the task, rather than real sex differences. Thus experimental task may be confounded with self-concept. Secondly, girls may also be more willing to accept a much broader range of responses and performance as being compatible with a healthy self-concept.

According to another report (Marsh *et al.* 1983), boys have significantly higher self-concepts in physical ability and mathematics, although girls have higher self-concepts in reading. This seems to be a well-established finding, and future research should endeavour to determine to what extent this is due to the influence of socialisation processes. Marsh and his colleagues also noted that self-concept scores varied according to the school the students attended (see also Chapter 5). Sex differences were accentuated in the public co-educational schools, thus maintaining traditional stereotypes. Although sex differences were also observed among the private school students, the effects were much smaller. This led Marsh and his colleagues (1983: 180) to conclude that:

reference groups that contain both boys and girls accentuated sex differences in self-concept in the direction of traditional sexual stereotypes.

## Sex-role Identity

The extent to which we adopt typical 'male' or 'female' behaviours has, with the advent of the women's movement, given rise to considerable research and theorising in psychology (Huston 1983). Out-dated values and perspectives on gender-appropriate behaviours have largely been abandoned. The prevailing view now seems to be that sex-role stereotypes are constraining to a large extent, and therefore limit one's identity exploration.

### Theories of Sex-role Identity Formation

There are a number of influential theoretical perspectives which are useful in explaining the formation of sex-role identities (Archer 1992, Huston 1983). Each will be briefly described.

*Social Learning Theories*
We noted in the previous chapter that one can learn behaviour through imitation and observation. We learn gender-appropriate behaviours in very much the same way. Traditionally, gender-appropriate behaviours have been reinforced, while unacceptable behaviours have been frowned upon. A young boy playing with his sister's dolls, for example, is unlikely to receive much encouragement and reinforcement from his father. On the contrary, his father is likely to be quite agitated, regarding this as gender-inappropriate play (Langlois and Downs 1980).

The previous chapter explained that social learning is distinguishable from more classic forms of learning, in that it highlights the importance of *observation*. Therefore, the girl who notices that it is only mother who keeps house, may come to believe that it is inappropriate for males to do such chores.

*Cognitive Developmental Theory*
According to this perspective, teenagers' *understanding* of masculinity and femininity is important, rather than their actual behaviour. Teenagers look for consistency between understanding and behaviour, and it is the former which seems to determine the latter (Archer 1992). Naturally, the understanding of concepts such as

gender is age-related. As a consequence, therefore, one progresses through various stages of sex-role identity formation with increasing age (Huston 1983, Archer 1992).

One exponent of this view of sex-role identity formation is Kohlberg (Hughes and Noppe 1985, Huston 1983). In the first stage, according to Kohlberg, young children of two to four years recognise that they are a 'boy' or a 'girl'. They learn from their parents or siblings about acceptable and gender-appropriate behaviours. Children interpret their daily experiences in accordance with their understanding of 'boyness' or 'girlness'. They also derive pleasure from gender-appropriate behaviour.

In middle childhood, individuals are aware that they possess gender constancy: that is, that they will one day grow up to be either male or female. At this age, children adhere rigidly to rules about being a member of a gender group and cross-sex behaviour is unacceptable.

During adolescence, individuals are asking the question 'Who am I?' Not only is the teenager confronting the psychological self, but also the sexual self, brought on by rapid physical and biological maturation (Hughes and Noppe 1985). Whereas early adolescents have quite fixed ideas about appropriate behaviours for the sexes, they become more flexible in their views as they get older. In late adolescence, it is believed that teenagers are much more willing to adopt either 'masculine' or 'feminine' traits in accordance with their own evolving personal identity. It is during the latter part of this psychological orientation period (Hughes and Noppe 1985: 48) that:

> Sex-stereotyped traits are not assumed to be crucial aspects of personal identity. Principles of equality and freedom are proposed as standards for behavior, and are used to define an ideal model of personal and interpersonal functioning.

### Gender Schema Theories

It was suggested that an important element of the cognitive developmental perspective is the adolescent's understanding of being male or female. Gender schema theories have extended this view by arguing that sex-role stereotypes set the framework within which much of our thinking about gender-related matters is conducted. Thus, we develop schema or cognitive frameworks which help organise our information and help us interpret and process stimuli. Schema are especially useful in new and unusual situations in that we draw on previous experience in helping us deal with current events. Schema, moreover, may be culturally driven or learned from parents, role models or friends.

Like most frames of reference, schema can bias our interpretation of information. It has been found, for instance, that individuals who tend to adhere to sex-role stereotypes are much more likely to distort or to reconstruct information to match their world view or schema. In one report (Archer 1992), research is highlighted which demonstrates how those holding traditional sex-role views reconstructed non-traditional pictures (e.g. a female doctor) into more traditional ones (e.g. a male doctor).

In summary, although schemas are useful in helping us process information quickly and deal with novel situations, they oversimplify our social world and are sometimes based on incorrect information.

## Sex-role Identity and Adjustment

Is there a relationship between sex-role identity and psychological adjustment? There are three models which make quite different predictions about the relationship between sex-role identity and adjustment. The first is referred to as the *congruence* model (Whitley 1983). It assumes that masculinity and femininity are opposite poles of a single continuum. According to this model, masculinity and femininity are mutually exclusive and incompatible. The model predicts that high self-concept is dependent upon one's sex-role orientation being congruent with one's gender. In its slightly reformulated version, the model predicts that high masculinity and low femininity in men, and high femininity and low masculinity in women are related to high self-concept.

The *androgyny* model suggests that individuals can incorporate both masculine and feminine traits to varying degree. This two-dimensional model (shown in Figure 2.3) gives rise to four sex-role types: androgynous, undifferentiated, masculine and feminine. It is therefore possible to fit into any one of the quadrants, irrespective of one's gender. The model predicts an association between androgyny and psychological well-being (Whitley 1983).

Finally, the *masculinity* model predicts that psychological well-being depends upon the masculinity component of androgyny (Whitley 1983). In other words, the femininity component makes only a very small contribution to overall well-being, suggesting that so-called masculine traits (e.g. dominance, assertiveness, etc.) are influential in explaining psychological adjustment.

Support for these models varies, and is largely dependent upon the samples studied and the measures used. Generally, most support has been found for the androgyny and masculinity models. In

**Figure 2.3** *The Two-dimensional Model of Sex-role Identity*

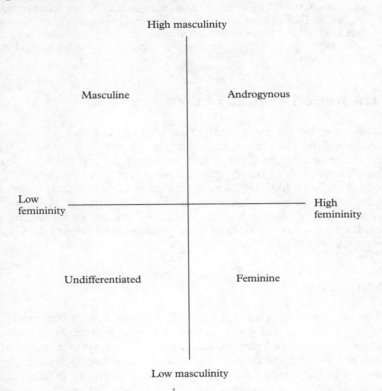

one study (Massad 1981), for example, it was found that, among adolescent females, both masculinity and femininity were related to positive self-esteem. Among adolescent males, high masculinity was associated with high self-esteem. It was also observed that androgynous and sex-typed males had higher self-esteem than cross-typed males. Androgynous females had higher self-esteem than either sex-typed or cross-typed females. Thus the results of this study suggest that adolescent females may be under more pressure than their male counterparts to adopt non-traditional sex-role traits.

A study among university students also found support for the androgyny and masculinity models. The authors (Orlofsky and O'Heron 1987: 1041) concluded as follows:

masculine qualities appear to have broadly positive implications for self-esteem and adjustment . . . Feminine qualities do not relate to self-esteem and adjustment indices as strongly or consistently as do masculine qualities . . . they do play a central role in more communal aspects of self-esteem while also contributing somewhat to more general aspects of adjustment.

## Theoretical Considerations

There can be no doubt that Erikson's (1968) views on identity formation have had an enormous impact on our thinking about the nature of adolescent identity and the search for self-meaning. His psycho-social stage theory (and the subsequent reformulations by others such as Marcia) have generated empirical research which has largely served to support its validity. Erikson broadened psychoanalytic theory to a considerable extent, and eloquently explained just how important social factors are in human development (Crain 1985).

## Summary

The development of one's identity is a crucial task for the adolescent. Of course, this process is not necessarily completed by the end of the teenage years. Indeed, some individuals continue with this task well into adulthood. Fortunately for many adolescents, by the time they leave school they have a fair idea of their sexual orientation and likely occupation. They have a fair sense of knowing just 'who I am' and 'where I am going'.

A vitally important aspect of identity formation is the development of a sexual identity. Thus by late adolescence, most teenagers are able to identify themselves as either hetero- or homosexual. This stage of the life span can be an agonising one as teenagers confront their sexuality and rapidly changing body. It is also quite clearly a time of excitement for many, as they contemplate life as an adult.

The development of a vocational identity is also seen as an integral part of the process of identity formation. For many teenagers, this process is much more difficult than it was only a generation ago. Most developed nations currently have relatively high levels of youth unemployment. Many manufacturing jobs have been lost, while the competition for university courses has become more acute. Thus governments and communities have an enormous responsibility to harness the talents of these teenagers and assist, as best they can, those who are at risk of long-term unemployment and its side-effects, such as depression and feelings of hopelessness.

As adolescents embark on identity formation, they are greatly influenced by their family and friends. Both act as sources of emotional support and psychological well-being. Both help mould teenagers' behaviour by setting the boundaries of what is acceptable. Sometimes these boundaries are contradictory. Most teenagers will accept them and experiment with a range of behaviours and roles. This is a natural part of growing up and helps define the self.

Another important influence on adolescent development and emotional adjustment is the family. It is to this important topic that we now turn.

## Additional Reading

Crain, W. (1985) *Theories of Development: Concepts and Applications*. Englewood Cliffs, N.J.: Prentice-Hall

Erikson, E. (1968) *Identity: Youth and Crisis*. New York: W.W. Norton and Co.

Marcia, J. (1966) 'Development and Validation of Ego-identity Status,' *Journal of Personality and Social Psychology* 3: 551–58

Muuss, R. (1988) *Theories of Adolescence* (5th edn). New York: Random House

## Exercise

1. To what extent are the development of a vocational and sexual identity during adolescence related to overall identity development? Can these develop in isolation from one another?

# 3 Family Influences

## Introduction

The young individual's first awareness and experience of other humans occurs in the context of the family. Indeed, it has been suggested that the quality of the attachment and bonding processes between parent and infant in the first few months of life are important for the later emotional health of the individual. The family is an important arena in which much learning about the world and general socialisation occurs. Research findings indicate that family relationships during adolescence have important flow-on effects for a number of domains, such as the autonomy and later independence of the individual (e.g. Coleman and Hendry 1990), adolescent self-esteem (e.g. Rosenberg and Kaplan 1982), individual pathology (e.g. Scott and Scott 1987), and problem behaviour (e.g. Barnes, Farrell and Windle 1990), to mention just a few.

The family is regarded by some as the most important support system available to the child and adolescent. Consequently, any dilutions of this support system through factors such as changes within the adolescent, parental separation or a particularly negative parenting style, have implications for adolescent functioning, adjustment and identity achievement. Indeed, changes in parent-adolescent relationships are of central concern to developmental psychology (Collins 1990).

In this chapter, several aspects of the parent-child relationship will be examined. Central to this discussion will be the extent to which these factors influence adolescent development. Of concern are the effects of parenting styles and control, and those of divorce and parental separation on adolescents' emotional adjustment. Attention will also be briefly paid to parent-adolescent communication, as well as the challenges teenagers face when they move into new families.

## Theoretical Perspectives

In an attempt to better understand family interactions, various theories of the family have been proposed. The following have been listed as particularly influential (Callan and Noller 1987): symbolic interactionism, social exchange theory and family systems theory.

Briefly, symbolic interactionism refers to attempts to view the world through the eyes of the adolescent. Key concepts (or symbols) include roles, categories, positions and definitions of situations. According to this view of the family, teenagers organise their behaviour and interact with others in terms of their perceptions of these symbols (Callan and Noller 1987). Adolescents and their parents fulfil quite different roles in the family and their interactions depend, to a large extent, on their definition of these roles. When adolescents respond to the actions of their parents, their response incorporates an *interpretation* of the parental action. According to this perspective, then, behaviour must be viewed in terms of perceptions and expectations of *other* family members.

Maximising rewards and minimising punishments is central to social exchange theory. Thus an adolescent may engage in some behaviours and not others in the hope that this might have some beneficial effect on someone else (e.g. smiling to gain approval). Such two-way exchanges occur in all person-to-person interactions.

Other writers have argued that the family should be viewed from a systems-oriented perspective, that is, the family is viewed as an integrated network of individuals and relationships. An underlying principle of this approach is that not only are all members of a system interconnected, but each has links outside it. Thus each element has the potential to have an effect on any other within the system and its immediate environment. According to Schneewind (1990), this perspective emphasises the organisation of the family in terms of relationships.

Likewise, Callan and Noller (1987: 33) have argued that:

> To see the family as a system, operating by system rules, with each part affecting the others in systematic ways is very different from seeing the family as a collection of individuals who happen to live in the same house.

According to the systems perspective, the family is regarded as an intricate arrangement of interconnecting relationships. Many family units are harmonious relationships, while some on occasion experience mild conflict. Although not all are characterised by conflict (see Noller and Patton 1990, Paikoff and Brooks-Gunn 1991), there appears to be no doubt that the *nature* of the parent-child relationship undergoes changes as the child approaches early adolescence. This is almost certain as the child faces, and parents witness, biological, cognitive and emotional change.

Three models implicating pubertal change as a determinant of parent-adolescent relationships have been proposed (Paikoff and

Brooks-Gunn 1991). It is possible to interpret these in the light of symbolic interactionism, social exchange theory and the systems perspective. In the first model, hormonal changes occurring within the child are likely to have an effect on his or her emotional lability, thus affecting interactions with parents. This has led some researchers to focus on such factors as depression and moodiness in adolescents, boys' increasing levels of aggression, and so forth.

Secondly, it is possible that the timing or rate of development of secondary sex characteristics in teenagers may influence the nature of parent-child relationships. This may occur by influencing individual perceptions. In one study, for instance, it was found that parents attached more importance to pubertal changes than did adolescents (Savin-Williams and Small 1986). No doubt, physical changes in the adolescent are a dramatic reminder to parents that their children are growing up and will soon take on new roles in society. The authors also found that parents were less apprehensive about early maturing sons and late maturing daughters. Such physical changes in the young adolescent symbolise the approach of adulthood and, according to Paikoff and Brooks-Gunn (1991: 51):

> are salient to both adolescent and parent, and they signal the incipient reproductive and social maturity of the child, an event laden with meaning.

Thirdly, pubertal changes interact with a number of other important factors to influence parent-adolescent relationships. Such factors may include social and cognitive changes in the child, particular individual and familial characteristics such as parenting styles and parent-child communication, perceptions of physical change by the adolescent and parents, and changes to the self-identity of the parent and child (Paikoff and Brooks-Gunn 1991).

## Models of Family Functioning

There are several different, although related, models of family functioning (Callan and Noller 1987, Walsh 1982). It is beyond the scope of this chapter to review these in detail. Suffice to say that some writers have proposed an *integrative* model of family functioning which combines elements and constructs of each of the major models. Accordingly, eight dimensions of healthy family functioning have been identified (Walsh 1982). These are:

- Individuation vs. enmeshment
- Mutuality vs. isolation
- Flexibility vs. rigidity

- Stability vs. disorganisation
- Clear vs. distorted perceptions
- Clear vs. role conflict
- Role reciprocity vs. conflictual roles
- Clear vs. diffuse generation boundaries.

Walsh (1982) stresses that these factors characterise normal family functioning, and that an improvement in one is likely to lead to an improvement in others. It is also important to bear in mind that 'normal' functioning is not the sole prerogative of the traditional family unit. This point will be emphasised at different times throughout this chapter.

Although the nature of the parent–child relationship in nearly all families will undergo some change across time, certain familial characteristics have been identified as crucial in predicting the psychological adjustment of adolescents. Some of these will now be briefly discussed.

## Parent-adolescent Influences

The family plays an important role in shaping child and adolescent behaviour (Jaccard and Dittus 1991, Bahr 1991). This is not to say that children are not influenced by other factors, like social experience or peer groups. Rather it is suggested that the influence of the family is pivotal. Parents influence their teenagers in several ways (Jaccard and Dittus 1991).

In the first place, parents serve as role models, and teenagers learn by observation and imitation. Secondly, parenting styles and child-rearing patterns have an important influence on teenagers' social and emotional development (see later). Thirdly, parents transmit their values and morals to their children. Included here are general belief systems about what constitutes acceptable behaviour. Finally, parents are an important source of information on a range of topics. Communication between parents and teenagers is therefore vital (see later).

### Parenting Styles

Notwithstanding the sex, social background or other characteristics of the adolescent, all teenagers confront major developmental tasks. As was noted in Chapter 1, some of these are adjustment to physical changes, establishing effective social and working relationships, coming to terms with one's sexuality, establishing an identity or preparation for a career. It has been argued that a crucial factor in assisting one attain these goals is the family (Conger and Petersen 1984).

In a now-classic study, Schaefer (1959) proposed his well-known two-dimensional scheme of parental behaviour patterns, namely, autonomy-control vs. hostility-love. He argued that parents in the hostility-control quadrant are likely to be demanding and authoritarian in their relationships with their children, while those in the autonomy-love quadrant are more likely to act in a democratic and co-operative way. Several schemes have been proposed by various theorists. Although the labels theorists use differ to some extent, two dimensions appear quite consistent. These have been referred to as *emotional support* and *parental control* (Amato 1990). Most parental behaviours vis-à-vis the child can be classified under these. Perhaps of greater importance, however, is that each of these styles has been shown to relate to adolescent adjustment to varying degrees.

In a recent review, for example, (Noller and Patton 1990) summarised the two basic parental strategies and their possible effects on the adolescent. The authors noted that, if parents are supportive and tend to use low levels of coercion, their adolescent offspring are more likely to be socially competent. On the other hand, coercion combined with lack of support is likely to result in behavioural problems among adolescents. Evidence suggests that these parental qualities can act in isolation, or in combination, in determining psychological adjustment (Conger and Petersen 1984, and see also next section).

Acknowledging that parenting qualities such as emotional support and control are useful devices for thinking about family interactions, one may question whether they coincide with adolescents' perceptions of family relationships. In other words, just how valid are these dimensions? In order to determine this, Amato (1990) interviewed 402 pairs of Australian children, including adolescents, and their parents. Respondents were asked a range of general questions about family processes. For instance, they were questioned about their perceptions of parental closeness and support, decision-making, punishment, family cohesion and how their parents reacted to misbehaviours. It was found that adolescents do indeed perceive two dimensions, namely, support and control (see Figure 3.1). This led Amato (1990: 618) to conclude that:

> . . . the dimensions researchers have used to guide their observations and analyses are very similar to the dimensions children use in cognitively organizing family events and relationships.

**Figure 3.1** *Dimensions of Parenting Behaviour*

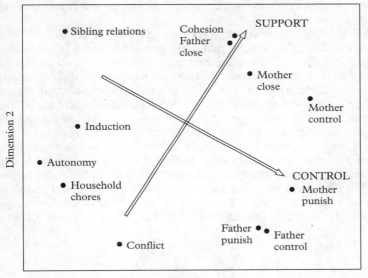

Source:    Amato 1990

It is worthwhile to note that not all children emphasise the same dimensions when thinking about their family. Adolescents tend to emphasise the control dimension, rather than the support one. Younger children are more likely to emphasise parental support (Amato 1990). Amato suggests that this is nothing more than a reflection of various developmental stages. Adolescents are more likely to view control and independence from parents as important issues since they tend to have support outside the family (e.g. peers). Thus, not all forms of parental behaviours may be suited to all children within one family.

## Parental Control

The effect of parental discipline on adolescent developmental outcome has received much attention in the research literature. Empirical studies have shown that teenagers who rate their parents as authoritative are likely to score higher on measures of competence, social development, self-esteem and mental health than those who rate their parents as permissive or authoritarian (Lamborn and associates 1991).

Following the earlier suggestion by Maccoby and Martin (1983), some writers have argued that 'permissive' parenting is too vague a concept. They differentiate between authoritative and authoritarian forms of control, as well as indulgent and neglectful permissiveness. Indulgent permissiveness refers to low parental control coupled with trust and a democratic attitude. Neglectful, by contrast, refers to low parental control coupled with disengagement from the responsibilities of child-rearing (Lamborn *et al.* 1991).

It has been empirically demonstrated that each of these styles has unique adolescent outcomes. The greatest differences have been observed between teenagers from authoritative and neglectful homes. The differences in outcome between authoritarian and indulgent homes tend to favour teenagers from authoritarian homes, although the differences are not always significant. Table 3.1 sum-

**Table 3.1** *Effects of Parental Control on Adolescent Outcomes*

| Parental control | Adolescent outcomes |
| --- | --- |
| Authoritative homes | High competence<br>High adjustment<br>High academic competence<br>High psychosocial development<br>Low problem behaviour<br>Fewer psychological and somatic problems than neglected youth |
| Neglectful homes | Lower on psychosocial development, but not significantly different from authoritarian homes on self-reliance, perceived social competence, and perceived academic competence<br>High on internalised distress<br>High on problem behaviour |
| Authoritarian and indulgent homes | Teenagers tend to perform between above two groups. Youth from authoritarian homes rate lower on school misconduct, drug use and somatic symptoms. Have positive orientation to school. Youth from indulgent homes score higher on social competence and self-confidence. Also higher on less serious deviant behaviours. |

*Source:* Lamborn *et al.* 1991

marises the main differences in outcome as a function of parental control. It shows that adolescent outcomes are most favourable for those from authoritative homes.

Teenagers from such homes appear to be better adjusted and more competent. They are also usually more confident about their abilities. Children from authoritarian homes conform and are obedient, yet are lacking in self-confidence. Although indulged teenagers are likely to engage in some deviant behaviours, these are not particularly serious. In addition, such youngsters are also likely to score quite high on measures of social competence. Lamborn and his colleagues (1991: 1062) concluded that indulged adolescents, although not high on serious misconduct:

> are especially oriented towards their peers and towards the social activities valued by adolescents – including activities not especially valued by adults.

## Family Communication

Implicit in parenting styles is the nature of communication between parents and adolescents. It is quite reasonable to assume that a warm empathic parenting style will result in communication with a teenager that is qualitatively different from that resulting from an autocratic and coercive style. In line with this view, some writers (e.g. Barnes and Olson 1985, Noller and Callan 1991) maintain that family communication is a pre-requisite for the healthy functioning of the family and its individual members. Healthy communication is likely to have beneficial effects on the adolescent's level of independence and self-esteem. Families with high levels of communication show more cohesion, adaptability and satisfaction (Barnes and Olson 1985).

Adolescent males and females differ with respect to their perceptions of communication within the family. Females report talking more often with their mothers than with their fathers, while males report talking more often to their fathers about sexual issues and general problems. Females report disclosing more to their mothers than to their fathers, although males report equal disclosure to both parents. Generally, mothers are seen by adolescents as more willing to listen and initiate conversations, while fathers are seen as more judgemental. Moreover, what adolescents actually disclose to their parents seems determined in part by the sex of both the adolescent and the parent (Noller and Callan 1990).

## The Psychological Health of Parents

In addition to parenting styles, there is much evidence demonstrating significant links between the psychological health of parents and their adolescent children. For example, an examination of the results of several longitudinal studies found evidence to support a link between pathological behaviours in parents and serious disorders (e.g. schizophrenia and depression) in their children several years later (Downey and Coyne 1990, Goldstein 1988).

In a separate study, a team of Australian researchers (Scott and Scott 1987) assessed the linkages between what they referred to as family and individual pathology in 724 members of 'normal range' families (including adolescents). They were interested in the extent to which manifestations of family pathology, that is, inter-member conflict, low solidarity and member dissatisfaction, were related to individual symptoms, namely, neurosis, self-esteem and dissatisfaction with life circumstances.

The results of this study indicated that the various manifestations of family pathology tended to be inter-related. That is, inter-member conflict tended to be associated with low solidarity, and so on. Moreover, most members of pathological families tended to perform their roles rather poorly. Of further interest was the finding that parent-reported family pathology was predictive of children's individual pathology. Thus evidence was found to support the view that the family acts as a strong socialisation agent, and that parental attitudes, values and behavioural manifestations are often reflected in the behaviour of the children (Scott and Scott 1987).

Other reports have commented upon the complex links which exist between parental self-esteem, child-rearing practices and adolescent behaviour. In one study, for example, Small (1988) suggested that parents who themselves feel they are of some worth are likely to raise children who have positive self-esteem and are socially competent. Small tested this view among 139 parent-child dyads in the United States. The respondents in his study were predominantly white and middle class. Parents were asked questions relating to their self-esteem, support for the child, communication and conflict, parental control over decisions involving the child and parental perceptions of the child's independence. Children were questioned about their perceptions of parental support, conflict, and control, as well as aspects of the child's deviant behaviour and autonomy.

Regardless of the age of the child, it was found that mothers with low self-esteem were more likely to punish their adolescent, and to have an adolescent with an increased desire for autonomy. Moreover, fathers with low self-esteem were more likely to resort to hitting their adolescent. Overall, positive parental self-esteem was associated with improved communication between parents and their children. In addition, mothers with high self-esteem were more likely to communicate better with their children and to view their children as independent. Fathers with positive self-esteem were less likely to use physical force when disciplining their children.

These findings demonstrate the many ways in which parental self-esteem interacts with parenting styles in determining adolescent adjustment. If physical punishment is a consistent response by the parent, it is quite likely to have negative effects on the parent-adolescent relationship and to increase the adolescent's desire for autonomy (Small 1988).

*Adolescent Depression*

Adolescent depression is an area of research which has recently received much attention, not least because of its hypothesised link with suicide (see Chapter 10 for a detailed discussion). Of interest to the present discussion is the influence of parental rejection and adolescent self-esteem on adolescents' depression. In one study which has examined this issue (Robertson and Simons 1989), it was observed that parental rejection, rather than factors such as family conflict, perceived parental control or perceived family religiosity were crucial in determining adolescent depression. Interestingly, parental rejection was observed to *interact* with adolescent self-esteem in a quite specific way. Parental rejection was important in predicting adolescent depression, *especially* in those homes where parents failed to nurture adolescents' self-esteem by providing love, understanding, or support. In other words, factors such as family religiosity and family conflict tended to become less important in understanding adolescent depression as parental rejection *increased*. Thus not only did parental rejection have a direct effect on adolescent depression, but it was also found to have an indirect effect through adolescent self-esteem. This study demonstrates the extent to which parenting styles and individual differences interact in determining adolescent adjustment; the model is illustrated in Figure 3.2.

# Adolescents' Attitudes to the Family

## The 'Ideal' Family

Although most adolescents have quite positive and favourable attitudes towards their families (Noller and Patton 1990, Payne and

**Figure 3.2** *A Model of Adolescent Depression*

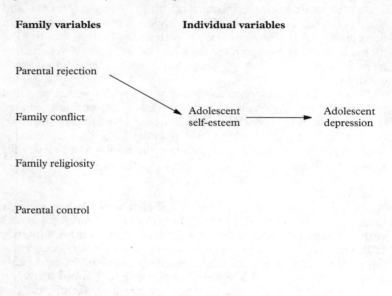

*Source:* Robertson and Simons 1989

Furnham 1990), they nevertheless identify a number of components as characteristic of the 'ideal' family (see Table 3.2).

Research among adolescents in Barbados found that girls, more than boys, considered family openness, expressiveness and co-operation to be the hallmarks of the ideal family. Girls, but not boys, appeared more concerned about getting various household chores completed. They considered these chores to play an important part in the day-to-day functioning of the ideal family – which may reflect their socialisation experiences. Adolescents who rated their family environment as 'open' with 'constructive communication' were more likely to be satisfied with their families (Payne and Furnham 1990).

## Adolescent Perceptions and Adjustments

Some scholars have focused on the associations between adolescent *perceptions* of family functioning and their adjustment (e.g. Dancy and Handal 1984, Kleinman *et al.* 1989). There are a

**Table 3.2** *Adolescents' Dimensions of the Ideal Family*

| Dimensions of ideal family | Example of questionnaire item |
| --- | --- |
| Problem-solving/decision-making | A family should get problems solved right away |
| Authority structure/division of labour | All family members should share in doing chores |
| Age and status | Older persons should have more privileges than younger ones |
| Co-operation/togetherness | Every member of the family should help each other |
| Individual rights | Every family member has a right to keep certain thoughts and feelings private |
| Emotional expressiveness | Children should be open and honest with parents |
| Extra-familial activity | Boys should have more privileges than girls |
| Positive/open relationships | Adults should be able to admit their mistakes to their children. |

*Source:* Payne and Furnham 1990

variety of measures of perceived family life. Perhaps the best known and most widely used is the Family Environment Scale (Moos and Moos 1986). It measures such dimensions as Relationships, Personal Growth (e.g. independence), and System Maintenance (e.g. control and organisation).

Hovestadt and colleagues (1985) constructed the Family-of-Origin (FOS) scale (see Table 3.3). Research with the FOS has found it to be a multidimensional instrument, measuring autonomy (e.g. responsibility, openness to others) and intimacy (e.g. empathy for others, trust). Of significance is that adolescents' perceptions of family life can be used to predict their level of distress. For example, one study of adolescents in the United States found that those who characterised their family as being low in cohesion, but high in conflict were much more distressed than one would expect by chance alone. Controlling for the effects of age and sex did not diminish their findings (Kleinman *et al.* 1989).

Not surprisingly, adolescent perceptions of family-induced trauma have also been found to be associated with more severe emotional disturbances. A recent study (Sanders and Giolas 1991) illustrates this very well. The authors were interested in the relationships between various forms of trauma (psychological, sexual, physical

**Table 3.3** *Subdimensions of the Family-of-origin Scale*

| Autonomy | Intimacy |
| --- | --- |
| Clarity of expression | Range of feelings |
| Responsibility | Mood and tone |
| Respect for others | Conflict resolution |
| Openness to others | Empathy for others |
| Acceptance of loss | Trust |

*Source:*　　Manley *et al.* 1990

etc.) and feelings of unreality in adolescents aged thirteen to seventeen years. They found that childhood trauma was indeed associated with dissociative experiences. Moreover, the trend was significant for all aspects of trauma that were measured, namely, physical, sexual, and psychological abuse, neglect and negative attitudes to the family.

## Reactions to Parental Separation and Divorce

Parental separation and divorce will affect an ever-increasing number of children. According to some estimates, two-fifths of children in the United States will experience these. It has also been suggested that 50 per cent of children in the United States will be affected by separation or divorce by the time they reach eighteen years of age. Moreover, about half the children involved in divorce will experience a second divorce (Bumpass 1984). Likewise, in other European countries as well as Canada, Australia and New Zealand, divorce rates have shown marked rises over the last few decades. As these rates have increased, so too has interest in the consequent psychological adjustment of former spouses and their offspring. This section will concentrate on the effects of parental separation and divorce on the adjustment of adolescents.

How do children and adolescents respond to divorce, separation, and remarriage? They may react with anger, resentment, anxiety, depression or aggression. They may be confused and apprehensive about the future and the changing relationships around them. This very often has negative consequences for scholastic performance. So-called 'easy' children, however, are likely to cope better with divorce and remarriage, while a support network for the child (understanding teachers, grandparents, etc.) is likely to ameliorate stress levels (Hetherington *et al.* 1989).

It is generally believed that parental separation and divorce is stressful for most adolescents, not least because of the disruption to daily routine, the structure of the new family and the associated financial, emotional, and social costs that are involved (Hetherington *et al.* 1989, Westman 1983). Westman estimates that up to one-third of adolescents and parents *do not* adjust to divorce. In similar vein, other authors (e.g. Fine, Moreland and Schwebel 1983) have noted the sometimes negative effects of divorce on adolescents' relationships with their parents, as well as a reduction of trust in, and increasing anger at, their parents. More recently, others have reported the adverse effects of divorce on adolescents' coping strategies (Irion, Coon and Blanchard-Fields 1988) and self-esteem (Harper and Ryder 1986). Still more have noted that family characteristics of enmeshment and disengagement, rather than cohesion, are associated with unsatisfactory social relationships among adolescents (Abelsohn, cited in Huang 1991).

## The Role of Cognition

It is perhaps not surprising that older children are cognitively better equipped than younger ones to cope with the effects of family disruption. Of course, this does not reduce the pain and anger they feel (Hetherington *et al.* 1989). This point has recently been demonstrated by Kurdek (1988–89), who considered whether there are differences in siblings' reactions to parental divorce. He examined this issue with forty-nine pairs of pre-adolescent and adolescent siblings, all of whom were white and middle class. Their parents had been divorced for less than twenty-four months. A review of siblings' self-reports, as well as the ratings of the custodial mothers showed the older siblings to be better adjusted than the younger ones.

A separate study found that younger children reacted differently to divorce than older children did (Neale 1983). It is suggested that this is largely due to the different abilities of the age groups to decipher the often subtle messages about divorce contained in day-to-day communication between parent and child. What is important, but largely unanswered by these reports, are the long-term emotional effects, if any, of divorce on adolescents (see later).

## Psychological Adjustment

There have been numerous studies into the effects of divorce on adolescent adjustment. Evidence to hand suggests particularly negative effects for adolescent girls, such as behavioural problems, lower self-esteem, and increased anxiety and depression. Evidence shows that boys from divorced homes tend to have higher self-esteem than girls (Frost and Pakiz 1990). Other researchers (Wallerstein 1984) have intimated that boys from such families are at greater risk from delinquency and drug use, while it has also been found that teenagers from divorced families are more likely than others to endorse defensive and less mature coping strategies (Irion *et al.* 1988).

A recent Australian study focused specifically on the effects of the absence of the father on male adolescents. Respondents were drawn either from intact families, families where the parents had separated, or father-deceased families. This is a noteworthy study, since all mother-son pairs were matched for age of son, IQ based on school records, socio-economic status, number of siblings and number of older siblings (Harper and Ryder 1986).

The authors were interested in the effects of the absence of fathers on sons' self-esteem, and how sons perceived their maternal bonding. Compared with intact families, boys from father-absent families perceived their mothers as less caring and more over-protective. Of further interest was the fact that the ratings of maternal bonding by boys from father-deceased families were similar to those of boys from intact families, but not from divorced families. Likewise, the self-esteem of boys from intact and father-deceased families was significantly higher than that of boys from divorced homes.

Harper and Ryder (1986) concluded that being in an intact, as opposed to a divorced, family has important implications for the self-esteem of male adolescents. They argued that (1986: 23–24):

> it is not the single parent family *per se* which has a detrimental effect upon the adolescent boy, but the long chain of possible adverse circumstances and the quality of the parental relationship he experiences . . . Low self-esteem may also be closely associated with feelings of guilt linked with conflict over loyalty to both parents.

## Time since Divorce

Another important factor when considering adolescent adjustment is elapsed time since the divorce. One research team (Frost and Pakiz 1990) recently followed a group of adolescents over a ten-year period, until they were about fifteen years of age. The authors found that adolescents who had recently (in the preceding five years) experienced marital separation, were more likely to suffer adjustment difficulties than were adolescents whose parents separated before they were six years old, or adolescents whose parents separated while they were six to nine years old. They found that girls from recently separated families were more likely to skip school and to be depressed. In addition, girls whose parents separated when they were young were more likely to engage in alcohol and drug use.

Satisfactory adjustment in children including adolescents is more likely to occur in those families where the restructuring took place when the child was quite young. Such children are more likely to regard the step-parent as 'real', although by the time they reach adolescence, children are more likely to become 'curious' about their biological parent (Ochiltree 1990).

There can be no doubt that, irrespective of the time family restructuring takes place, it is the quality and style of parenting that has an important effect on adolescent adaptation and functioning. A warm, cohesive, and emotionally supportive family, irrespective of its structure, is important for the psychological health of the adolescent.

## Family Conflict

Not all writers emphasise the negative consequences of parental separation. Some (e.g. Barber and Eccles 1992) have cogently argued the benefits of children living in conflict-free environments, and suggest that adolescents adjust better in serene one-parent families than in conflict-ridden intact ones. In one study (McLoughlin and Whitfield 1984), sixty-four adolescents were questioned about their views regarding the separation or divorce of their parents. Based on their findings, the writers concluded that divorce may in fact be of some benefit to particular children and that it does not necessarily impede children's psychological adjustment. Adolescents appear to prefer one-parent families to conflict-ridden intact ones. Provided that parents keep their children informed about their intentions pertaining to possible divorce, and remain friendly towards each other after the event, adolescents will adjust quite well to the disintegration of their family.

Relationships have been found between adolescent personality traits and the level of conflict in the home. In one study, self-esteem, locus of control and perceptions of the family among 150 high school students were examined (Slater and Haber 1984). It was found that continuing parental conflict in intact *and* divorced families had deleterious effects on adolescents' anxiety, self-esteem and feelings of personal control. These findings suggest that adjustment is not necessarily negatively affected by divorce, but rather by the amount of inter-parental conflict the adolescent experiences. Thus the influence of divorce on adolescents' adjustment is not an isolated factor, but is affected by a range of others.

Positive self-esteem among adolescents seems to be related to the perceived happiness of their biological parents. One study found that the self-esteem of girls in intact happy homes was higher than that of those from unhappy intact homes and those whose parents had separated (Long 1986). These findings lend added support to the view that actual family *structure* is less important than whether the family is conflict-ridden or not (see also Long *et al.* 1988, Forehand *et al.* 1988). It is now clear that inter-parental conflict increases stress in adolescents which impacts negatively on their adjustment and academic performance. It is also likely that inter-parental conflict results in an atmosphere of neglect, and that adolescents witness inappropriate methods of conflict resolution. Thus, Long and colleagues concluded their research as follows (Long *et al.* 1988: 469):

> The present study cannot address which of these factors may be the active mechanism; however, the results do indicate that interparental conflict is an important mediating variable in young adolescent response to divorce.

Another important aspect of inter-parental conflict influencing adolescent adjustment is the extent to which adolescents feel 'caught between parents'. Such adolescents, it is suggested, are likely to adjust poorly to divorce and parental separation (Buchanan, Maccoby and Dornbusch 1991). The strongest predictor of feeling 'caught' is the continuing nature of the relationship between mother and father. Specifically, conflict, high discord and poor and uncooperative communication between parents *after* separation are more likely to result in poor adjustment by the adolescent. There do appear to be some exceptions, however. For instance, when parents who are in conflict refrain from quizzing their adolescent about the other parent, adolescents are less likely to feel caught and therefore adjust better to the disintegration of their family (Buchanan *et al.* 1991).

## Summary

Important reviews (Amato and Keith 1991, Barber and Eccles 1992) of the literature on adjustment following divorce have noted inconsistencies in many of the findings. This may be due, they suggest, either to methodological variations or to the characteristics of the children studied (e.g. social class differences). Amato and Keith conducted a review of almost 100 research reports in this area. They concluded that children from divorced families were more likely to report lower levels of psychological well-being than were children from intact families. Although they found the differences between the groups of children to be significant, they were, in fact, not large.

It has therefore been suggested that emotional adjustment in children and adolescents following divorce is a 'short-term' consideration. What is really needed is for researchers to conduct longitudinal studies in which the children of divorces are followed up into adulthood. By so doing, it might be possible to examine the long-term quality of life outcomes of these children as adults (Amato and Keith 1991). Such sentiments are echoed by Barber and Eccles (1992), who suggest that we must consider the long-term effects of family transitions on adolescent adjustment. They add that we must dispense with the outmoded view of adopting a 'negative crisis orientation' when thinking about family transitions. Rather, we should consider the *quality* of parenting in all types of families.

## Adolescents in New Families

There has been such a marked increase in marital separation and divorce over the last few decades that one might be tempted to view new families (that is, step-parent families, one-parent families, blended families, etc.) as the norm (Visher and Visher 1982). Nonetheless, much research evidence would suggest that adolescents find it difficult, at least in the short term, to adjust to the new family structure, particularly one with 'new' siblings (Hetherington *et al.* 1988). Although divorce or separation may end years of bitter inter-parental dispute and conflict, the result is fractured relationships (Montalvo 1982) and a new family with changed norms and expectations. This poses a variety of emotional and social challenges for the adolescent.

Not all new families are dysfunctional (Visher and Visher 1982). As has been pointed out (Goldsmith 1982), an unhealthy family environment is not a necessary consequence of divorce and separation. Although members of divorcing families may indeed experience some stress, for many the break-up of the family unit presents those concerned with new opportunities for personal growth (Barber and Eccles 1992). It has been suggested that, sociologically, the new family takes on the same roles and responsibilities as the former, although tasks may now be assigned to different members (Goldsmith 1982). The new family (including the adolescent) is presented with its own set of unique developmental tasks (Visher and Visher 1982), successful completion of which will launch the family and individual members along the path to psychological adjustment.

New families face unique developmental tasks. These are (Visher and Visher 1982):

- Mourning of losses: New families involve change. To a certain extent, all members mourn the loss of the familiar
- Negotiation and development of new family traditions
- Formation of new alliances and preserving those that are still regarded as important
- Stepfamily integration: it takes up to two years for stepfathers to form a friendly relationship with stepchildren.

## Problem-oriented vs. Normative-adoptive Frameworks

Two general frameworks or paradigms have guided past research on children in new families, namely, the *problem-oriented* and the *normative-adoptive* (Barber and Eccles 1992, Coleman and Ganong 1990). Most studies seem to fit the first, although research adopting the second began to appear in the second half of the 1980s (Coleman and Ganong 1990). Table 3.4 shows the two perspectives and the different approaches that can be adopted within each.

From Table 3.4 it appears that the so-called problem-oriented perspective has been most emphasised. Thus researchers have assumed that adolescents in new families are likely to be deficient in certain attributes compared with adolescents in intact families. As Coleman and Ganong (1990: 927) suggest:

> this approach has been primarily influenced by clinical writings, but it may also be that it simply reflects societal attitudes toward stepfamilies.

The stress hypothesis emphasises that family restructuring is stressful and, accordingly, has negative influences on the social-psychological adjustment and development of the adolescent. Thus these adolescents suffer from lowered self-esteem and particular behavioural problems. According to one view, this may include depression, anxiety, school-related problems, and alcoholism (Coleman and Ganong 1990). The authors also, however, note inconsistencies in some results. For example, according to the first

**Table 3.4** *Two Perspectives on Research into Children in New Families*

| Problem-oriented | Normative-adaptive |
| --- | --- |
| Deficit-comparison | Parent-child relationships |
| Stress-hypothesis | Stepparent-child relationships |
| Self-esteem | |
| Problem behaviour | |
| Cognitive functioning | |
| Parent-child relationships | |
| Socialisation hypothesis | |
| Biological discrimination | |
| Incomplete-institution hypothesis | |

*Source:*   Coleman and Ganong 1990

perspective, children in new families are likely to perform below expectations at school. Yet in a British study which highlighted the importance of controlling for social class, no differences in academic performance were observed between children in new and intact families.

With respect to parent-child relationships, some studies report few differences in terms of level of support and conflict between new and intact families (Coleman and Ganong 1990). Most research studies focus on structural differences between families rather than on stressful family transitions (see also Goldsmith 1982). Thus, intact families have their own stressors (e.g. financial considerations, unemployment, parental pathology) affecting the adjustment of adolescents. The first perspective also posits inadequate family socialisation experiences for children in new families, compared with others. It is suggested that family disintegration limits the child's exposure to adequate role models. It is further assumed that inadequacies in stepparent-adolescent relations may also be due to the fact that biological or genetic ties are absent. Moreover, it is argued that new families lack guidance regarding their roles and how problems should be dealt with, the so-called incomplete-institution hypothesis (Coleman and Ganong 1990).

According to the normative-adaptive perspective, parental separation or divorce and the resultant creation of a new family, whether it be blended or single-parent, is not an unusual phenomenon in most industrialised nations (Barber and Eccles 1992, Coleman and Ganong 1990, Demo 1992, Goldsmith 1982). Thus researchers adopting this perspective have ceased to focus on assumed 'pathological' behaviours, and begun to study *family process* (Coleman and Ganong, 1990). Research interest is therefore focused on parent-child and stepparent-child relationships. The quality of parent-child relationships varies depending on the children involved, changes in parent-child contact over a number of years, custody arrangements and so forth. Although relationships between stepparent and child have the potential to be less close than parent-child relationships, they need not necessarily be characterised by stress and conflict. Should the biological parent be absent, stepparent-child relationships have the potential to be rewarding (Coleman and Ganong 1990).

These sentiments are shared by Barber and Eccles who concluded (1992: 113) thus:

> Divorce research must now go beyond the narrow conceptualization of a family transition as a crisis-potentiating event. New frameworks must be constructed that describe normal development in single-parent families.

## Theoretical Considerations

The research findings reviewed here have implications for theories of the family as well as theories of adolescence. The research results appear to lend support to the view that the family is an integrated system and that change in one element has consequences for other elements of the system. Thus, parenting style has implications for adolescent adjustment, while the nature of parent-adolescent communication is an important predictor of teenagers' behaviour and psychological health. Likewise, restructuring the family is important in understanding changes in adolescent behaviour.

With respect to theories of adolescence, elements of several of them appear to be germane here. Adaptation to parental separation appears to be related to level of cognitive development. Perhaps not surprisingly, evidence suggests that older children have the cognitive capacity better to understand and adjust to family disruption. They are able to reason abstractly and consider the likely consequences of remaining in what is usually an unhappy family. Certain parenting styles and family communication patterns facilitate adolescent adjustment. Both, no doubt, have implications for adolescent identity formation. Finally, biological changes in puberty and beyond have been shown to be related to changes in parent-child relationships and, consequently, to psychological adjustment.

# Summary

This chapter has examined family influences on the psychological adjustment of adolescents. A number of crucial factors were identified, each important in shaping adolescents' emotional health. These were parenting styles; communication; parental pathology; separation or divorce; family conflict; adolescent perception of the family; as well as the reactions of adolescents who find themselves in new families. The research evidence at our disposal suggests that particular parenting styles (such as lack of emotional support) are less conducive than others to healthy psychological adjustment among adolescents. Moreover, parenting styles interact with particular characteristics of adolescents such as self-esteem to determine personality characteristics in teenagers.

Perhaps one of the most crucial factors influencing the emotional health of adolescents is family pathology. Research evidence is quite clear on this. Parents manifesting personality and behavioural disorders can expect their adolescents to be emotionally and behaviourally maladjusted. What is not quite clear from the evidence is just how much family pathology an adolescent can tolerate. For example, are everyday mood swings in a parent as influential a factor in determining adolescent adjustment as major affective disorder in the parent? If not, what is the critical threshold, if any?

It is interesting to note that, whereas many studies suggest negative emotional consequences of divorce for adolescents, a meta-analysis of research suggests otherwise (Amato and Keith 1991). Adolescents in new families may be disadvantaged in terms of their emotional health and development, but the effects are not large. This is an important finding and worthy of consideration by psychologists, other professionals and parents. Perhaps of far greater importance, as Amato and Keith (1991) have suggested, are the *long-term* effects of divorce on the emotional health of the individual. What are needed, therefore, are longitudinal studies of adolescents over several years in which their adjustment as adults is examined. Of further importance is the finding that being in a new family *per se* is not a necessary precursor to maladjustment. Of greater import is the *quality* of family life. Adolescents prefer a happy new family to an unhappy intact one. As Demo (1992: 114) explains:

> Children's well-being depends much more on enduring parental support and satisfying family relationships than it does on a particular family structure.

What does appear to be beyond dispute is the fact that divorce or parental separation is a complex event. Not only is there the splintering of delicate inter-relationships, but also the challenges of forming new ones. Intertwined are the personality characteristics of all concerned, as well as other social and economic pressures. Many research designs cannot, because of their inherent limitations, hope to disentangle all of the possible causes from the many effects. Careful attention to methodological detail and design should be a priority for future research.

## Additional Reading

Amato, P. and Keith, B. (1991) 'Parental Divorce and the Well-being of Children: A Meta-analysis,' *Psychological Bulletin* 110: 26–46

Barber, B. and Eccles, J. (1992) 'Long-term Influence of Divorce and Single Parenting on Adolescent Family- and Work-related Values, Behaviors, and Aspirations', *Psychological Bulletin* 111: 108–26

Callan, V. and Noller, P. (1987) *Marriage and the Family*. Sydney: Methuen

## Exercises

1. Plan a study to investigate the effects of parental separation on adolescent adjustment. Operationalise your dependent and independent variables and give details of your research design.
2. Describe how you would construct a measure to assess adolescents' perceptions of their family. Provide details about your reliability and validity checks.

# 4 Friendships and Peer Groups

## Introduction

In addition to the family, close friends and the wider peer group have a significant influence on the teenager's social development. As individuals move from late childhood into adolescence and beyond, peer influences and the social network begin to play an increasingly important role in the life of the teenager. The adolescent is undergoing rapid cognitive and biological development, and it is reasonable to assume that these are a major impetus for change to his or her self-concept as well as changes to family and social relationships (Cole and Cole 1989, Paikoff and Brooks-Gunn 1991). It is the peer group that forms a vital and often useful avenue by which the adolescent makes the transition from the family to the wider world (Dunphy 1963). Research has shown quite clearly that as children move into early adolescence, an increasing amount of time is spent with other members of peer groups, while the amount of time spent with the family decreases (Larson and Richard 1991).

We find ourselves in social relationships with others at every stage of the life span. Indeed, even infants and toddlers are aware of the presence of others of different ages. Infants express interest in one another and react differently to other infants than to adults (Parke and Asher 1983). They are also capable of differentiating social contexts in which a mother might be present or absent. Likewise, during the teenage years peer interaction forms an integral part of everyday social relationships and is an important part of social and emotional development as well as the development of social competence (Parke and Asher 1983, Parker and Asher 1987). The view that peers are an essential part of adolescent development is echoed by Johnson (cited in Parker and Asher 1987) who noted that (p. 357):

> Experiences with peers are not superficial luxuries to be enjoyed by some students and not by others. Student-student relationships are an absolute necessity for healthy cognitive and social development and socialization.

Theorists have noted that belonging to a peer group and its associated youth culture is important in the transition from childhood to adulthood (Fasick 1984). Such a group is an important vehicle by which the teenager achieves a sense of identity and independence. Close identification with the youth culture is temporary, however, and is abandoned once full autonomy is acquired (Fasick 1984).

Forming satisfying relationships with close friends and one's peer group is an important developmental task of adolescence (see Chapter 1), which also has implications for so-called life tasks (Manaster 1989). The successful completion of this task will have significant implications for general tasks relating to friends and the general community, as well as one's sense of self and the ability to get on with others.

We turn now to particular aspects of friendships and peer groups. We begin by considering the nature of friendships.

## The Nature of Friendships

Having well-liked and close friends is not a new experience for the young adolescent. Friendships are formed early in primary school. In addition to a network of somewhat closer friends, the adolescent may also have several companions drawn from school, sporting teams and clubs. As adolescents undergo cognitive, social and emotional development, the nature and quality of friendships change too. New interests are developed, and ideas about the self change. In addition, adolescents' views about a range of issues are being challenged and altered in a myriad of ways. Not surprisingly, some friendships may lose their appeal, while new ones will be formed, particularly during early adolescence.

### The Formation of Friendships

The formation of friendships in childhood and adolescence proceeds through various developmental stages (Hartup 1983). One of the earliest and clearly identifiable stages is the *reward-cost* stage. This occurs around the second or third grade in school and is characterised by the sharing of common activities and similar expectations. The second stage, referred to as the *normative*, develops during the fourth or fifth grade. Its main feature is a commitment to sharing. The *empathic* stage occurs in early adolescence. It is characterised by understanding, self-disclosure and shared interests.

Friendships in adolescence appear to be qualitatively different from childhood ones. They are formed on the basis of interpersonal relations, physical attributes and achievement. Various age groups regard interpersonal relationships as an important basis for friendships, although this appears to be more important for older than younger adolescents.

The development of friendships in late adolescence is like a gradual unfolding process. Longitudinal studies (e.g. Hays 1985) have found that friends first tend to share jokes or discuss local events. As the friendship becomes more intense and meaningful, individuals are more likely to discuss personal problems, exchange gifts and visit relatives. Some writers have noted exceptions to this *general penetration* approach to friendship formation. Adolescents at boarding school who share the same dormitory, for example, are much more likely to progress through the stages of friendship at a quicker pace.

It has been reported that someone who is initially disliked only rarely (about three cases in ten) becomes a close friend (Richey and Richey 1980). Becoming close friends does not happen suddenly; rather it can take up to several months. Sometimes the friendship is not idyllic, of course. Most friends report having quarrelled at least once (Richey and Richey 1980).

It would seem that the basis for friendship formation among boys is the sharing of common activities. They are likely to go camping or form a rock band. An essential feature seems to be the sharing of attitudes and 'having fun' together (Richey and Richey 1980). Boys' friendships are likely to be less intimate and more guarded than girls'. Girls, on the other hand, are likely to form friendships on the basis of verbal communication about themselves. They, too, 'have fun', but the nature and essential features of their activities are slightly different. Girls are more likely to self-disclose and characterise their friendships as mutually intimate and understanding. Boys tend to de-emphasise affection. Instead, they stress the instrumental aspects of friendship, such as being supportive (Sharabany *et al.* 1981). Friendship bonds appear to be equally strong for both sexes, although males and females have different ways of expressing their friendship (Hays 1985).

Same-sex and opposite-sex friendships exhibit different developmental patterns. It has been shown that girl-girl relationships are more intimate (in terms of aspects such as self-disclosure) than boy-boy friendships. Opposite-sex friendships, as viewed from the girl's perspective, rapidly increase in intimacy over time, compared with boys' perceptions of such friendships. However, by the time adolescents leave school, major differences between same-sex and opposite-sex friendships have diminished (Sharabany *et al.* 1981).

Same-sex friendships change over time in some fundamental respects. Characteristics such as trust remain relatively stable, while others tend to increase (Sharabany *et al.* 1981). These changes are listed in Table 4.1.

Finally, adolescents are able to differentiate between friendships and romantic relationships (Hays 1988). Late adolescents view same-sex friendships as having fewer fluctuations than romantic relationships. Same-sex friendships are also perceived to level off at a lower magnitude than romantic relationships. Moreover, the intensity of friendships were viewed by adolescents in one study to increase more gradually than were romantic relationships (Hays 1988).

## Functions of Friendships

Friendships, even in adolescence, serve an important socio-emotional function. It is now well established (Hays 1988) that friendships are intrinsically satisfying since they provide companionship, stimulation, a sense of belonging and emotional support. Not having friends can be an important source of stress and low self-esteem. It has been suggested that there is an increased need for emotional intimacy during early adolescence and that close friends help fulfil it. Should the need not be met, loneliness, psychosocial disturbance and alienation may result (Buhrmester 1990).

A characteristic feature of a close friendship is involvement, reciprocity and commitment (Hartup 1989) as well as trust and loyalty (Dusek 1991). During adolescence, friendships will evolve around leisure activities and the sharing of beliefs, values, and information about books, movies and who is dating whom. Very

**Table 4.1** *Developmental Changes in Aspects of Same-sex Friendships*

Stable over time
- Trusting the friend
- Preferring to do things with friend
- Feeling free to take from, or impose on, friend

Increasing over time
- Knowing and being sensitive towards
- Conveying one's own thoughts and feelings frankly and spontaneously
- Ability to know others' point of view

*Source:*    Sharabany *et al.* 1981

often, adolescents will offer advice to their close friends on a range of topics. In short, close adolescent friends are confidants and allies (Richey and Richey 1980).

Close friendships share a range of other functions as well. Friends are reliable and act as allies. They also give moral support in times of emotional crisis. Friendships embody trust, loyalty, equality, consideration, mutual understanding and intimacy. Friendships encourage spontaneity as well as open and honest exchanges of feelings and ideas (Mannarino 1978). If friends argue, their friendship forces them to show some self-restraint, while also encouraging them towards quick reconciliation (Richey and Richey 1980).

Although they are all likely to share private information, girls are perhaps more likely than boys to disclose intimate information (Hays 1988). Not only do friends share attitudes, values, and information but also behaviours. In this regard, Kandel (1990) has suggested that behaviours such as illicit drug use are often shared by close friends. She found that when best friends did not use marijuana, only 15 per cent of adolescent respondents reported smoking it. However, when best friends reported using marijuana once or twice, 50 per cent of adolescent respondents reported using it. These findings suggest, therefore, that close friends can play an important role in shaping each other's behaviour. They are important in initiating a range of behaviours and helping form attitudes.

Friends are also important in determining adolescents' emotional adjustment. Numerous research reports have indicated the strong relationships that exist between having a good friend and psychological health. Having a close friend has been found to be related to higher self-esteem, feelings of being relaxed and being 'myself', and psychological maturity. In one study, for example, the relationship between having a close friend or 'chum' and preadolescents' self-esteem was examined (Mannarino 1978).

Boys in the sixth grade were asked to nominate other children in their class whom they would like to play with, and with whom they would participate in group activities. From these nominations, the author compiled a 'chum checklist,' and divided the sample into those boys who had a close friend and those who did not. Results showed that having a best friend was positively related to higher self-esteem (Mannarino 1978) (see Table 4.2).

The findings emphasise the importance of close friendships for psychological health. Friends act as a support network, raising one's feelings of self-worth, and acting as a buffer against daily stressors. Having a close friend reinforces one's own ideas and beliefs about things, enabling the individual to resolve personal uncertainty. As Mannarino (1978: 108–9) explained:

As two youngsters communicate openly, the preadolescent realizes that he shares certain ideas and feelings with his chum and begins, perhaps for the first time in his life, to appreciate the common humanity of people.

**Table 4.2** *Mean Self-esteem Scores for Best Friend Groups*

| Groups | Self-esteem | |
| --- | --- | --- |
| | Mean | Standard deviation |
| Having a best friend | 61.1 | 8.11 |
| No best friend | 53.3 | 11.05 |

*Note:* Group means differ significantly: $F_{(1,58)} = 9.70$, $p < 0.01$

*Source:*    Mannarino 1978

## Peer Groups

We have so far seen that friendships provide a sense of belonging and emotional support in that friends very often feel comfortable sharing private information. Friends generate feelings of trust and well-being. Peer groups, on the other hand, have as their members individuals of the same age who may be known to the adolescent, but who might not necessarily be a close friend. Peer groups, comprising companions and other acquaintances, embody the wider cultural norms and values that are important to the adolescent. Strict normative codes often exist, with those who deviate from these norms being rejected by other members of the group (Gavin and Furman 1989). Peer groups dictate the rituals that members should perform (Coleman and Hendry 1990). Rituals refer to a variety of activities, including modes of dress, codes of conduct, hairstyles and general attitudes.

It is also possible that, within an age category in one school, for example, several peer groups may co-exist, each with slightly different cultural values and modes of conduct. Some authors (see the review by Downs and Rose 1991) have identified a 'fun' group, for which the main concern is dating, drinking and generally having a good time. There is usually also an 'academic' group, concerned with achieving in school work. Another group is the 'delinquent' one, characterised by discipline problems in school and behaviour which defies authority.

Not surprisingly, there is much pressure to conform to group norms. Some writers have suggested that group conformity is strongest during middle adolescence (Costanzo and Shaw 1966), although others dispute this by suggesting that conformity pressures increase linearly over the adolescent years (Gavin and Furman 1989). What is beyond dispute is that the adolescent comes under pressure to experiment with new roles and behaviour. This forms a natural part of the identity formation process (see Chapter 2). Quite often, teenagers look to the peer group not only for guidance about such things as fashion, but also for acceptance. According to some writers (e.g. Tedesco and Gaier 1988), much energy is expended by the adolescent in making friends and winning a place in a group.

## Functions of Peer Groups

Peer groups serve several important functions. They provide a context for sociable behaviour, the exploration of personal relationships and a sense of belonging. Furthermore, they foster learning and a concern with the integrity of the self (Zarbatany, Hartmann and Rankin 1990). The peer group is a source of self-esteem and helps build one's reputation. It facilitates the achievement of identity and is also a source of companionship, since it helps avoid loneliness and generates various social activities (Brown, Clasen and Eicher 1986). Peer groups also serve an important function when adolescents have been rejected by their parents. In these instances, the group provides valued support and friendship. Peer groups, then, form a major context in which the adolescent learns social skills and strategies. The peer group very often serves as an emotional anchor (Tedesco and Gaier 1988). Coleman and Hendry (1990: 107) argue that during adolescence

> Peer groups become more important in determining interest and influencing the behaviour and the personality of the individual.

Gavin and Furman (1989: 827) explain it this way:

> Without being connected to the peer group, one may be left without an important source of support during a period of physical, emotional, and social upheaval.

Peer groups are an important source of affiliation (Kandel 1990). Schools play a vital role in the formation of such groups, and facilitate affiliative behaviour in a number of important ways. Firstly, schools are age-graded. This results in concentrated numbers of adolescents at similar levels of cognitive development. Thus they are easily able to share ideas and values. Secondly, they are at similar levels of biological development, sharing similar physical experiences. Spending large amounts of time in the presence of others, teenagers are increasingly reliant on one another (Kandel 1990).

Another important function of the peer group is to provide the teenager with a sense of status, which can be either *earned* or *derived* (Ausubel, Montemayor and Svajian 1977). Because the relationship with parents is slowly changing, and the adolescent is not yet fully a member of adult society, he or she experiences a loss of status. By filling this important gap, peer groups can provide adolescents with earned status in the group. A close relationship with the peer group, based on group interests and approval, enhances the teenager's self-esteem, thereby providing derived status.

Ausubel and colleagues (1977) have noted two other closely related functions of the peer group. As the adolescent moves beyond the familiar realms of childhood, the peer group provides a welcome frame of reference. This provides the adolescent with security and heightens the feeling of self-determination and emancipation. As the authors explain (p. 350):

> The creation of peer group norms rescues [the adolescent] from [a] no-man's-land of orientation and provides relief from uncertainty, indecision, guilt, and anxiety about proper ways of thinking, feeling, and behaving.

Peer groups also protect the individual from adult authority by acting as a pressure group (Ausubel *et al.* 1977). In other words, parents are very often likely to find themselves negotiating acceptable attitudes and behaviour with the close friends of their teenager. Parents therefore need to develop the skill to have their opinion considered without alienating their adolescent. The peer group can also be viewed as a socialising agent, transmitting those norms and values not usually transmitted by parents. Finally, Ausubel and colleagues note that peer groups act as a stabilising force during a transition period, when the adolescent is undergoing fundamental social, emotional, and physical change.

In summary, it is apparent that peer groups reduce the dependence of the adolescent on the family by facilitating the development of new social skills (e.g. dating) and the restructuring of teenagers' values and attitudes (Dunphy 1990).

## The Structure of Peer Groups

Peer groups can be categorised as cliques, crowds or gangs (Dunphy 1963, 1990). A clique consists of a relatively small number (from five to nine) of same-sex teenagers. They are usually close friends and share many leisure activities. They quite probably attend the same school, and are of similar age. In most urban centres, cliques also share residential proximity (Dunphy 1990).

Cliques serve important functions (Dunphy 1963). Their main function (like that of close friends) is to talk and share information, as well as to plan social activities. A clique is cohesive and closely-knit and, given its small size, it is very often difficult for a stranger to gain access. Cliques have leaders and followers, and it is the leaders who are more likely to date sooner and more frequently than the followers. Dusek (1991: 310–11) suggests that leaders

> tend, by their example, to push the other members toward more advanced levels of development.

Crowds are larger, contain members of both sexes, and may comprise several cliques, although not all cliques need necessarily be represented in a crowd. All individual members of crowds are also members of cliques, while it is possible for a clique member not to be a member of a crowd (Dunphy 1963). Crowds tend to be less intimate than cliques (Dusek 1991). Dunphy also notes that crowds are characteristic of middle adolescence and are born of a need to make heterosexual contact. As such, they facilitate the transition from single-sex to heterosexual interactions. According to Dunphy, boys tend to be slightly older than girls in a crowd, with most socialising occurring over weekends. Crowds provide the adolescent with an opportunity to meet others with different attitudes and values, and are therefore an important source of social comparison (see later).

Crowds can form quite spontaneously. Opposite-sex class mates, for example, who happen to be neighbours and on good terms with each other, might introduce the members of their respective cliques, thus forging heterosexual contact (see Figure 4.1). As Dunphy (1990: 174) has indicated, a clique is a prerequisite for crowd formation and serves as the

> pivotal point in the change in the adolescent's association structure from unisexual to heterosexual groupings and is the structural base for the development of a new heterosexual role.

Figure 4.1 represents just the first step in the formation of heterosexual cliques (see the various stages listed). In this first stage, members of the various cliques occasionally meet for heterosexual leisure activities, like a school dance. For the most part, however, cliques function independently of one another, and remain single-sex.

**Figure 4.1** *Early Stages in the Formation of Heterosexual Cliques*

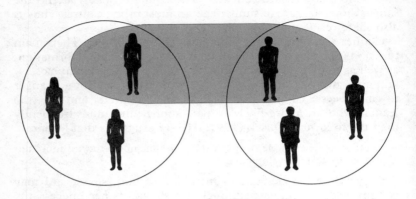

Dunphy (1963, 1990) has proposed an elaborate theory of group development from early to late adolescence. According to his model, there are five stages of group development (see Figure 4.2). These can be summarised as follows:

Stage 1:  This is the primary stage of development consisting of same-sex isolated cliques.

Stage 2:  Same-sex cliques engage in tentative heterosexual inter-action. All heterosexual activity is conducted from the safety of the clique (see Figure 4.2).

Stage 3:  Formation of the heterosexual clique. Some members engage in dating and retain membership of the same-sex clique.

Stage 4:  Same-sex cliques slowly being re-organised into hetero-sexual cliques.

Stage 5:  Disintegration of crowd. Loosely associated groups of couples who are dating or engaged.

From Dunphy's theory, it seems clear that structural change of groups can and does occur. The first change is the merging of young individual adolescents into same-sex cliques. This is fol-lowed by sporadic heterosexual contact which is later followed by the formation of a heterosexual clique, and so on.

**Figure 4.2** *The Stages of Group Development*

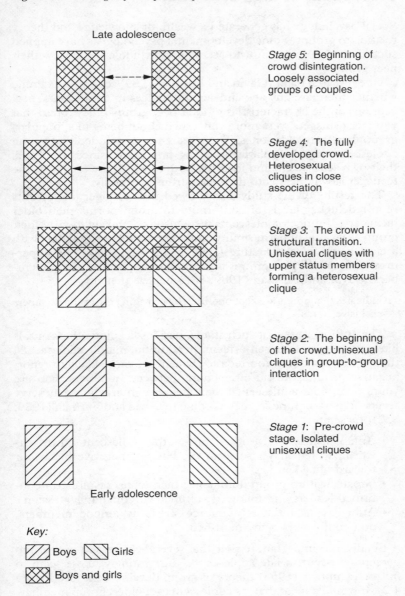

Late adolescence

Stage 5: Beginning of crowd disintegration. Loosely associated groups of couples

Stage 4: The fully developed crowd. Heterosexual cliques in close association

Stage 3: The crowd in structural transition. Unisexual cliques with upper status members forming a heterosexual clique

Stage 2: The beginning of the crowd. Unisexual cliques in group-to-group interaction

Stage 1: Pre-crowd stage. Isolated unisexual cliques

Early adolescence

Key:

Boys   Girls

Boys and girls

*Source:* Dunphy 1963

## Perceptions of the Peer Group

Social psychology has generated a wealth of knowledge and theory relating to groups. Some developmental psychologists have applied such theory in an attempt to ascertain how adolescents view their peer group.

One research team (Gavin and Furman 1989) set out to examine whether there are any age and sex differences in adolescents' perceptions of the characteristics of their peer group. They found that younger teenagers were more concerned about being in a 'popular' group than were older ones. The researchers concluded that young adolescents view popularity as being important, since it bolsters their own self-esteem and identity, both of which are crucial as the teenager slowly begins to disengage from the family.

The results of the study also showed that younger adolescents reported higher levels of conformity to group norms than older teenagers. Younger adolescents were also more likely to view their group as lacking in permeability, and as being relatively stable, with a clear hierarchical structure (leaders and followers). The impermeable nature of peer groups is deemed important by group members. Gavin and Furman (1989: 832) believe that this

> indicates that others are kept out, thereby providing the group members exclusive status.

The authors note that such status, besides keeping others out, is likely to enhance their self-esteem. In addition, middle adolescents, that is, those of about fourteen to sixteen, are more likely to report negative or antagonistic interactions between members than are younger or older adolescents. Such negative interaction may serve several important functions. According to Gavin and Furman (1989: 832), these are:

- Antagonisms toward others boosts the adolescent's own self-worth, which may also form the basis of negative behaviour toward outsiders
- Greater within-group dominance hierarchies resulting in confirmed leaders and followers, ultimately reducing aggression
- Antagonisms ultimately enforce similarity among members, non-conformers being punished.

Finally, it is important to note that several changes in peer group perception occur in late adolescence. Interestingly, these seem to mirror Dunphy's (1963) theory of group development (see Figure 4.2). It would appear that, as adolescents get older, group membership *per se* is viewed as less important by its members. This might explain the reduction in antagonism among older adolescents that was previously noted. Increasingly, groups are viewed as more permeable, while the pressures to conform are reduced. Moreover, whereas very young adolescents perceive peer influence as primarily concerned with friendships, older adolescents are able to think more abstractly about the group, realising that it symbolises certain attitudes and values (O'Brien and Bierman 1988). Younger adolescents are more likely to define groups in terms of activities and social behaviour, while older adolescents tend to view group-influences as far-reaching, influencing dress style and illicit acts but also attitudes and values. Whereas young adolescents view the group as a source of friendship, older adolescents are more likely to describe it in terms of their own self-esteem (O'Brien and Bierman 1988).

## Summary

Perceptions of the peer group mirror adolescents' cognitive development. In the early years, perception includes belonging and friendship. In later years, the peer group is viewed more abstractly: it remains a source of friendship, but also comes to symbolise values and personal esteem.

## Perceptions of Peer Pressure

It is generally accepted that adolescents tend to conform to peer norms and values (Gavin and Furman 1989, Costanzo and Shaw 1966). When asked to nominate the peer pressures they experienced, adolescents in one study indicated that peer pressure tends to cluster in five broad categories, as listed in Table 4.3 (Brown *et al.* 1986). These categories include social activities (such as going to parties), misconduct (such as drug use or sexual activity), conformity (such as dress style), school-related activities (such as attitudes to academic matters) and family issues (relationships with parents, curfews, etc.).

Since it is not clear precisely to what extent peer pressure induces adolescents to perform behaviours which they otherwise would not, various researchers have examined these issues. Evidence suggests that adolescents are more likely to follow their peers and engage in 'neutral' or pro-social behaviours than in anti-social behaviours, although males are more likely to engage in the latter than females (Berndt 1979, Brown *et al.* 1986). Contrary to popu-

**Table 4.3** *Peer Pressures Encountered by Adolescents*

Peer social activities
  • Spending time with friends
  • Going to parties
  • Concerts and school events
  • Pursuing opposite-sex relationships
Misconduct
  • Drug and alcohol use
  • Sexual intercourse
  • Petty theft
  • Vandalism
  • Minor delinquent activities
Conformity to peer norms
  • Dress and grooming
  • Musical preferences
  • Involvement in school
  • Academic matters
  • Extra-curricular activities
Involvement with family

*Source:*    Brown *et al.* 1986

lar stereotype, evidence indicates that adolescents feel pressured to
be *involved* with their peers and do not necessarily feel pressured
towards misconduct (Brown *et al.* 1986). However, it would seem
that older adolescents report experiencing more pressures in this
regard than do younger ones. Not surprisingly, adolescents who
experience peer pressure and conformity dispositions report more
peer involvement, misconduct and anti-social behaviour. Peer
pressure appears to be an important component of adolescent
misconduct, particularly among those who are more susceptible to
conformity.

*Susceptibility to negative peer pressure*
Why are some teenagers more likely to succumb to peer pressure of
a negative kind? One body of research has investigated the consequences of adolescents who are left to care for themselves after
school while their parents are still at work.

   Although it has been suggested that those who care for themselves after school are more likely to be involved in anti-social
behaviour than those who have a parent at home, some writers
dispute this. According to one study (Steinberg 1986), there are a
variety of after-school experiences, and it is possible for teenagers
to be supervised by their parents *in absentia*, thus reducing the
susceptibility to anti-social peer-induced behaviour. It appears that
teenagers most at risk of anti-social behaviour are those who are

not supervised after school and are also not at their homes, so-called 'hanging out' teenagers. It is possible for working parents to supervise teenagers by phone, thereby helping to eliminate unacceptable behaviour. Research findings also indicate that teenagers who have been raised by authoritative parents (see Chapter 3), are less likely to succumb to anti-social peer pressure. Thus, *parenting style* acts as a buffer against the ill-effects of lack of after-school supervision.

The importance of family and school experiences in childhood in helping us understand the susceptibility to negative peer pressure during adolescence should not be understated. A *social interaction* model has been proposed to explain these linkages (Dishion *et al.* 1991). It consists of the following three stages:

Stage 1: Begins with maladaptive parent-child interactions which are likely to result in anti-social behaviour. This has flow-on effects for school performance. This is also likely to lead to rejection by peers

Stage 2: Failure in school. Individual also does not succeed with the peer group

Stage 3: The failing, disliked and anti-social child selects those social settings that maximise social reinforcement. This appears to be exacerbated in those high schools that stream adolescents on the basis of academic performance

This model makes quite explicit the fundamental role that parent-child relationships play in determining adolescent behaviour and emotional adjustment. We noted some of these aspects in the previous chapter. They include parenting style, communication between parent and teenager, parental maladjustment and family disruption.

A second avenue of research has dealt with family structure and susceptibility to anti-social peer pressure. Teenagers living with both natural parents are least likely to be at risk for deviance.

There does appear to be some disagreement among writers, however, about the effects of other family structures on adolescent deviance. One report, for example, indicates that living in a single-parent household is particularly risky, although the presence of an additional adult in such families reduces the risk of teenagers succumbing to anti-social peer pressure (Dornbusch *et al.* 1985). Such a view is not shared by all researchers. One author found that an additional *biological* parent was a stronger buffer against peer pressure than the addition of a stepparent (Steinberg 1987).

## Peer Rejection

Why are some adolescents rejected by their peers? Are there particular behavioural and emotional characteristics that lead some to be rejected?

Before considering these questions, it is important to note that some writers distinguish between those who are neglected and those who are rejected by their peers (Asher and Dodge 1986). Neglected adolescents, although not disliked by their peers, do not have friends. Rejected teenagers are disliked by their peers. Some important behavioural differences have been noted between these groups (Asher and Dodge 1986). Firstly, rejected teenagers appear to be disliked wherever they are. They are also likely to manifest aggressive and disruptive behaviour. Neglected adolescents, on the other hand, very often make a new start when they move to a new school or neighbourhood. It has also been found that rejected children are likely to report higher levels of loneliness and social dissatisfaction than neglected teenagers.

It has already been suggested that rejection of individuals in late childhood and early adolescence is associated with relatively high levels of aggression (see also Parkhurst and Asher 1992). Some theorists have questioned this claim, suggesting, rather, that rejected children can be categorised either as aggressive and disruptive, or as socially unassertive, with low social interaction. Such a pattern of behaviour is referred to as *social withdrawal*. Socially unassertive teenagers have been described (Parkhurst and Asher 1992: 231) as

> avoiding confrontations, as making few and highly deferential requests, and as being 'easy marks'.

Such teenagers, therefore, tend to be easily victimised and bullied.

It is possible to gain a broad picture of the rejected adolescent by considering the characteristics of the popular teenager. In one study, young adolescents were administered a range of questionnaires, such as positive and negative sociometric nominations, measures of loneliness and social dissatisfaction and a measure of interpersonal concerns. Adolescents who were described as having low aggressive and disruptive behaviour were generally considered to be kind, trustworthy and co-operative (Parkhurst and Asher 1992). The best-liked students were viewed as co-operative and compassionate. Rejected adolescents were thought of as aggressive, disruptive and lacking in qualities. Some teenagers were thought of as 'controversial' by their peers. They tended to be rated high on negative interactional qualities.

Aggressive-rejected and submissive-rejected adolescents dislike being teased by their peers. Evidence shows that the former group tends to over-react to teasing; they see it as a form of provocation. Submissive-rejected teenagers experience teasing as a form of criticism by their peers, which no doubt increases their feelings of loneliness, and their tendency to be withdrawn.

Finally, research evidence (Boivin *et al.* 1989, Parkhurst and Asher 1992) suggests that submissive-rejected individuals are more likely to suffer from loneliness and social dissatisfaction. Peers usually describe such teenagers as 'sad'. It also seems that aggressive-rejected teenagers are at risk for later behavioural problems such as delinquency and dropping out of school, while submissive-rejected adolescents are more likely to be at risk for later depression (Parkhurst and Asher 1992).

## Parents vs. Peers

A popular belief is that parents and peers have quite opposite demands and influences on the adolescent, and that there is an underlying tension between the two. This is not a surprising thesis given that the peer group is seen as providing a context for sociable behaviour and is seen as providing an emotional anchor for the teenager. Indeed, some writers (e.g. Burlingame 1970: 143) have gone so far as to suggest that adolescents

> must reject their parents' dictates and, occasionally, their values.

The view that adolescents 'choose' to conform to peer pressure, while abandoning the ways of their family, has lately been challenged. Such an 'either-or' process is not necessarily true, and parental and peer influences are not always contradictory (Coleman and Hendry 1990). Indeed, there is a surprising amount of overlap between parental and peer values and standards. It has been suggested that so-called negative peer pressure is not as influential as previously thought. Some go as far as to suggest that the peer group may, in many instances, exert a positive influence on the adolescent (Foster-Clark and Blyth 1991).

This view is shared by Noller and Patton (1990) who suggested that most adolescents are not likely to reject their family, but would prefer to maintain warm and close emotional relationships with their parents. As they suggest (p. 62):

Adolescents will not be told what to do, but they are generally willing to talk things over with and listen to parents who are prepared to try and understand their position. They want to have more independence and autonomy, but within the context of a supportive family.

Although adolescents slowly become emotionally autonomous from their parents and spend increasing amounts of time away from the family, some evidence suggests that the *quality* of time spent alone with mother or father does not change substantially. At the same time, adolescents may also begin to spend more time *alone* at home. This may take the form of studying, reading, watching television or listening to music. Some writers suggest that the ability to spend some time alone is an indication of psychological well-being (Larson and Richards 1991). Too much time alone, of course, may also be an indication of depression.

That adolescents abandon the advice of parents and embrace totally the values and norms of the peer group is not entirely accurate. We now know that teenagers seek advice from both peers and parents depending on the dilemma that they are faced with. Thus it has been found that adolescents tend to value the judgements of their parents with respect to weighty matters such as possible careers, decisions regarding further study, and so forth, while peers are important sources of information about dating, money, drinking, life style and such matters (Noller and Patton 1990, Sebald 1989).

One research study (Sebald 1989) attempted to shed further light on this. The author compared the responses to identical questionnaires administered to samples of high school students in the United States in 1963, 1976 and 1982. He noted some fluctuations over the years in peer orientation. Generally, the teenagers were least susceptible to peer pressure in 1963, and most susceptible in 1976. Sebald also found that girls had become increasingly susceptible to peer pressure compared with boys. The author does not discuss the significance of these findings to any great extent, and one must accept them with some caution. In the first place, the findings were based on the responses of a relatively small number of mostly white students. One must therefore question their representativeness. Secondly, it is not clear to what extent they apply to groups of teenagers in other cultures. This question needs to be addressed in future research. Thirdly, the author does not discuss contextual issues affecting his findings. For instance, were the 1976 students affected by particular social events?

# Bullying at School

Bullying has been identified as a significant problem in schools in the United Kingdom, the United States and Australia (Rigby and Slee 1991). Surveys of students estimate that up to 10 per cent of school students can be identified as victims of bullying, although the prevalence appears to be slightly lower in high schools than junior schools. Boys are generally more likely to experience bullying than girls.

Following the work of Olweus, authors like Perry and colleagues (1988: 807) have identified bullying as a form of aggression involving verbal or physical harrassment of a child who is usually much weaker (the 'whipping boy'), by a child who is usually much stronger (the bully).

Bullying can take different forms. One study among junior and high school students in Australia (Rigby and Slee 1991) revealed four types of bullying: being called names, being picked on by other kids, being hit and pushed around by other kids and being made fun of. The survey revealed that boys were more likely than girls to experience physical bullying, while most teenagers were more likely to be called names. The main results of this study, showing the different experiences of boys and girls, are shown in Table 4.4. It shows that boys were more likely to be the victims of different types of bullying, although sex differences were significant for the physical dimension only. Thus boys were more likely than girls to report being hit or pushed around by other kids.

Most youngsters are opposed to bullying at school. Certainly, there is much opposition to bullying, with much support for the victim in junior school. However, opposition, as well as support for the victims of bullying, gradually decreases as teenagers move through high school (Rigby and Slee 1991). The authors explain such diminishing support for victims thus (p. 626):

> schools tend to inculcate stereotypically male values, which run counter to the development of empathic responses to others. Arguably increased exposure to such values may result in a lessening in sympathy for the victims of bullying.

Just why does bullying occur at school? Can one predict with some certainty who is likely to bully or be bullied? Or does bullying occur in a rather haphazard fashion?

## The victim

One report (Perry *et al.* 1988) suggests that one is able to identify those youngsters likely to be bullied. They note that victims tend to

**Table 4.4** *Experiences of Boys and Girls being Bullied (%)*

| Victimisation item | Never | | Once in a while | | Pretty often | | Very often | | Sex differences |
|---|---|---|---|---|---|---|---|---|---|
| | Boys | Girls | Boys | Girls | Boys | Girls | Boys | Girls | |
| 1. I get called names by other kids | 11.5 | 13.6 | 61.8 | 67.7 | 15.9 | 12.5 | 10.8 | 6.2 | n.s. |
| 2. I get picked on by other kids | 27.7 | 31.4 | 54.5 | 55.8 | 11.8 | 7.9 | 6.1 | 4.8 | n.s. |
| 3. I get hit and pushed around by other kids | 39.5 | 61.2 | 45.9 | 31.2 | 10.2 | 5.1 | 4.5 | 2.5 | < 0.01 |
| 4. Other kids make fun of me | 27.1 | 31.7 | 55.4 | 57.5 | 11.1 | 5.9 | 6.4 | 4.8 | n.s. |

*Source:*   Rigby and Slee, 1991

have a history of yielding to the bully's demands and usually do not offer resistance. Sometimes victims may resemble others that the bully has observed being bullied, or it is possible that the victim may, in some way, be provocative. Some victims reward bullies by actually acquiescing to their demands. Finally, the authors note that there is some evidence which shows that victims tend to have low self-esteem, are socially isolated, are physically weak or are afraid to be assertive.

One must distinguish between provocative (aggressive) and passive (non-aggressive) victims (Perry *et al.* 1988). Aggressive victims (those who deliberately start a fight) are most at risk for rejection by peers. These youngsters tend to be the most disliked members of a group, and are likely to suffer later maladjustment.

### The aggressor

Several research studies have identified hormonal and social influences on the aggressive behaviour of children and teenagers (see also Chapter 1). In an important review of the literature (Parke and Slaby 1983), a link was noted between plasma testosterone levels and self-reports of physical and verbal aggression in sixteen year-old Swedish boys. The higher the testosterone level, the more impatient and irritable the boys were. Although some links between testosterone levels and agression have also been noted in females, the effect is much weaker.

Evidence also indicates that aggression in youngsters may have social antecedents. Parke and Slaby (1983) note as influences the family, the peer group and the effects of television viewing. Thus it has been demonstrated that the family sets the context in which children and teenagers learn to be aggressive. Excessive use of physical force on the child, or husband-wife violence may induce the child to act in an aggressive manner.

It is also possible that children and teenagers learn aggression from their peers. Peers may *elicit* aggression, or may serve as role models to other children who have a predisposition to act aggressively (see Chapter 1, social learning theory). Moreover, peers may reinforce aggressive behaviour. Research has also suggested that the viewing of violent television programs may be linked to aggressive behaviour. Although countries differ in their regulation of the portrayal of violence on television, it remains a powerful socialising agent. When violence (however subtle) is portrayed, it is usually committed by a male figure. More often than not, victims tend to be females or males in much weaker positions, such as members of minorities (Parke and Slaby 1983).

In conclusion, it is doubtful whether bullying will ever be completely eradicated in school. There are strong influences on children and adolescents acquiring aggressive behaviour, such as biological changes and social learning effects. Perhaps school authorities can attempt to counter those influences by rewarding children's acceptable behaviour more positively.

## Theoretical Considerations

Two theoretical approaches appear to have important implications for this discussion. In the first place, close friendships as well as the larger peer group fulfil an important role in assisting the adolescent with the process of identity formation. Friends serve as a sounding board in a way quite different from parents. They reflect contemporary attitudes and values as well as dress and hairstyles. Friends and peers therefore act as a barometer against which the teenager is continually measured. Very often, parents and peers differ in their ideas about a whole range of issues. This serves a useful function for the adolescent, who must consider alternative arguments and propositions. This is a crucial aspect of identity formation.

Secondly, it has been argued that maladaptive parent-child relations are implicated in rejection by peers (Dishion *et al.* 1991). It was noted earlier that biological changes may be a strong influence on changed parent-child relations. Thus, biological changes are linked to peer rejection and, perhaps, bullying. What is required are longitudinal studies over several years to plot biological change in youngsters and associated parent-child relations and aggressive behaviour at school.

Thirdly, social learning theory is implicated in bullying in that children and teenagers are likely to learn such behaviours from others (parents or television shows) while still relatively young. For them, violence becomes an acceptable response, a way of dealing with a threatening situation or uncertainty. Finally, we noted that the peer group plays a crucial role in the adolescent's journey to adulthood. In this sense, it fulfils an important psycho-social function: assisting teenagers break the close emotional attachments to their parents.

## Summary

This chapter has highlighted the important role that friendships and peer groups play in the psychological development of the adolescent. As individuals move into adolescence, the peer group becomes increasingly important as a vehicle of social comparison. At the same time, the peer group is crucial in assisting the teenager become emotionally autonomous of the family and thus gradually assert his or her own independence. For those who do not have a warm relationship with their family, the peer group very often serves as an emotional anchor.

This chapter also discussed the importance of close friendships. A close friend acts as a confidant, someone to whom the adolescent can turn in the event of a problem or crisis. In short, close friends can be 'trusted'. Important sex differences were also noted in the nature and formation of close friendships.

Many of the studies reported here, as elsewhere in this volume, are based on English-speaking (mainly American) samples. There is a dearth of data using non-English-speaking non-Western people. It would be interesting, for example, to replicate some of the studies reported here among Chinese teenagers. The family traditionally has a very important place in Chinese life. What is the role of the peer group in such situations? Are its functions similar to that reported for Western teenagers? Moreover, are there differences in the functions of the peer group between Hong Kong and People's Republic Chinese? Questions such as these need to be addressed in future research.

## Additional Readings

Dunphy, D. (1963) 'The Social Structure of Urban Adolescent Peer Groups', *Sociometry* 26: 230–76

Hays, R. (1988) 'Friendship', in S. Duck (ed.), *Handbook of Personal Relationships: Theory, Research and Interventions*. Chichester: John Wiley and Sons

## Exercise

1. To what extent do adolescents use their parents and friends as a 'sounding board' for various issues? Interview five sixteen-year olds and question them about this. Cover topics such as dress style, musical preference, dating, future career options, religious beliefs and political attitudes. Include other topics too, if you wish.
   Are there differences in the sorts of issues that adolescents believe parents and friends are qualified to deal with?

# 5 Educational Processes

## Introduction

Schools have a major influence on adolescent development. Not only are many friendships formed there but, as society becomes more complex, with increasing emphasis placed on the acquisition of specialist skills and training for jobs, so the importance of the school as a social institution is likely to increase. Some believe that this will happen at the expense of the influence of other social institutions such as the family and the church (Conger and Petersen 1984).

More and more adolescents are choosing to complete high school. For instance, by 1985, 80 per cent of high school students in the United States completed their studies. In Canada, the school retention rate in 1982–83 was 84 per cent, while in Japan in 1981 it was 89 per cent (Blakers 1990). In Australia, retention rates rose from 60.3 per cent in 1989 to 71.3 per cent in 1991 (Australian Bureau of Statistics 1992). Such encouraging retention rates seem to be characteristic of most developed nations. Perhaps this is symptomatic of relatively high youth unemployment rates (see Chapter 8). On the other hand, such high retention rates may simply be a reflection of a view that higher levels of education are associated with higher social status and better-paid jobs (Blakers 1990).

As the workforce becomes more sophisticated, more parents and teenagers see distinct advantages in completing high school. Parents may view staying on at school as a means whereby their children can improve their prospects both socially and economically. Although many teenagers hold negative attitudes towards school and the curriculum (Poole 1983, 1990), they nonetheless see a link between completing their studies, better qualifications and the increased likelihood of finding a job (Blakers 1990).

This line of thought has been echoed by the results of two large-scale surveys of adolescents, one in the United Kingdom (Furnham and Gunter 1989) and the other in Australia (Poole 1983). It was noted that 57 per cent of the British sample and 86.5 per cent of the Australian one agreed with the statement: 'An educated person stands a better chance in life than an uneducated person.' Fifty-nine per cent of the British sample and 72.2 per cent of the Australian agreed with the statement 'A lot of schooling is necessary to avoid a dead-end job.' In both, there appears to be some recognition by adolescents that by completing high school they enhance their job prospects. It is difficult to explain the quite large differences between the results of the two samples. Perhaps it reflects sampling or cultural differences, or simply the fact that the surveys were conducted five years apart.

In this chapter, various important psychological issues relating to school life and academic attainment will be discussed. It will begin by examining the transition to high school, before exploring some of the psychosocial correlates of academic performance and motivation. Attention will also be paid to high school dropouts and the effects of gender and type of school on academic performance.

## The Transition to High School

The transfer from primary to high school is a potentially stressful time for the young adolescent, and has the potential negatively to affect emotional adjustment (Dowling 1980). The move to high school is often accompanied by a move away from close friends and familiar surroundings, and is associated with new expectations and teaching methods. Not only is the new high school student surrounded by teenagers who appear to be a lot older and more confident, but there are also new curricula to select from, taught by unfamiliar teachers. Thus many young adolescents may experience strain and loss of self-esteem (Wall 1977).

Writers such as Wall have suggested that the first few weeks of high school are crucial in many respects. For many new students, this period may set the basis for future attitudes and behaviour. For instance, moving into a large and impersonal high school separated from old friends and what is familiar may serve to lower the adolescent's self-esteem and confidence. This may then influence his or her approach to interpersonal relationships and academic performance, at least for the immediate future.

Wall (1977) has noted several other crucial factors which impinge on the adolescent's adaptation to high school. He notes, for example, that the family plays a crucial role in helping adjustment to high school (see later). It is also clear that young teenagers are at different stages of cognitive development with some, but not all, capable of abstract and formal reasoning. It is at this time, too, that teenagers are characterised by rapid physical and emotional changes, thus presenting them with a variety of challenges and developmental tasks. The new high school student is therefore confronted by a range of different and complex challenges: interpersonal, academic, cognitive and biological.

One study (Dowling 1980) examined the relationship between adjustment one year after entering high school and various assessments of children made towards the end of primary school. Before entering high school, students were administered measures of verbal reasoning, sentence reading comprehension, personality and teacher's ratings of adjustment such as: 'I think that this child will make a satisfactory social and emotional adjustment in secondary school'. A year after entering high school, Dowling assessed the adolescents' attitudes toward school, their behaviour and general adjustment. He found that personality factors such as extraversion and introversion were weakest in predicting adjustment. The best predictors were teachers' ratings of adjustment to high school. It should be pointed out, however, that the various predictive factors only explained 17 per cent of the variance in teachers' adjustment ratings. This suggests that other factors not considered in the research may contribute to such adjustment. Some of these, no doubt, include the personality of the adolescent, attitudes towards school and parental support.

Educational systems differ across the world. Students who move from junior school to junior high and then on to senior high school, experience disruption twice. Research findings indicate that the transition in early adolescence has negative consequences for girls' self-esteem and the participation of both sexes in extra-curricular activities. These students are just coming to terms with their transition when they need to change schools again. The later adolescents make their first transition, the better able they are to cope (Blyth and colleagues 1983). This option is, of course, not available in all educational systems.

Although adjustment to high school has not generated much psychological research, this is not the case as far as the psychosocial correlates of academic attainment are concerned. It is to these and other issues that we now turn our attention.

## Attitudes to School

Evidence indicates that there are differences in the ways boys and girls perceive school. It appears that, overall, girls have a much more positive attitude than boys. Moreover, there is cross-cultural support for this view.

In one study conducted in the United Kingdom, over 2000 teenagers aged between 10 and 17 years were asked to share their views about school (Furnham and Gunter 1989). Some questions were specifically directed at what adolescents expected from school.

Table 5.1 shows the responses of all the respondents to a selection of questions. Generally, boys were found to be *less* optimistic and to have slightly higher negative expectations about school than girls. Boys, for instance, were more likely than girls to lower their expectations about school in order to avoid disappointment. Boys were also more likely to expect teachers to dislike them.

Similar findings were obtained in an Israeli study of over 2600 students (Darom and Rich 1988). As predicted, the authors found that girls tended to have more positive attitudes to school than boys. Moreover, teachers perceived the attitudes of girls to be more positive than those of boys, although teachers tended to over-estimate these sex differences. To what extent boys' relatively negative attitudes are determined by teachers' negative perceptions, or vice versa, has yet to be established.

Teenagers have well developed views about the structure and organisation of schools. Australian studies have shown that many are dissatisfied with the ways schools are run. They are not viewed as particularly inviting or supportive, and are seen to be organised along authoritarian lines, with an emphasis on discipline. Many adolescents find schools alienating and impersonal. Whereas prim-

**Table 5.1** *Sex Differences in Attitudes to School*

| Attitudes | | Respondents | | |
|---|---|---|---|---|
| | | All | Male | Female |
| 1. You should not expect too much from school, for you would only be disappointed | Agree | 45 | 49 | 41 |
| | Neither | 25 | 25 | 25 |
| | Disagree | 30 | 25 | 35 |
| 2. Students should not expect teachers to like them | Agree | 41 | 49 | 33 |
| | Neither | 30 | 28 | 33 |
| | Disagree | 29 | 23 | 34 |
| 3. Most of the subjects I take are interesting | Agree | 55 | 50 | 59 |
| | Neither | 22 | 25 | 18 |
| | Disagree | 23 | 25 | 23 |
| 4. It really doesn't matter how well you do at school | Agree | 22 | 26 | 18 |
| | Neither | 15 | 17 | 12 |
| | Disagree | 63 | 57 | 70 |
| 5. I get bored and fed up with school and do not really enjoy anything connected with it | Agree | 39 | 41 | 37 |
| | Neither | 27 | 28 | 25 |
| | Disagree | 34 | 31 | 38 |

*Source:* Furnham and Gunter, 1989

ary schools are usually characterised as more supportive, high schools, with their system of rotating teachers, are not (Poole 1990).

According to one review, adolescents are critical of the selection of subjects generally available to them. For many, the selection is 'too academic', with many desiring more vocationally oriented and practical subjects (Poole 1990). As we approach the next century, schools face the challenge of producing well-educated individuals who will be able to meet the social, intellectual, and technological challenges of our times. Schools need to adapt their ethos, subject choice and organisational structure accordingly.

## Psychosocial Correlates of Academic Performance

Academic performance at school is not only dependent upon the child's academic ability. There are many other psychological and social factors which help determine achievement. This section will review just some of them.

### The Importance of Family Life

Like so many other aspects of adolescent development, the family plays an important role in offering emotional support to adolescents and socialising them to do the best they can academically. Connell and his colleagues (1982) concur with this viewpoint by suggesting that (pp. 185–86):

> Families are thought to shape the educational careers of their young members in a wide range of ways: the extent to which parents care about schooling, the manner in which family members relate to each other . . . (methods of discipline), their material provision (for example, of a quiet place to study), and their internal structure (especially the state of the parents' marriage).

The extent to which the family can play a supportive role in the adolescent's school career depends very much on a range of factors such as parenting styles and the nature of the communication process between them, the personality of the adolescent, and other factors such as the family's social status and financial situation. In the United States, for example, black adolescents living in single-mother households very often have to cope with factors such as large family size, father's absence, crowding and mother's relatively low educational level (Scheinfeld 1983). In Australia, Poole (1983) has confirmed the importance of social class. She found that higher social status families are likely to have children who remain at school for a longer period of time and obtain higher status jobs. She refers to this process as *cultural and social reproduction* (p. 111).

In her longitudinal study of 1600 adolescents, Poole (1983) found support for the importance of social class factors in academic aspiration. She found that fathers in professional occupations were much more likely than fathers in white collar or blue collar jobs to strive for university education for their children. There were also striking differences between the aspirations of the adolescents *themselves*. For instance, those with professional fathers were more likely to strive for university education than were adolescents with white collar or blue collar fathers (63.9, 43.4 and 32.1 per cent respectively). The reverse was true regarding adolescent aspirations for completing high school: more adolescents from blue collar than white collar or professional families aspired to a high school education only (19.1, 14.7 and 12.0 per cent respectively).

Of some import is the fact that similar findings have been noted in an African study (Cherian 1991). The author examined whether an association existed between the academic achievement of 1021 Xhosa-speaking students aged thirteen to seventeen years and parents' aspirations. The parents were subdivided in terms of their level of education, occupation, income and socio-economic status. The findings supported the hypotheses: higher parental occupation, education, income and socio-economic status were associated with higher parental aspirations which, in turn, were associated with higher academic performance by the students.

Various writers (e.g. Masselam *et al.* 1990, Steinberg *et al.* 1989) have noted the nature of family functioning and adolescent achievement at school. It is clear, for instance, that adolescents who are making academic progress compared with those who are not, perceive their families quite differently. Those who are achieving academically tend to see their familes as exhibiting cohesion and expressiveness, while those who are underachieving are likely to describe their family as conflict-ridden and 'pressuring'.

Researchers have identified family cohesion and adaptability as important facets of family functioning (Masselam *et al.* 1990). Cohesion refers to the emotional bonding that the family displays, while adaptability refers to the extent to which family members are able to adapt to changing roles. Masselam and colleagues conducted a comparative study of two groups of matched adolescents. One comprised students who were not making academic progress at school, while the other comprised successful students. It was noted that significant differences existed in the perception of family functioning between the two groups of teenagers and their parents.

With respect to cohesion, adolescents making academic progress, as well as their parents, characterised their family as being significantly more cohesive than did adolescents who were not making progress. The two groups did not differ significantly with respect to adaptability. Respondents were also asked to give their *ideal* family rating on cohesiveness and adaptability. Significant differences emerged between the successful and unsuccessful students with respect to their *actual* and *ideal* scores. Table 5.2 shows that the discrepancy scores for the group making academic progress were much smaller than for the group which was not successful. Thus for the successful group there was greater congruence between actual and ideal family functioning.

Parenting style has also been shown to be related to academic achievement. Research indicates that authoritative parenting is best associated with academic achievement, while authoritarian and permissive styles are not (Dornbusch *et al.* 1987). This theme has been extended in further research by Steinberg and his associates (1989). They argued that three components of authoritative parenting are influential in academic performance. These are parental acceptance or warmth, psychological autonomy and behavioural control. These aspects of parenting *facilitate* rather than simply accompany academic performance.

**Table 5.2** *Mean Discrepancy Scores between Real and Ideal Family Functioning by Adolescents and their Parents*

| Measure | Successful students | Unsuccessful students | F |
|---|---|---|---|
| **Adolescents** | | | |
| Cohesion | 17.15 | 29.85 | 10.17* |
| Adapability | 30.10 | 44.13 | 12.64* |
| **Mothers** | | | |
| Cohesion | 12.33 | 29.22 | 18.09* |
| Adaptability | 27.13 | 28.70 | 0.20 |
| **Fathers** | | | |
| Cohesion | 9.74 | 24.42 | 25.30* |
| Adaptability | 23.31 | 23.19 | 0.00 |
| **Families** | | | |
| Cohesion | 13.50 | 28.43 | 26.11* |
| Adaptability | 27.29 | 33.60 | 7.83* |

*Note:* *Means differ significantly at 0.05 level

*Source:*    Masselam *et al.* 1990

It has been suggested that an authoritative parenting style, in which much parental warmth and support is present, generates psychosocial maturity in adolescents (Steinberg *et al.* 1989). Psychosocial maturity is characterised by several features, one of which is a positive attitude to school work. Steinberg and colleagues found that psychosocial maturity increased the chances of academic performance in those homes classified as authoritative.

The model showing the relationship between parenting style and academic performance is shown in Figure 5.1. It also acknowledges the importance of other factors, such as family structure, the sex of the child, the socio-economic position of the family and achievement test scores on final academic performance.

## Influence of Family Disruption

The impact of family separation and divorce on the adjustment of children is well documented (e.g. Hetherington *et al.* 1989, Amato

**Figure 5.1** *Relationships between Parental Warmth, Adolescent Maturity and Academic Outcome*

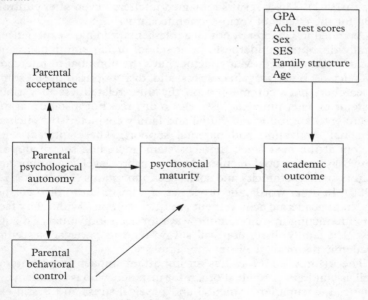

*Source:*    Steinberg *et al.* 1989

and Keith 1991; see also Chapter 3). Numerous studies have been conducted examing the effects of family disruption on various adjustment domains such as psychological and social adjustment, general conduct and self-esteem. In this section, the effect of family disruption upon academic performance will be considered.

Most research evidence in this area indicates that adolescents whose parents have separated or divorced do not perform academically as well as those from intact families. For instance, Bisnaire and associates (1990) noted the negative impact of father's absence on boys' academic performance. They also reported that children from one-parent families tend to be characterised by poorer socioemotional development and lower academic achievement. An independent analysis (Wood, Chapin and Hannah 1988) also highlighted the important role that the home environment plays in adolescents' academic success.

These findings were borne out by a separate longitudinal study (Zimiles and Lee 1991) which examined the academic attainment of high school students from intact, single-parent and remarried families. It was noted that students from intact families significantly outperformed those from other families, although the differences between the groups were not large (see also Amato and Keith 1991). These results remained unaltered even after controlling for the effects of socio-economic status.

As noted in Chapter 3, not all adolescents who have experienced family disruption underperform at school or are emotionally and socially maladjusted. Many factors have the potential to intercede and act as buffers against stress and disruption. Indeed, some researchers have commented on the inter-relatedness of various systems in determining adjustment to divorce. For instance, at the micro level are found individual and family characteristics such as personal motivation and parental support. These interact with factors at the next level, the ecosystem, including social support networks and school factors. At the macro level are important factors such as ethnicity and socio-economic status (Mednick *et al.* 1990). In other words, the processes of adjustment to divorce and resultant academic achievement are quite complex with many factors interacting in quite unique ways for each individual. To suggest that family disruption will always tend to lower adolescents' academic performance is far too simplistic.

The divorce *experience* has an important impact on parents as well as children. A single mother, for instance, who is experiencing financial, occupational, mental and physical stress and is still experiencing conflict with her ex-partner, may find it extremely difficult to cope. Furthermore, it is unlikely that she would be able to conceal this fact from her child. Such visible stress is likely to have a negative effect on adolescent academic performance (McCombs and Forehand 1989, Mednick *et al.* 1990).

Other researchers have examined the role of factors such as mother's level of contentment and adolescent-peer relations. For example, one team conducted an eighteen-year longitudinal study of the academic achievement of Danish adolescents who had experienced family disruption and divorce (Mednick *et al.* 1990). The authors examined reading and mathematics proficiency in the last two years of school and related these to various social and family matters. After partialling out the effects of socio-economic status and mother's educational level, several factors were found to predict academic performance. Table 5.3 shows that lower reading proficiency was related to mother's discontentment and adolescent's poor peer relations. Lower mathematics proficiency was associated with mother's discontentment, mothers' disorderliness, maternal employment instability and number of school changes.

The evidence indicates that mathematics proficiency may be more sensitive to family disruption and mother's level of adjustment than is reading proficiency. The authors argued that the ability of the single mother to cope with her situation is an important factor in determining the academic performance of her children (see also Barber and Eccles 1992). Mednick and colleagues (1990: 82–83) state that

> a decrease in the mother's ability to deal with her situation has a rather pervasive influence on her children's academic performance.

**Table 5.3** *Correlations between Social and Family Factors and Achievement in Reading and Mathematics*

|  | Reading | | Mathematics | |
| --- | --- | --- | --- | --- |
| Social and family factors | r | p | r | p |
| Stepfamily unification problems | −0.19 | n.s. | −0.18 | n.s. |
| Mother's discontentment | −0.24 | 0.05 | −0.31 | 0.01 |
| Mother's disorderliness | −0.17 | n.s. | −0.28 | 0.01 |
| Maternal employment instability | −0.17 | n.s. | −0.36 | 0.01 |
| School changes | −0.11 | n.s. | −0.26 | 0.05 |
| Poor peer relations | −0.29 | 0.01 | −0.11 | n.s. |

*Note:* Socio-economic status and mother's level of education have been partialled out

*Source:* Mednick *et al.* 1990

## The Role of Personality Factors

To what extent do personality factors predict academic attainment and achievement motivation? This is an area of enquiry that has generated substantial research endeavour (for a recent review see Byrne and Byrne 1990).

A large body of literature has evolved which has examined the link between achievement motivation and academic performance on the one hand, and their personality correlates on the other. Research has yielded some interesting, albeit seemingly contradictory, results for primary school students and late adolescents. For example, extraversion has been shown to be an important factor in academic attainment among primary school students, whilst introversion is important for older students (Entwistle 1972). There are a variety of possible explanations for this. Perhaps able students become more introverted as they get older, while students who are less able become more extraverted. It is also possible that some extraverted students, perhaps because of excessive socialising, could fall behind as more complex academic skills develop (H. Eysenck and M. Eysenck 1985).

Entwistle (1972) also showed that the relationship between personality traits such as extraversion and academic attainment is complicated by the effects of students' intellectual level, type of institution and the subject being studied (see also Seddon 1977). In a later study among various groups of Bulgarians (Paspalanov 1984), extraversion was found to be related to achievement motivation for groups of high school students and skilled industrial workers, gifted and talented high school students, and eminent musicians and artists, although the associations were stronger for the latter group.

Other research has looked at the effects of levels of anxiety, low self-esteem and locus of control on achievement motivation. In a study of 512 Indian adolescents, for instance, it was found that a significant negative relationship exists between achievement motivation and anxiety (Jindal and Panda 1982): that is, those who were achievement-motivated tended to be less anxious. Interestingly, this relationship only held for males, and could be attributed to different socialisation patterns for male and female Indian adolescents. On the other hand, a study among Bulgarians found some evidence of a positive significant relationship between anxiety and neuroticism and achievement motivation among groups of high school students and eminent musicians, but not among gifted and talented high school students (Paspalanov 1984).

Another factor shown to be related to academic outcome is

'locus of control'. Those who are said to be internally controlled believe that what happens to them does so as a result of their own efforts. In other words, they feel in control of the events of their lives. Externals, on the other hand, believe that fate and chance factors play a large role in their lives. It has been found that those who are internally controlled score higher academically than do 'externals' (e.g. Fry and Coe 1980, Heaven 1990). In addition, research in the United States has shown this relationship is more complex among black than white students. 'Internal' blacks seem to perform best when competing against a white, or when collaborating with other black students (Fry and Coe 1980).

Another personality factor shown to be important in explaining academic performance among adolescents is social competence. It has been noted that prosocial and responsible forms of behaviour are associated with academic attainment, whereas those who are rejected by their peers tend to be underachievers. On the basis of her research among 423 twelve and thirteen-year-olds, Wentzel (1991) highlighted the importance of three aspects of social competence to academic attainment. These are: socially responsible behaviour (such as adhering to social rules and expectations), sociometric status (having friends), and self-regulatory processes (such as planning and setting goals).

As predicted, it was found that all aspects of social competence were related to academic attainment. Of some import, however, was the finding that socially responsible behaviour mediated the relationship between academic performance and factors such as peer status, social responsibility, goals, interpersonal trust and interpersonal problem-solving. There are three possible explanations for these findings (Wentzel 1991). Firstly, it is possible that socially responsible behaviour is itself an end goal of the educational process, and therefore associated with academic performance. Secondly, teaching strategies may influence socially responsible behaviour in adolescents. Thirdly, it is possible that academic performance is a direct result of socially responsible behaviour. Further longitudinal research would be required to determine such cause-effect relationships.

## Causal Attributions for Success and Failure

The study of attributions or 'lay explanations' enjoys a central position in social psychology. Lay theories exist for most social events that we encounter in our daily lives. Thus, we each have particular beliefs about the possible causes of alcoholism, poverty, success, failure and so on. The study of attributions is important to psychologists, since attributions link the stimuli we encounter to individual behaviour (Ross and Fletcher 1985). Attributions, therefore, have implications for behaviour.

It was earlier proposed that three dimensions underlie our attributions for success and failure (Weiner 1979). These are controllability, locus and stability. Locus refers to internal dimensions (such as motivation) on the one hand, and external dimensions (such as ability or luck) on the other. Stability refers to how persistent the cause is (e.g. 'Am I always lucky?'). For example, intelligence is an important factor in explaining academic success. It is an internal and stable attribute. Table 5.4 shows that these dimensions can be further classified in terms of controllability or uncontrollability.

Research evidence shows that success in a task is usually attributed to internal stable causes, while failure is attributed to external causes. In an Australian study, students who passed a course exam explained their success in terms of their ability. Students who failed, however, were more likely to explain their failure by resorting to external factors, such as bad luck or task difficulty (Simon and Feather 1973). Some exceptions to these general principles have been noted. Low-achieving individuals tend to attribute success to *external* causes (Chapman and Lawes 1984). Research has also indicated that there are sex differences in attributional processes. Females, for instance, are more likely than males to make external attributions for success and failure: they are, that is, more likely to view their fate as being determined by external rather than personal reasons.

*Expectations* of success and failure are also important. Irrespective of whether one expects to succeed or fail, research has shown that expected outcomes are usually attributed to stable causes, and unexpected outcomes to unstable ones. So a student who expects

**Table 5.4** *Causal Dimensions for Success and Failure*

|  | Internal | | External | |
|  | Stable | Unstable | Stable | Unstable |
| --- | --- | --- | --- | --- |
| Controllable | General effort | Attention Immediate effort | Teacher bias | Help from others |
| Uncontrollable | Ability health ('I'm sickly') | Mood Maturity | Task difficulty Family | Health ('flu') Luck |

*Source:*   Derived from Weiner 1979

to pass, but does not, is more likely to attribute failure to bad luck than to lack of effort (Simon and Feather 1973).

According to expectancy-value theories of motivation, students' motivation to succeed is determined by their expectations for success as well as the value they attach to this. These two factors, therefore, are closely related in predicting motivation to succeed. Research, however, has yielded inconsistent findings on the predictive value of these components. There appears to be some debate as to which is most closely related to academic performance. Recent evidence shows that actual achievement may be more strongly related to expectations for success than to values about it (Berndt and Miller 1990).

# High School Dropouts

High school retention rates in many developed nations are higher than 70 per cent. As noted earlier, it is not clear whether this is due to limited employment prospects for teenagers, or to a perception that high school education will ultimately enhance one's future job prospects. In an expanding economy, higher educational qualifications are normally associated with better occupational prospects (Power 1984). However, this is not necessarily the case during a severe economic contraction or recession.

Maintaining high retention rates, particularly during a time of limited employment, is a social and political imperative. As Power (1984: 116) noted:

> Early school leavers face a greater risk of being unemployed than those successfully completing secondary school. Low retention rates have contributed to increases in the youth labour supply and hence to higher levels of youth unemployment.

What are the factors associated with the decision to stay on at school? This question has been reviewed by several researchers (e.g. Ainley, Foreman and Sheret 1991, Pittman 1991, Poole 1983, Power 1984, Zimiles and Lee 1991). Power (1984) studied over 2000 high school students in thirty schools in South Australia. He showed that school retentivity was determined by factors such as the type of school attended, parental encouragement and academic self-esteem. Perhaps unexpectedly, he found no evidence that parental socio-economic status and satisfaction of students with school were directly related to adolescents' decision to remain there. Instead, parental socio-economic status was directly linked to type of school and to parental encouragement. Both these factors were significantly related to the decision to remain at school.

A related model has been proposed by Ainley and his colleagues (1991; see Figure 5.2). They propose that several background or antecedent variables and intervening variables are related to school retention. The antecedent variables are factors such as socio-economic status of the family, parental expectations about whether a teenager should complete school, non-English-speaking background and type of school. Their evidence suggests that teenagers from higher socio-economic backgrounds are more likely to complete high school than students from lower ones. Moreover, some teenagers from non-English-speaking backgrounds (e.g. Hispanics in the USA.) are more likely to complete high school than native English speakers. Thus, these antecedent factors may have direct effects on educational plans, while intervening variables such as achievement level and satisfaction with school and curriculum may mediate the decision to remain in school. Unlike Power (1984), Ainley *et al.* (1991) found that satisfaction with school is an important factor in determining retentivity.

The role of socio-economic status in the decision to remain at school is an interesting one. It appears that this factor impacts on the decision in a unique way. It is the 'social' aspect rather than the 'economic' that determines the decision to remain at school (Ainley *et al.* 1991). That is, parents of high socio-economic status have certain attitudes, expectations and beliefs about the need to complete high school. Consequently, they socialise their teenagers accordingly. They seem to encourage them in a way that parents from lower socio-economic groups do not. The role of this factor is particularly evident in Power's (1984) research, which found that parental encouragement has a direct influence on the decision to stay at school.

Adolescents who decide to stay at school differ in their perceptions of what their parents expect of them from those who leave. In one survey of Australian adolescents, for example, it was found that those who stayed at school were more likely to believe that their parents wanted them to enter lower or upper professional occupations. Adolescents who decided to leave school were more likely to believe that their parents were in favour of them following skilled manual or white collar vocations (Poole 1983).

Other writers have focused on the effects of family structure on high school dropout rates. One major longitudinal study examined over 10,000 adolescents (Zimiles and Lee 1991). The researchers divided their sample into either intact, single-parent or stepparent families. They found that students from intact families were up to

**Figure 5.2** *Ainley's Path Model for School Retentivity*

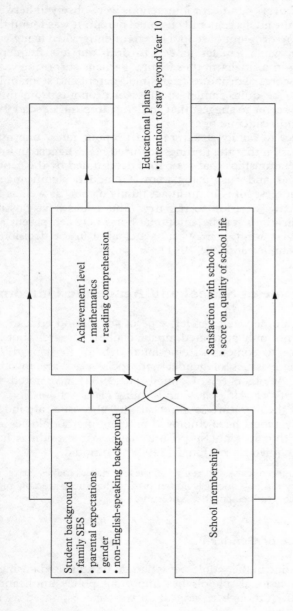

*Source:*   Ainley *et al.* 1991

three times less likely to drop out of school than those from other families. Moreover, significant interactions were observed between the gender of the adolescent and custodial parent. It was found that males tended to drop out of school less frequently when living with single fathers, while females tended to drop out less frequently when residing in a single-mother family. Perhaps surprisingly, the achievement scores of dropouts from single-parent and stepfamilies were found to be quite similar to those of dropouts from intact families. This seems to suggest that students drop out of school for reasons beyond academic ones.

With respect to family structure and dropout rates, one must note in conclusion that the findings reported here suggest an intricate web of relationships that are partly determined by the gender of the teenager and custodial parent. Of added significance is whether the adolescent is in an intact family or not, as well as the custodial parent's decision to remarry. This could have possible negative implications for the emotional bond between parent and teenager. In that event, it may act as a catalyst in the decision to quit school (Zimiles and Lee 1991).

## Gender, Type of School and Academic Outcome

The relationship between gender, type of school and educational outcome has not only generated much scholarly research, but has also given rise to sometimes emotional debate. Perhaps this is inevitable where issues of gender and social class are involved (Jones 1990). As others (e.g. Connell *et al.* 1982) have noted, the debate concerns 'working class' and 'ruling class' schools.

A review of the literature soon reveals that the issues are indeed complex. Researchers have employed different methodologies and samples, and thus it is not surprising that research findings have tended to be equivocal. As Jones (1990: 153) noted,

> The intersection of class and gender in these variables makes the task of research very difficult and it is not surprising that there are now many studies which produce conflicting results.

### The Influence of Gender

The question of whether adolescents should be educated in single-sex or co-educational schools has important policy implications (Marsh 1989). Although co-education was first espoused as the ideal environment in which equal opportunity between the sexes could be made manifest, there is now some doubt among feminists and other writers as to whether girls perform optimally in such schools (e.g. Byrne and Byrne 1990, Jones 1990, Marsh 1989, Rowe 1988). Jones, for example, has argued that class ideology is transmitted from the social structure of society into co-educational schools. As a consequence, class and gender interact to lower the academic and career aspirations of girls in such schools. By contrast, girls in single-sex (usually wealthy private) schools have access to better facilities, smaller classes and generally seem to perform better.

Much research has focused on school type and gender differences in academic performance in subjects such as mathematics and science. Results have shown that boys in co-educational schools tend to outperform girls, while girls in government co-educational schools are less likely to enrol in higher level mathematics and science subjects (Jones 1990). Some evidence has shown that girls from single-sex schools are more likely to prefer science subjects and rate their performance in mathematics and science higher than girls from co-educational schools. Girls from mixed schools, however, are more likely to prefer subjects like English. Boys from co-educational schools tend to prefer science subjects compared with boys from single-sex schools. On the other hand, boys in single-sex schools prefer subjects like English, although they are more likely to have higher self-esteem than males in co-educational schools (Foon 1988). Thus, Foon concluded as follows (p. 52):

> The type of school attended does seem to have differential conse-quences for students in terms of their stated preferences and rated achievement in subjects: those attending single sex schools seem to be less rigidly attached to traditional views . . . By contrast, attendance at co-educational schools appears to be associated with traditional subject preferences and related assessments of achievement in those subject areas.

Various explanations for girls' relatively lower performance in science-related subjects in co-educational schools have been ad-vanced (Byrne and Byrne 1990, Jones 1990). Factors include school ethos, community attitudes, low aspiration, and negative teacher attitudes. Although some would argue that there are bio-logical differences between the sexes with respect to mathematical ability, this has been disputed (see Byrne and Byrne 1990). As most school principals and department heads in co-educational schools are male, girls lack adequate role models (Byrne and Byrne 1990, Jones 1990). It has been argued that mixed classrooms have a negative impact on girls' self-esteem so that they tend not to take subjects such as mathematics and science offered at advanced levels. It is not clear whether lowered self-esteem is the result of being in a mixed class or not. Nonetheless, there is evidence to suggest that boys in such schools are much more confident in their ability to learn mathematics (Rowe 1988). Future research should determine the source of this confidence, so as to initiate intervention strategies for girls.

There also appear to be particular classroom dynamics in operation whereby boys demand and receive more teacher attention (Jones 1990, Rowe 1988). This has led some researchers to conduct studies in which girls *within* coeducational schools have been placed in single-sex classes. One study (cited in Jones 1990) conducted in Britain found that girls in such single-sex classes achieved better results in mathematics and science than did girls in traditional mixed classes. Support for this view also comes from an Australian study which found significant gains in confidence over time for students in single-sex rather than mixed classes in a coeducational school (Rowe 1988).

## Changing the Nature of the School

Notwithstanding the fact that some research studies have found academic benefits for girls in single-sex schools, it has been the policy of some educational departments to convert public single-sex schools into co-educational ones. During the 1980s, for example, two single-sex schools (one for boys, one for girls) in a suburb of Sydney, were converted into co-educational schools. A team of researchers (Marsh, Owens, Myers and Smith 1989) conducted a longitudinal study extending over five years in which they examined teachers' perceptions of the effects of the transition, students' performance and their self-esteem. Over 2000 students were involved in the research.

According to teachers' perceptions *after* the transition, boys were advantaged by co-educational schooling in terms of their social and academic development. It was thought that they improved in English, the social sciences, art, music and home sciences. Teachers perceived that co-educational schools advantaged girls in social areas such as maturity, dress sense and general appearance, but that they were disadvantaged with respect to mathematics, science and computer studies. However, an examination of students' final scores in various subjects revealed that overall performance in English and mathematics remained largely unaltered for both gender groups. Only with respect to self-esteem were any changes noted. The authors found that, across all dimensions of the self-concept, students in co-educational schools obtained higher scores than students in single-sex ones.

The results reviewed here suggest that teachers' perceptions do not always mirror the actual academic performance of students. As the authors (Marsh *et al.* 1989: 171) remind us:

> teacher perceptions may reflect aspects of academic achievement, behaviour and motivation that do not show up in the . . . grades.

## Private vs. State Schools

The issue of private vs. state schools and students' educational outcomes should not be divorced from our discussion so far. In a sense, they are closely intertwined, since many private schools are, in fact, single-sex schools. However, whereas the previous section focused primarily on issues relating to gender, this section will concentrate on the academic performance of students in private and state schools irrespective of adolescents' gender.

It now appears to be a well-established fact that students who attend private schools are more likely than their state counterparts to complete more schooling and to attend university (Jones 1990, Byrne and Byrne 1990). Support for the view that private school students perform better than their state school counterparts comes from a large-scale survey of Australian students (Graetz 1990). This study found that private school students, on average, tend to spend more years at school (11 years) than state school students (9.6 years). It noted too that 58 per cent of independent school students were likely to proceed to university compared with 36 per cent of state school students. The main results are summarised in Table 5.5.

It is important to remember that it is not clear to what extent observed differences in outcome are due to *pre-existing* differences between students at co-educational and single-sex schools (Marsh 1989). Some single-sex schools, it has been argued, are academically selective, attracting students with above-average ability. It is therefore difficult to attribute any differences in outcome to actual school type.

Of considerable interest are the changes which have occurred in academic outcome between different types of schools over the last few decades. There has been considerable educational expansion. New schools and universities are associated with population growth

**Table 5.5** *Academic Attainments at Different School Types*

|  | Type of school | | |
|---|---|---|---|
|  | State | Catholic | Independent |
| **Basic schooling** | | | |
| Percentage completed | 20 | 30 | 58 |
| Mean years completed | 9.6 | 10 | 11 |
| **Higher education** | | | |
| Percentage participation | 36 | 43 | 58 |
| Mean years completed | 2.9 | 3.2 | 3.8 |

*Source:*   Graetz 1990

and a question that arises is whether this expansion has benefited all segments of the population. Australian research has demonstrated that those who attend private schools have benefited most from educational expansion (Graetz 1990). Graetz divided his sample into three cohorts, namely, pre-war (before 1950) post-war (between 1950 and 1969) and more recent (after 1970). The results of his analysis are shown in Table 5.6. It is clear, for instance, that completion rates for basic education have increased by 29 per cent in the state sector for the whole period, but by almost 50 per cent in the private sector. There have been similar changes with respect to participation in higher education and completion of first degrees.

In conclusion, Graetz (1990) makes an important observation about the long-term benefits of private schooling. He comments

**Table 5.6** *Academic Attainment and School Type over Time*

|  |  | School type | | |
|---|---|---|---|---|
|  |  | State | Catholic | Independent |
| **Basic schooling** | | | | |
| Percentage completed | pre-1950 | 6 | 10 | 28 |
|  | 1950–69 | 12 | 19 | 55 |
|  | post-1970 | 35 | 52 | 77 |
| **Higher education** | | | | |
| Percentage participated | pre-1950 | 18 | 19 | 30 |
|  | 1950–69 | 33 | 38 | 58 |
|  | post-1970 | 50 | 65 | 72 |
| **Highest attainments** | | | | |
| Degree | pre-1950 | 5 | 5 | 19 |
|  | 1950–69 | 9 | 11 | 29 |
|  | post-1970 | 19 | 34 | 50 |

*Source:*   Graetz 1990

**Figure 5.3** *Profile*

David was born into a professional family. His father was a solicitor in a large provincial city. His mother, somewhat withdrawn and shy, believed quite firmly that they were a cut above the rest of the community. After all, they paid more than their fair share of taxes, drove expensive cars and sent their children to a private primary school.

It was a foregone conclusion that David, the eldest child, would be sent to an expensive and elitist boarding school in the city when it came time for him to enter high school. The several thousand dollars it would cost every year was neither here nor there; an education from one of the local high schools was simply not good enough. Naturally, one got more than an education from one of these 'good' city schools. An important motive on the part of David's parents was the conviction that David would meet boys from like-minded, well-to-do families. Thus would begin, at an early age, the formation and cementing of friendships and a network of connections that might well prove useful in later life

that up to the final year of school a private education bestows definite benefits and that, generally, adolescents attending such schools are distinctly advantaged. For academic performance beyond that, say at university level, school type makes little difference to academic outcome. Instead, according to Graetz, ability and social background are more important predictors of academic success.

## The Transition to University

The relatively high rate of youth unemployment coupled with an increasing demand for a sophisticated and well-educated workforce have increased the demand for university education. Of course, not all high school students make it to university, and even then some students will drop out. Who is likely to proceed to higher education? Are other factors besides academic ability important in predicting entry?

It is likely that many factors play a role in the decision to attend university. Some of these are economic, such as financial expectations and labour market opportunities. Others are sociological, such as peer group influence and teacher encouragement. Recently, Hayden and Carpenter (1990) also identified the following factors:

- Attracted by certain features of higher education system
- Did well at school (especially in science)

- Received encouragement from parents and teachers
- Attended non-government high schools
- Have better-off and better-educated parents

Similar observations have been made in a longitudinal study of several hundred school leavers over several years (H. Winefield *et al.* 1988). The adolescents were surveyed towards the end of their high school careers and then four years later when they were in one of four comparison groups, namely, at university, unemployed, in satisfactory employment or in unsatisfactory employment. Of the adolescents rated 'definitely capable' of university study by their teachers, 43.4 per cent of the males and 32.9 per cent of the females proceeded to university. The authors noted that more males with high-status fathers than with low-status ones proceeded to university (46.3 per cent vs. 22.0 per cent), while for females the trend was 42.7 per cent vs. 28.1 per cent respectively.

This study also examined the effects of certain psychological factors. While at school, males in the four comparison groups were found not to differ significantly on measures of self-esteem or locus of control. However, females who proceeded to university had higher self-esteem and internal locus of control than other groups of females. Differences between the groups were also observed with regard to reported parental rearing patterns. Although there were no significant differences between the groups of males, females who entered university were much more likely than other groups of females to have a father who encouraged university education and the achievement of success. The decision of females to attend university is therefore more closely related to certain personality attributes than it is among males. Thus H. Winefield *et al.* (1988: 189) noted that

> the pattern of sex differences found here suggests that the process of taking on a 'student' identity is, for young women, dependent on considerable psychological resilience.

## Theoretical Considerations

Schools act as an important socialising agent in the lives of most adolescents. As such, they play an important role in the acquisition of social competence and adequate interpersonal skills, as well as friendships. Parallel with this influence is the role of the family. Supportive, yet authoritative parenting is likely to increase adolescents' psychosocial maturity, competence and self-esteem. This, in turn, is likely to enhance academic performance. Both the family and school, therefore, play an important role in academic performance and identity formation. The development of a vocational identity as well as the development of positive attitudes to work will, no doubt, be facilitated in those schools which are supportive and which encourage independence among students. These processes, moreover, are facilitated by families which are characterised by open channels of communication.

## Summary

More and more adolescents in developed countries are staying on to complete high school. This is no doubt due to the increasing technological sophistication of society, with its greater demands for a well-educated workforce. Other factors such as limited job opportunities for youth also increase school retention rates.

The transition to high school can be a difficult period for some adolescents. This chapter reviewed some of the key factors crucial to academic performance in high school. It was made clear, for instance, that supportive parenting styles assist teenagers in the transition to high school, thus enabling them to adjust to new demands with relative ease. The chapter also noted some of the most important socio-demographic characteristics of academic attainment, as well as the sometimes negative effects of family disruption.

Personality and attitudinal factors, it was noted, are also important in differentiating those who achieve academically and those who do not. There is a large body of literature which has reviewed the role of certain personality factors in academic achievement. Findings are not always straightforward. Thus, for example, it was noted that extraversion may be an important factor for younger adolescents, while internal locus of control is not equally important for all racial groups in the United States. In addition, there are individual attributions, expectancies and values which also need to be considered when explaining academic performance among adolescents.

Attention was also paid to the critical issue of gender and school type. This is a delicate matter, since it touches on matters of ideology, social policy and social class. It is doubtful whether the last word on this topic has been written. There is much scope here for further longitudinal research into the inter-relationships between these factors. Attention needs also to be paid to matters of policy such as the implementation of single-sex classes within co-

120 Contemporary Adolescence

educational schools, as well as changing teachers' and students' expectations regarding academic attainment.

## Additional Readings

Connel, R., Ashenden, D., Kessler, S. and Dowsett, G. (1982) *Making the Difference: Schools, Families and Social Divisions*. Sydney: Allen and Unwin
Graetz, B. (1990) 'Private Schools and Educational Attainment: Cohort and Generational Effects', *Australian Journal of Education*, 34: 174–91
Poole, M. (1983) *Youth: Expectations and Transitions*. Melbourne: Routledge and Kegan Paul

## Exercise

1. After reading Poole (1983), interview a number of adults in full-time employment in your community. Select people from a wide range of occupations: professionals, white collar workers, blue collar workers. Talk to them about their schooling and other background factors. For instance, did they attend private or public schools? What schools did their parents attend? Did they or their parents attend university? Determine whether there is a link between certain types of schooling and current occupation. Were respondents more likely to attend university if their parents did? Test for any other hypotheses you might have formulated.

# 6 Sexuality

## Introduction

We live in an age in which we are overwhelmed by material and information of a sexual nature. The AIDS epidemic has raised the consciousness of many adults and adolescents about sexually transmitted diseases, 'safe sex' practices and so on. Sexually explicit material, not available a generation or two ago, is now freely obtainable. Glossy magazines depict the 'perfect' female body or the 'handsome' male. Understandably, some adolescents may feel pressurised to make themselves as sexually appealing as possible.

The onset of sexual awareness coincides with puberty. Whereas boys begin to show an interest in girls in a *sexual* way, girls are more interested in boys in a *romantic* way (Harris and Liebert 1987). It is during puberty that the body undergoes rapid change in terms of size, height, weight and distribution of body hair. The various hormones being released into the bloodstream at this time prepare the child physically for adult sexuality (Gallois and Callan 1990). The young female will also experience her first menstruation, while the male will experience his first ejaculation. These are major psychological events for the adolescent; they herald the end of childhood and signal to the young adolescent the imminence of adulthood. In this move towards adulthood, the adolescent is not only engaged in identity formation, but must also come to terms with his or her own sexuality. This needs to be meaningfully integrated into the self-identity with as little conflict and turmoil as possible (Conger and Petersen 1984).

Writers like Furnham and Stacey (1991) contend that puberty and its associated rapid changes also have implications for self-perceptions of attractiveness and sexual desirability. They explain as follows (p. 106):

> Further, the mass media constantly present fashionable types of beautiful people for adolescents (as well as adults) to compare themselves with. Adolescents often worry about their looks and physical attractiveness, and their capacity to appeal sexually. If there is a failure to meet current standards of acceptable looks, then this may well become an important personal problem.

Why is it that some adolescents engage in sexual intercourse at an earlier age than others? Are there specific identifiable causes of such behaviour? Are such teenagers more affected than others by hormonal, family or other social influences? Or is it simply a matter of chance as to who is likely to engage in sexual intercourse? These and other issues will be discussed in this chapter.

## Sexual Initiation

Introduction to sexual intercourse appears to be a gradual process. According to some authors (e.g. Harris and Liebert 1987), adolescents first experiment with kissing and hugging before they proceed to 'light' and then 'heavy' petting. There also appear to be racial and cultural differences in this regard. For instance, one research team observed a developmental sequence from necking, to feeling parts of the body directly, to sexual intercourse for white 12–15-year olds in the United States. Among blacks, however, fewer seemed to engage in the various petting activities that precede intercourse (Miller and Moore 1990).

It would seem that adolescents are becoming sexually active at an increasingly younger age. Several studies support such a view. For instance, a representative sample of Danish teenagers aged 16–20 showed that about one-third had experienced sexual intercourse by age 16 (Wielandt and Boldsen 1989). Another report indicated that, whereas 30 per cent of never married females aged 15–19 had experienced sexual intercourse in the United States in 1971, this figure had risen to 50 per cent by 1979 (Baker *et al.* 1988). Moreover, it would seem that rates among black adolescents in the United States are higher. One report noted that more black adolescents experienced sexual intercourse at a slightly younger age than whites (Zelnik and Kantner 1980).

Although most adolescents initiate sexual activity voluntarily, for some this is not the case (Erickson and Rapkin, 1991; Miller and Moore 1990). In one study (Erickson and Rapkin), 15 per cent of the adolescents who were surveyed reported having had an unwanted sexual experience. Most of these were females. About half of the respondents had such an experience between the ages of 13 and 16. According to the researchers, unwanted sexual experiences can be categorised as 'forced' or 'unforced'. Under 'forced' sex are included rape and child abuse. Under 'unforced' sex are included sex due to the effects of alcohol or drug use, or partner and peer pressure. Almost 60 per cent of the females in the survey had experienced forced sex, compared with 20 per cent of the males. Many more males than females (80 vs. 42 per cent) reported having had 'unforced' sex. Of these, 32 per cent reported regret at having had sexual intercourse. These figures display quite dramatically the differences in power relations between the sexes.

## Learning about Sex

How do teenagers first learn about sex? Is the motivation to engage in sexual intercourse due to hormonal influences, or do social factors such as the influence of family and friends play an important role in shaping adolescent sexual behaviour? Let us consider some of these issues.

### The Influence of Family and Friends

Numerous studies have examined the relative effects of family and friends on adolescent sexual behaviour. Although both factors are important socialisation influences (Miller and Moore 1990), it has been argued that the family sets the social context within which the adolescent will learn about sexuality (Tucker 1989: 270). Factors such as mother's adolescent sexual experience, the educational level of parents, the sexual activity of older siblings, communication within the family and parents' attitudes and values towards adolescent sexual intercourse have all been linked to the sexual behaviour of adolescents. Thus, for example, it has been found that early sexual experience of an adolescent mother may increase the likelihood that her adolescent daughter will also engage in sexual intercourse at a relatively young age.

In addition, adolescents with sexually active older siblings, adolescents in single-parent (particularly single-mother) families, or adolescents in families with little communication about sexual matters are also more likely than others to engage in sexual intercourse (Miller and Moore 1990).

Research evidence to date suggests that parents' *marital status changes* may determine adolescents' transition to sexual behaviour. It appears that teenage males and females incorporate family structure and family disruption is different ways as manifest in their transition to sexual activity. For instance, on the basis of a longitudinal study among several hundred white teenagers in the United States, it was found that girls who remained in intact families had a 15 per cent chance of beginning sexual activity. Girls who moved from intact families to single-mother families increased their risks of sexual activity to 31 per cent. Boys who remained in intact families had a 24 per cent chance of beginning sexual activity, while boys who moved to single-mother families were much more likely to initiate sexual activity (a 70 per cent chance) (Newcomer and Udry 1987).

From Table 6.1 it is clear that the transition effect for boys *remaining* in single-mother families is small, which leads one to conclude that it is the *disruption* of family life rather than the *type* of family which is an important predictor for male adolescents. Among girls, furthermore, moving into blended families appears especially risky for the initiation of sexual behaviour (Newcomer and Udry 1987).

The data reported in Table 6.1 lead one to conclude that the break-up of the family unit, rather than its type, is the important key to understanding adolescents' transition to sexual behaviour. It is quite likely that during marital or family break-up, partners are too concerned with their own personal problems to adequately supervise their children. It is also likely that single mothers (most of whom have custody), are sexually active and dating men, thus providing a particular role model for their adolescents. Newcomer and Udry (1987) conclude as follows:

> For boys the loss of control is associated with the *disruption* inherent in the loss of the father from the household, while for girls the loss of control is associated with the *state* of not having a father in the household and not the disruption per se.

Single fathers who have custody of their teenagers are also presumably sexually active. Because most children are in the custody of single mothers, few research studies have examined the sorts of role models that single fathers provide for their adolescents.

**Table 6.1** *Adolescent Virgins' Transition to Sexual Intercourse from Time 1 to Time 2, by Parental Marital Composition*

| Marital composition, Time 1 | Marital composition at Time 2 | | |
|---|---|---|---|
| | Orginal parents | Blend | Single mother |
| | Boys (%) | | |
| Original parents | 24 | 25 | 70 |
| Blend | – | 18 | 50 |
| Single mother | – | 20 | 25 |
| | Girls (%) | | |
| Original parents | 15 | 100 | 31 |
| Blend | – | 23 | 50 |
| Single mother | – | 100 | 38 |

*Source:*   Newcomer and Udry 1987

*Parent-adolescent Communication*

Several studies have highlighted the importance of parent-adolescent sex communication (e.g. Jaccard and Dittus 1991, Mueller and Powers 1990, Tucker 1989). They note that the mother is the primary source of information regarding the menstrual cycle and contraception, at least as far as the daughter is concerned. Parents also appear to differentiate between their sons and daughters with respect to the *content* of their sexual discussions. For example, there are some matters of a sexual nature that fathers simply don't discuss with their daughters. On the basis of several research studies, Mueller and Powers (1990) recently summarised these differences in content, which are shown in Table 6.2. It is clear that mothers tend to discuss a whole range of issues with their daughters. With her son, a mother discusses matters related to sexual morals, bodily changes and birth. Fathers discuss birth and abortion as well as homosexuality with their sons, although fathers' discussions with daughters tend to be much more superficial.

That parents are likely to discuss matters of a sexual nature with daughters rather than sons is borne out by an independent study of intact families with a teenager aged between twelve and sixteen (Jaccard and Dittus 1991). Parents were much more likely to have *extended* discussions with daughters. Mothers, moreover, were more likely than fathers to discourage premarital sexual relationships, particularly for daughters.

The studies reviewed here suggest that a double standard is operative, with parents directing much more communication re-

**Table 6.2** *Parent-adolescent Communication about Sex*

| Mother with daughter | Mother with son |
|---|---|
| • Menstruation | • Sexual morals |
| • Dating and boyfriends | • Bodily changes |
| • Sexual morality | • Birth |
| • Conception | |
| • Sexual intercourse | |
| • Birth control | |
| • Bodily changes | |
| • Homosexuality | |
| • Abortion | |
| | |
| Father with daughter | Father with son |
| • Least intense and least intimate discussions about sex | • Birth |
| | • Homosexuality |
| | • Abortion |

*Source:*   Mueller and Powers 1990

garding sexual matters towards their daughters. As some writers (e.g. Jaccard and Dittus 1991) have noted (p. 77):

> In our opinion, both males and females should be made aware of the potential consequences of their actions . . . The implications of a sexual relationship and a possible pregnancy should be explored thoroughly with both genders and responsible behavior should be encouraged for adolescent males and females alike.

To conclude this section, little research has been done on parent-adolescent sex communication in single-parent families. Do fathers with custody of adolescent daughters, for instance, provide the sex information that is usually provided by the mother in intact families? More research is needed in this area.

### Influence of Friends

Adolescents' perceptions of peer norms and expectations about sexual behaviour as well as the behaviour of friends are important

---

**Figure 6.1** *Profile*

Janet was born to working class parents. Her mother was seventeen when she had her first child, Janet's brother. Janet's childhood was like that of many other girls in her neighbourhood, with the exception that she was clearly not her mother's favourite: that honour was reserved for her brother. Janet and her parents always seemed to be quarrelling over clothing styles, who Janet was going out with, where she was going or what time she would be back. Notwithstanding this conflict, Janet always managed to do what she wanted to, anyway.

Although of above-average intelligence, Janet never performed well at school. Besides not receiving much encouragement at home, she was more interested in dating boys. She had sexual intercourse by the age of fifteen. She skipped school periodically, and it wasn't too long before her grades began to suffer.

She decided to leave school at age sixteen. Her parents would have preferred her to stay on, yet they didn't make much fuss. She found a job as a shop assistant, but quickly grew tired of the monotony. Very often she would stay out all night and arrive home too tired to go to work. So she would fake illness and spend the day in bed.

Janet left her job and home before she was seventeen. Together with her twenty-year-old boyfriend at the time, Rod, she made it to the city, several hundred kilometres away. She had met Rod at a friend's house, and had sex with him soon after. Living on welfare assistance, they were just able to survive in the city. They could not, however, get public housing, and found rents expensive. Not much was left for day-to-day living, and both were unsuccessful in finding work. They would have taken anything on offer, but the recession made it difficult. It was then that Janet discovered she was pregnant.

in predicting adolescent sexual activity. Boys are more likely to learn about menstruation from their friends than from their parents, while girls are more likely to learn about menstruation from their mothers and friends than from their fathers (Amann-Ganotti 1986, Mueller and Powers 1990).

It would seem that peer group pressure rather than parental norms and values is an important factor in the adolescent's *decision* to engage in intercourse for the first time. Friends assume an important influence over his or her behaviour. Indeed, there is evidence of a close relationship between reported sexual behaviour of adolescents and their friends, although it has been suggested that the importance of how friends are perceived may be overstated (Smith, Udry and Morris 1985). It could be that peer influence *interacts* with pubertal development in determining teenage sexual behaviour. This will be discussed in more detail below.

Once adolescents are sexually active, it would seem that parental views are important as far as the continued use of contraception is concerned. Parents who are tolerant of adolescent sexual activity are more likely to have adolescents who use contraception. Adolescents with more tolerant parents are less likely to experience stress about engaging in sexual intercourse, and are therefore more likely to use contraception (Baker *et al.* 1988).

## Hormonal vs. Non-hormonal Influences

According to one viewpoint, an increase in sexual activity during adolescence is not learned, but is rather the result of uncontrollable endocrinological influences (Paikoff and Brooks-Gunn 1990, Udry *et al.* 1985). Endocrinological changes occurring during puberty are the result of two processes. These are *adrenarche*, by which androgens are produced, and *gonadarche*, by which the hypothalmic-pituitary-gonadotropin-gonadal system is reactivated (Paikoff and Brooks-Gunn 1990). Not only do these changes in endocrinological levels have the capacity to lead to early sexual intercourse, but they have also been used to explain other changes in behaviour and mood (Buchanan, Eccles and Becker 1992, Paikoff and Brooks-Gunn 1990).

Changes in hormone level can affect adolescent behaviour in four possible ways (Buchanan *et al.* 1992). Firstly, hormone levels simply rise in concentration and have a direct and overwhelming impact upon behaviour. Secondly, it is possible that, as these hormone levels rise (notably sex steroids and gonadotropins), the adolescent adapts by adjusting behaviour. Thirdly, it is possible that there are 'irregular' effects. In other words, the rise in hormone levels could be inconsistent or spasmodic, resulting in mood swings and rapid changes of behaviour. Finally, the authors note that each of these factors may interact to varying degrees with one another, as well as with numerous social factors (e.g. family, peer and school relations) in influencing behaviour.

The view that early sexual activity, notably intercourse, is determined primarily by hormonal influences is not entirely endorsed by all social scientists. Psychologists with a more psychoanalytic bent have tended to explain behavioural change during adolescence by focusing on the individual's internal drives. A range of emotional conflicts, sexual instincts, and Oedipal complexes motivate the adolescent to enagage in various 'deviant' behaviours, ranging from compulsive eating to sexual intercourse (Buchanan *et al*. 1992).

Writers such as Miller and Moore (1990), remind us that there are racial and cultural differences in the extent to which adolescents enagage in sexual intercourse, and that hormonal levels alone cannot explain societal changes in sexual attitudes. Their line of reasoning seems to suggest that other non-hormonal factors are also important in understanding why adolescents engage in sexual intercourse. This view is also endorsed by several other writers (e.g. Paikoff and Brooks-Gunn 1990, Brooks-Gunn and Furstenberg 1989). They suggest that even if hormonal effects on sexual behaviour are clearly demonstrated, one still needs to consider the effects of social and other contextual factors. They argue that hormonal and non-hormonal factors interact in a variety of complex ways to produce behaviour.

Acknowledging the importance of non-hormonal factors, it has been argued that a biosocial model is most useful for understanding adolescent sexual behaviour (Udry 1988). Both biological and social factors are important in predicting whether adolescents will engage in early sexual intercourse. Hormonal factors act as social signals, heralding that the adolescent is now physically ready to engage in sexual activity. However, a variety of factors co-jointly determine the propensity of a teenager to enage in intercourse. Included are motivation (e.g. hormones, libido, etc.), physical attractiveness and social control (e.g. restrictions, familial controls, opportunities, etc.) (Udry and Billy 1987).

Udry's (1988) biosocial model, shown in Figure 6.1, combines hormonal and non-hormonal influences. Each of these may, of course, have direct effects upon sexual behaviour. What the model also suggests is that the factors interact in predicting adolescent sexual behaviour. For instance, it has been found that early maturing girls (a biological influence) are much more likely than other

**Figure 6.1** *Biosocial Model of Sexual Behaviour*

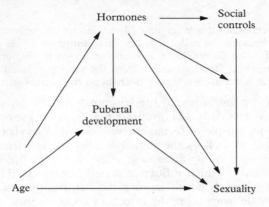

*Source:* Udry 1988

girls their age to have older friends (perhaps generating implications for social control). It is believed that this increases the risks of early initiation into sexual activity, smoking, drug use and so on (Brooks-Gunn and Furstenberg 1989).

The biosocial model was tested among a large sample of teenagers in the United States (Udry and Billy 1987). The respondents were asked a wide range of questions about their behaviour and attitudes, while parents and friends were asked to rate the teenagers on various behavioural and other dimensions. Important sex and race differences were observed. For example, the authors found that social controls were not as important in predicting sexual intercourse for white males and black females, while the sexual behaviour of white males was found to be strongly related to hormonal effects (namely androgens). There was, however, a strong social effect for white females, although their non-coital sexual behaviours seemed determined by androgenic hormones. It was also found that white females who participated in sports and had a father living at home were less at risk for early sexual intercourse than others. An important predictor for black females' transition to sexual intercourse was found to be attractiveness. In addition, black girls were found to engage in sexual intercourse at an earlier age than their white counterparts, although the authors are at a loss to explain this.

Results such as these lend support to the biosocial approach to understanding sexual behaviour among adolescents. Not only are hormonal levels important, but they interact with social factors in unique and important ways. Udry and Billy (1987: 852) conclude that:

> The effects of hormones on males' behavior are much stronger than on females because, as males mature, their androgen levels go up by a factor of 10 to 20, while, in females, androgen levels hardly double, with males and females starting from the same prepubertal levels. In males, the hormone levels may overwhelm the social controls.

Support for the biosocial model comes from a separate study (Smith *et al.* 1985). It was observed that increased sexual motivation among a sample of teenagers was related to levels of pubertal development as well as the sexual activity of best friends. Thus there is an important interaction effect between the social and biological factors which influence sexual behaviour. The authors noted that research which ignores the contribution of biological factors may be overstating the effects of social factors.

## Attitudes to Sex

Adolescents have quite clearly formed beliefs about sex-related matters. This has been demonstrated in a number of surveys. In a large-scale study of over 2000 British adolescents aged 10 to over 17 years, respondents were asked about the desirability of a range of sexual matters such as premarital sex and heterosexual relationships. Almost half of all respondents felt that society should tolerate all types of sexual relationships, not just heterosexual ones. Almost three-quarters approved of premarital sex. Just over 20 per cent of adolescents agreed that the main reason for having sexual relations should be to have children (Furnham and Gunter 1989).

Are there differences in sexual attitudes between young males and females? In one study (Wilson and Medora 1990), over 600 university students in the United States were surveyed to determine their attitudes towards premarital sex, masturbation, homosexuality, extramarital sex, oral-genital sex, anal sex and sexual fantasising. Overall, both males and females approved somewhat of premarital sex when the couple is in love or engaged. They were also approving of oral-genital sex and sexual fantasising, although males and females disapproved somewhat of homosexuality and extramarital sex. There were, however, significant differences in attitude between the sexes. Males and females differed significantly on premarital sex for casual couples, extramarital sex, oral-genital sex and anal sex. On all of these, males reported more favourable attitudes. The findings are summarised in Table 6.3.

**Table 6.3** *Attitudes of Undergraduates (N = 641) towards Sexual Behaviour*

|  | Mean scores | |
| --- | --- | --- |
| Sexual behaviours | Males | Females |
| Premarital sex – couple casually acquainted | 2.90 | 3.76* |
| Premarital sex – couple in love | 2.36 | 2.56 |
| Premarital sex – couple engaged | 1.89 | 1.99 |
| Masturbation | 2.96 | 3.16 |
| Homosexuality | 4.11 | 4.13 |
| Extramarital sex | 3.86 | 4.11* |
| Oral-genital sex | 1.76 | 2.28* |
| Anal sex | 2.80 | 3.36* |
| Sexual fantasising | 1.66 | 1.79 |

*Males and females differ significantly. Low scores indicate favourable attitude

*Source:*   Wilson and Medora 1990

## Condom Use and the Threat of AIDS

Contraception has traditionally been important in the context of adolescent pregnancy. Although teenage pregnancy continues to be of major concern, the focus has shifted somewhat in recent times. With the advent of the AIDS crisis, one particular form of contraception, namely condom use, has become the focus of re-newed research attention and is considered to be paramount in the prevention of HIV infection and other sexually transmitted diseases (STDs).

According to one report, female adolescents have the highest rates of gonorrhea, cytomegalovirus, chlamydia cervicitis and pel-vic inflammation (Brooks-Gunn and Furstenberg 1989). These diseases are likely to be exacerbated by early sexual activity and inconsistent condom use. Thus it has become imperative that adolescents be educated about the risks of 'unprotected' sex. Al-though the number of adolescents infected with HIV is relatively small (Rosenthal and Moore 1991), it is quite possible that failure to reduce risky sexual behaviour among adolescents may dramat-ically increase the number of adolescents diagnosed as HIV-positive.

Recent survey results suggest that condom use by adolescents rose sharply during the 1980s. For example, use by females be-tween 15 and 19 years of age in the United States doubled between 1982 and 1988. Among males in metropolitan areas, condom use more than doubled between 1979 and 1988 (Pleck *et al.* 1991). Although rates have risen sharply in recent times, they are still relatively low (Brooks-Gunn and Furstenberg 1989), and vary between ethnic and racial groups (Strunin 1991). Many adolescents seem to be apathetic and irresponsible about condom use and the risks associated with unsafe sex (Barling and Moore 1990).

This is borne out by a recent survey among Australian high school students. It was found that 83 per cent of respondents agreed that condoms generally prevent the spread of AIDS and STDs (Barling and Moore 1990). However, 38 per cent of them also agreed that AIDS was something they had not thought a lot about, while 30 per cent felt that it was of no concern to them, since their best friends were unlikely to be HIV-positive.

Several studies have examined the correlates of contraceptive non-use among adolescents (see Balassone 1991, Brooks-Gunn and Furstenberg 1989, Morrison 1985 for reviews). Factors affecting this can generally be classified as demographic, individual differences, interpersonal, and clinic characteristics. For example, there is now evidence to suggest that contraceptive non-use is likely to occur among adolescents who are younger, black and who come from lower socio-economic groups. They are likely to have initiated intercourse at a younger age and to have had sisters or friends pregnant as teenagers. Moreover, they are likely to have low self-esteem, external locus of control, lack future aspirations, and misconceive pregnancy risks. Such adolescents are also less likely to accept responsibility for sex and to lack information about birth control. They are likely to have poor communication with their parents about sex-related matters and not attend birth control clinics (Balassone 1991).

There are two major theoretical approaches to understanding contraceptive behaviour among adolescents. These are cognitive or decision-making models and socialisation models (Balassone 1991). Let us briefly review the decision-making model.

**The Decision-making Model**

The practice of contraception among sexually active adolescents has been quite firmly linked to cognitive development (Gordon 1990). The decision to use contraception is affected by various aspects of formal reasoning. In the first instance, it would appear that some adolescents do not comprehend the different forms of contraception that are available. Secondly, some do not properly evaluate the consequences of their actions. Quite often, therefore, pregnancy is 'unexpected' and unanticipated. Furthermore, it is clear that some adolescents do not take partners' needs into account. It seems as though some males fail to appreciate the risks of pregnancy to their female partners (Gordon 1990: 348–49), while

> adolescent females may romanticize their boyfriends' position by perceiving unprotected intercourse as an affirmation of love and commitment to a relationship.

Evidence also indicates that some adolescents cannot adequately reason about chance and probability (Gordon 1990). In other words, these teenagers seem to think that a single act of unprotected intercourse is less risky than several such acts.

Again, they appear quite surprised at the 'unexpected' pregnancy or infection. Such deficits in cognitive functioning have been referred to as *global developmental delay*. These teenagers also very often underachieve at school, which may be suggestive of an environment which is deficient in opportunities for abstract thinking (Gordon 1990).

These views are supported by the results of a study in the United States (Pete and DeSantis 1990). The authors conducted in-depth interviews with pregnant black fourteen-year-olds. These teenagers were asked about their sexual experiences, and how they viewed their pregnancy. All reported that their first sexual encounter had been unexpected, and that they had been unprepared for sex. It appears that the girls attempted to establish a relationship that they perceived was based on mutual 'trust' and 'love', and that sexual activity occurred afterwards. The perception among them was that the relationship was somehow 'special' and different. The researchers noted that such perceptions seem to act as an insurance (at least in the minds of the girls) against being abandoned by their partner or against pregnancy. Very often young females are surprised to discover themselves pregnant, believing that they are 'too young', or that simply by having sex once, they will not fall pregnant (Gordon 1990).

The importance of various cognitive strategies in decision-making about contraception has also been emphasised by several other writers (e.g. Barling and Moore 1990, Crawford, Turtle and Kippax 1990, Moore and Rosenthal 1991a, Pleck *et al.* 1991, Rosenthal and Moore 1991). However, they suggest that teenagers make decisions about contraception in different *social contexts* and that these need to be taken into account when predicting condom use. Thus, adolescents' perceptions about risk and responsibility for pregnancy as well as their subjective feelings about embarrassment are important factors in contraceptive decision-making. These costs-benefits, as perceived by male adolescents, are summarised in Table 6.4.

**Table 6.4** *Males' Costs-benefits of Condom Use*

Preventing pregnancy: personal costs-benefits
  • Concern about pregnancy increases condom use
  • Belief that female uses pill reduces condom use

Preventing pregnancy: normative belief
  • Belief that males have responsibility for reducing pregnancy increases condom use

Avoiding AIDS
  • Concern about AIDS increases condom use

Partner expectations
  • Request by females raises condom use
  • Belief by females that they can get males to use condoms increases use

Embarrassment and reduction of pleasure
  • Perception of not being embarrassed increases condom use
  • Belief that sexual pleasure will not be negatively affected increases condom use

*Source:*    Pleck, Sonenstein and Ku 1991

The costs-benefits involved in contraceptive decision-making among males have received some empirical support. For instance, in a survey of almost 2000 15 to 19-year-old males in the United States, it was found that normative beliefs predicted condom use (Pleck *et al.* 1991): that is, males who believed it is the male's responsibility to prevent pregnancy were more likely to use them. Their *personal* concerns about pregnancy were found to be less important. In other words, concern about fathering a child *per se* was less important than normative beliefs about pregnancy prevention. Males who believed that their partner was not using the pill, were also more likely to use a condom. In addition, frequency of worry about AIDS, rather than actual perceived risk of HIV infection, was more likely to lead to condom use. Males who perceived their partner as wanting them to use a condom and as being appreciative of this, were more likely to use one. On the other hand, males' embarrassment or belief that pleasure would be reduced was likely to reduce condom use (Pleck *et al.* 1991; see also Pendergrast *et al.* 1992).

Not all males of course suggest using a condom during sexual intercourse. Very often it may be up to the female to suggest some form of contraception. Others might not even discuss the question of contraception, and appear to blatantly disregard the risks of pregnancy and STDs. It is this attitude of denial and irresponsibility which has been noted by some researchers, and led Moore and Rosenthal (1991a) to comment as follows (p. 164):

> Adolescents are reputed to be highly susceptible to this kind of thinking, that is, the illusion that although others may suffer the consequences of dangerous and risky actions they are somehow immune.

## Risky Sexual Behaviours

Some writers have noted a discrepancy between adolescents' knowledge of safe sex and their actual behaviour. In a survey of Australian university students (Turtle *et al.* 1989), it was found that, although the respondents were aware of AIDS precautions and safe sex practices generally, their sexual *behaviour* was regarded as risky.

Another survey among undergraduate non-virgins (mean age = 18.5 years.) found that almost 10 per cent were engaging in unprotected vaginal intercourse with casual partners, while 15 per cent were engaging in withdrawal. Among regular partners, the frequencies were 13 and 27 per cent respectively (Rosenthal, Hall and Moore 1992). Thus teenagers are engaging in more risky behaviours with partners described as 'regular'.

Similar findings have been observed in Canada (Maticka-Tyndale 1991) and the United States (Roscoe and Kruger 1990). One study found that only 34 per cent of respondents in late adolescence reported changing their sexual behaviour in the light of the AIDS crisis. Of those who had changed, about 19 per cent reported being 'more selective' (Rocoe and Kruger 1990). This is a risky strategy. Very often, adolescents look for physical signs of AIDS, or believe that someone who is 'nice' is unlikely to be HIV-positive. These are serious misconceptions which put adolescents at risk no matter how 'selective' they believe they are (Roscoe and Kruger 1990).

Attitudes to AIDS precautions are linked to the likelihood of engaging in risky sexual behaviour. Moore and Rosenthal (1991b) recently found some interesting sex differences in this regard among Australian adolescents. Generally, females were more positively disposed to AIDS precautions than were adolescent males, although females with negative attitudes to precautions were more likely to engage in risky sex. Males were more accepting of condom use while females were more likely to view this as interfering with their relationships with their partner. Males with a more fatalistic attitude towards AIDS, however, and those with multiple partners, were more likely to engage in risky sexual behaviour (Moore and Rosenthal 1991b).

## Implicit Personality Theories and Risky Behaviour

A question that often arises is why adolescents engage in risky sexual behaviours even though they are knowledegable about HIV transmission. A noteworthy qualitative study (Williams *et al.* 1992), using focus group discussions, found that college students use *implicit personality theories* when judging the riskiness of potential sexual partners. They use several strategies, as summarised in Table 6.5. From the information provided, it is clear that the respondents judge the HIV status of partners in ways that are usually uninformative. Such strategies are unreliable – and can prove fatal (Williams *et al.* 1992).

### *Personality Traits and Risky Behaviour*
Evidence indicates that a link exists between personality disposition and the likelihood of engaging in risky sexual practice. One

**Table 6.5** *Implicit Personality Theories used in Judging HIV Status of Potential Partners.*

**Judgements of riskiness of sexual partners**
1. Known and liked partners are viewed as not risky
   ('I knew my partner really well before we had sex, so I didn't have to worry about her sexual history')
2. Risky people dress provocatively, hang around bars, tend to be older, are from large cities, and are keen for sex
   ('If they're dressed up like a slut . . . they're usually a slut')
3. Respondents tend only to use condoms with partners they don't know well
   ('If you just met, then you use a condom . . . if it's long term you aren't going to worry')

**Assessments of personal risk**
1. Respondents often thought themselves generally not at risk
   ('Personally, I'm not really worried about AIDS on this campus')
2. Respondents feel personally not at risk.
   ('I'm not gay')

**Reasons for unsafe sex**
1. Alcohol
2. Lust
   ('In the heat of the moment you don't think about it [AIDS]')

**Beliefs about condoms**
1. Condoms interfere with sex
2. Condoms are unpleasant to use
3. Condoms are inconvenient
4. They have undesirable implications – that is, you don't trust your partner

*Source:* Williams *et al.* 1992

recent study, for example, examined the link between sexual behaviours and beliefs about personal control and self-efficacy (Moore
and Rosenthal 1991a). The authors found that only 6 per cent of
the late adolescents in their study thought that they could *moder-
ately* control their chances of getting AIDS, while 17 per cent
thought they could *completely* control them. Of particular interest
was the finding that belief in personal control was related to various
types of sexual behaviour. The researchers found that a perception
of low personal control accompanied moderate- to high-risk sexual
behaviour. In other words, adolescents who took a more fatalistic
approach to diseases such as AIDS were less likely to employ safe
sex strategies.

The importance of a sense of control has been alluded to in
several other reports (e.g. Crawford *et al.* 1990, Heaven, Connors
and Kellehear 1992). Crawford *et al.* 1990 suggested that females
are especially at risk for HIV infection. It was found that female
respondents were less likely to insist on condom use with regular
partners than with casual ones, the implication being that females
tend to shift the burden of responsibility (or control) on to their
partners. Male respondents tended not to distinguish between
casual and regular partners, perhaps because they view HIV infection largely as a problem for homosexuals rather than heterosexuals
(Crawford *et al.* 1990).

How is one to understand these findings? One argument is that
females are represented as *traditionally* more dependent and less
proactive in sexual matters than are many males (Heaven *et al.*
1992). For example, males may be relatively more comfortable
with the practice of buying condoms (or asking for them from a
clinic) as a preventive measure in sex. This attitude is probably less
common among females. Traditional sex roles which encourage
males to be active and females to be passive and supportive in
dating and sexual practises may predispose females with a lower
sense of control to take less preventive measures against risk of
infection. Indeed, as Seeman and Seeman (1983) found, lower
sense of control may also be associated with less self-initiated
preventive care.

## Summary

It can be argued that several factors are related in complex ways
in determining adolescent use of condoms. Certainly, decision-
making is dependent upon cognitive skills such as the ability to
predict possible consequences, to weigh the pros and cons of a

situation, and so on. It is also clear that other personal and contextual factors are also important, such as how one views the threat of AIDS, normative beliefs about pregnancy prevention on the part of the male, and perception of personal control.

## Adolescent Sex Offenders

In a recent review it was reported that about 20 per cent of all rapes and some 30–50 per cent of all child sexual abuse cases are committed by adolescents (Davis and Leitenberg 1987). Alarming as these statistics are, the authors suggest that they may, in fact, under-represent the true picture. As they point out, not all offences lead to convictions and not all victims and their families report assaults. This may be because the offender is very often known to the victim and the family. Indeed, some parents may even regard the incident as 'insignificant', thinking of it as mere 'sexual exploration' and 'experimentation'.

Most adolescent sex offenders are male. Studies reveal that the most common offence is fondling ('indecent liberties') accounting for about 59 per cent of cases. This is followed by rape (about 23 per cent of cases), exhibitionism (11 per cent), and other non-contact offences (e.g. indecent phone calls, 7 per cent). Assaults against similar-age adolescents or those who are older usually involve rape (67 per cent of offences). Among younger children, however, rape only accounts for 24 per cent of offences (Davis and Leitenberg 1987).

According to many reports, victims are often known to the offender. In one study of incarcerated adolescents, for example, it was found that in 55 per cent of cases the victim was known to the offender in some way. Moreover, child victims rather than older ones are more likely to be known to the offender. Indeed, very often victims may be family members (20 per cent in one report) (Davis and Leitenberg 1987). Sex offenders also manifest other behavioural and adjustment deficits. Evidence suggests that many adolescent sex offenders have been charged or convicted of other delinquent offenses as well.

Adolescent sex offenders can be described in terms of a particular family history, social and psychological maladjustment, and a record of physical and sexual abuse (Davis and Leitenberg 1987, Fehrenbach *et al.* 1986). A recent report (e.g. Steele and Ryan 1991) elaborated on some of the family and personal characteristics of juvenile sexual offenders. Their life histories share many common themes such as lack of empathic experience and lack of available coping models. Others like Ryan (1991), note low levels of family affect, family secrets and distorted attachments, while the offender's role in the family appears to be as a focus for others' guilt and shame.

Not all children with these sorts of experiences, of course, are likely to sexually offend. More often than not, the offender has also been the recipient of physical or sexual abuse, may have witnessed family violence, or been subjected to other inappropriate sexual stimuli.

A recent study (Blaske *et al.* 1989) examined the individual functioning, family and peer relations of four groups of father-absent boys aged thirteen to seventeen. The four groups were sex offenders, assaultive offenders, non-violent offenders and non-delinquent adolescents. The researchers found that, compared with the other groups, the sex offenders evidenced less emotional bonding to peers and felt estranged in their relations with others. Sex offenders also reported higher rates of anxiety. It was also noted that the mother-son relationship of these adolescent boys showed poor levels of communication and that, generally, their families could be described as 'dysfunctional' (Blaske *et al.* 1989).

As not many adolescent sex offenses are committed by females, there is a dearth of research in this area. One exception is the recent report by Fehrenbach and Monastersky (1988). According to their observations, it appears that sexual offences among females do not form part of a syndrome of delinquent behaviour, as so often seems to be the case with boys. Most offences are against a younger victim who more often than not is someone known to the offender. Whereas a sizeable proportion of male offenders commit acts of exhibitionism, indecent phone calls, and so forth, this does not appear to be the case among female offenders. Finally, whereas male offenders quite often have a history of physical or sexual abuse, this tends not to be a causative factor for female offenders. As the authors note (Fehrenbach and Monastersky 1988: 151):

> prior sexual abuse alone does not explain why a girl would become an offender. Many more girls than boys are sexually abused as children, yet most offenders are male.

## Adolescents in Prostitution

Juvenile prostitution has shown a steady increase over recent years. It is estimated that in the ten-year period 1970–80, juvenile prostitution increased from 24 to 74 per cent in New York City (Schaffer and DeBlassie 1984). Large increases have no doubt also occurred in all other large cities across the world. Of concern are the enormous physical and emotional risks involved, such as rape, murder, STDs including HIV infection, and pornography (McMullen 1987). Some of the psychological risks are increased feelings of alienation and lowered self-worth.

Social scientists have speculated on the reasons for adolescent prostitution. The following have been suggested (McMullen 1987, Schaffer and DeBlassie 1984): alienation from the family; rejection by the family; parental abuse (psychological, sexual, physical and spiritual); and limited employment opportunities for lower class women. Some teenagers might also be attracted to prostitution through economic need, a sense of hostility (for example, anger at being rejected by their family), a sense of adventure and drug abuse.

Because of their age, adolescent prostitutes are relegated to the streets, and tend not to work in hotels and parlours. Most are under supervision of a pimp who, in a limited number of cases, might provide a sense of security and some shelter (Schaffer and DeBlassie 1984).

Although young male and female prostitutes may be in prostitution for for similar sorts of reasons, they also differ in some very important ways. Whereas female prostitutes engage in heterosexual intercourse, most male prostitutes participate in sex with other (usually older) males, even though they would normally regard themselves as heterosexual (Schaffer and DeBlassie 1984).

## Sexual Orientation

Although this chapter has focused chiefly on heterosexual relationships, a relatively large proportion of teenagers will, at some stage, adopt a homosexual orientation. It has been estimated that up to one-third of male adolescents beyond sixteen years of age had had at least one homosexual experience up to orgasm (cited in Remafedi 1987).

There is some doubt as to whether a homosexual orientation can be established or identified in adolescence (e.g. Savin-Williams 1991, Remafedi 1987). According to this view, homosexual experience is part of normal sexual experimentation and growing up. Any inclination to be attracted to someone of the same sex, it is argued, will in most cases be outgrown. Glasser (1977) asserts that it is only possible to be labelled gay or lesbian *after* adolescence.

According to this view, there is very little relationship between homosexual experience during adolescence and self-description as a homosexual during adulthood.

An alternative view is that it is indeed possible to identify a homosexual orientation in the teen years. Although many such adolescents may not directly label themselves as gay or lesbian, they experience a feeling of 'being different' and of being attracted to others of the same sex. This can be a time of great confusion for these teenagers. Very often they are not able to understand their inner feelings, which seem to run counter to general social norms and expectations. Among these youth, the label homosexual, gay or lesbian is only used later (around 19 years of age). It is not until some years later (around 23–28) that many will disclose their homosexual orientation to significant others (Remafedi 1987). It is perhaps only a very small proportion of young teenagers who actually label themselves as homosexual, but this can occur as young as 14 years of age (Remafedi 1987).

It has recently been reported (Garnets and Kimmel 1991) that males and females are first aware of being erotically attracted to members of the same sex at different ages. For males, this can occur between the ages of 12 and 13, while for females it can happen between 14 and 16. Table 6.6 highlights the developmental milestones for homosexual identity development.

The awareness of being attracted to others of the same sex can, for some, be a traumatic experience. Very often there is no-one in whom to confide – least of all friends and parents. These teenagers' sexual urges do not fit with social or personal expectations. They are often very confused and suffer emotional distress. This may impact negatively on school performance, and emotional upheaval may also lead to other behavioural problems, such as drug and alcohol use, and running away from home.

**Table 6.6** *Developmental Milestones for Homosexual Identity*

| | Age (in years) | |
| --- | --- | --- |
| Identity development | Lesbians | Gay men |
| Initial awareness of same-gender affectional-erotic feelings | 14–16 | 12–13 |
| Initial same-gender sexual experience | 20–22 | 14–15 |
| Self-identification as lesbian or gay | 21–23 | 19–21 |
| Initial same-gender sexual relationship | 20–24 | 21–24 |
| Positive gay or lesbian identity | 24–29 | 22–26 |

*Source:* Garnets and Kimmel 1991

As we move into the next century, there seems to be a growing awareness of, and openness to, different sexual orientations. Discrimination against people on the basis of sexual preference has been outlawed in some countries, and gay support groups have been established in many centres. Compared with previous generations, society seems more accepting of gay people, and it is now much easier for gays and lesbians to come to terms with their own sexuality and 'come out'.

Should one attempt to modify the behaviour or attitudes of an adolescent who 'comes out' or is suspected of being gay? Most writers would say no. Although techniques for behaviour change were attempted in the 1950s and 1970s, their effectiveness was always disputed. As Remafedi (1991: 505) explains:

> conventional wisdom suggests that sexual orientation is resistant to change and that attempts to change should be resisted, so as not to compound identity confusion, shame, and intrapsychic injury.

## Theoretical Considerations

Although few researchers actively set out to test the major theories as described in Chapter 1, three relate to the work examined in this chapter. These are biological theory, Erikson's identity formation theory and cognitive development. There is clear evidence that biological changes occur during puberty. These take on various forms, including endocrinological and physical changes. They impact not only on the teenager's emotional state (e.g. moodiness or depression), but also on parent-child relationships and sexual behaviour. Research evidence points to the influence of both hormonal and non-hormonal factors in sexual behaviour, suggesting that both are intricately related.

Synonymous with adolescent sexuality is identity formation. With biological change comes an awakening of sexual feelings and urges, an awareness of a sexual force within the adolescent. It is both exciting and intriguing and, at first, shrouded in mystery. An important developmental task is the exploration of this new dimension of the self and the discovery of just who one is sexually. Sexual identity cannot be divorced from one's self-identity, and in this regard, a loving and supportive family is important in facilitating self-discovery.

During the adolescent years, the teenager is undergoing cognitive development. As we noted, this has implications for sexual decision-making. Younger adolescents, it seems, are less able to reason about risk and probability and are therefore more likely to engage in sexual behaviour regarded as risky for HIV infection and pregnancy.

## Summary

In this chapter we considered some important issues relating to adolescent sexuality. From the evidence reviewed here, it is clear that adolescents are engaging in sexual intercourse at an increasingly young age. Sexuality is an important issue affecting all adolescents, and it was argued that they must come to terms with their own sexuality and incorporate it into their self-identity with as little disruption as possible.

This chapter reviewed findings which point to the importance of hormonal and non-hormonal factors (particularly the influences of family and peers) in explaining why some adolescents become sexually active. It seems clear that hormonal factors alone cannot explain sexual behaviour among adolescents and that a range of non-hormonal ones may need to be considered as well. Some reports have suggested that hormonal and non-hormonal factors interact in complex ways in determining adolescent sexual behaviour.

AIDS is a major crisis which all of us, including adolescents, must confront. Unfortunately, many adolescents seem unperturbed by the risks of unprotected sex. Indeed, many appear irresponsible. According to some reports, many adolescents do not practise safe sex and are putting themselves at risk for HIV infection and other STDs. Although adolescents appear knowledgeable about safe sex strategies, this is not matched by their behaviour.

Of further importance is the observation of links between risky behaviours and attitudes to AIDS precautions and certain personality traits, such as perceptions of personal control. Those adolescents adopting a more fatalistic attitude are more likely to engage in risky behaviour and therefore increase their risk of HIV infection. What is also noteworthy is the finding that males appear more accepting of condom use than females (Moore and Rosenthal 1991b). It would seem that females view condom use as an intrusion into the relationship with their partner. Future research should concern itself with how all adolescents might be encouraged to change their behaviour and adopt safe sex practices.

## Additional Reading

Brooks-Gunn, J. and Furstenberg, F. (1989) 'Adolescent Sexual Behavior', *American Psychologist* 44: 249–57

Miller, B. and Moore, K. (1990) 'Adolescent Sexual Behavior, Pregnancy, and Parenting: Research through the 1980s, *Journal of Marriage and the Family* 52: 1025–44

Newcomer, S. and Udry, J. (1987) 'Parental Marital Status Effects on Adolescent Sexual Behavior,' *Journal of Marriage and the Family* 49: 235–40

## Exercises

1. The literature suggests that, although adolescents are aware of the risks of HIV infection, they tend not to practise safe sex. Can you think of some strategies to encourage sexually active teenagers to take precautions against HIV infection?
2. Replicate the Wilson and Medora (1990) study referred to in the chapter (see also Table 6.3). If you obtain similar findings, what can you conclude? What about if you obtained different results?

# 7 Adolescents as Parents

## Introduction

We noted in the previous chapter that adolescents are becoming sexually active at an increasingly young age. Perhaps as a consequence, pregnancy rates have increased. Whereas in 1974, 9.9 per cent of all United States females aged 15–19 years became pregnant, by 1985 this figure was 11 per cent (Miller and Moore 1990). This rise in pregnancy rates has all sorts of ramifications. For instance, most teenage parents need welfare assistance (Miller and Moore 1990), while women who had their first child in their young teens are more likely to suffer educational, employment and income deficits (Grindstaff 1988, but also see Furstenberg *et al.* 1987).

Although these rates may have risen over recent years, it would seem that actual birth rates have fallen among teenagers in some Western nations. In Australia, for instance, birth rates for women under nineteen have dropped quite sharply (Australian Bureau of Statistics 1991a). This is not to suggest that Australian adolescents are now less sexually active than they were a few decades ago. These trends, reflected in Figure 7.1, may simply reflect the availability of legalised abortion in some Australian states.

A quite different picture emerges from some East European countries. In Hungary, for instance, the teenage birth rate is higher than it was a decade ago, notwithstanding the availability of legalised abortion there (Jakobovits and Zubek 1991). Table 7.1 shows the rate of teenage childbirth in relation to all deliveries in Hungary from 1946 to 1988. The data show that a peak was reached in 1984, whereafter birth rates began to decline.

Australian studies have documented different fertility rates for white and Aboriginal teenagers (e.g. Hart *et al.* 1985). For instance, whereas the reproduction rate for all teenagers aged 15–19 years in South Australia in 1981–82 was some 25 births per 1000 women, the Aboriginal rate was 140.4. Ethnic differences in fertility have also been noted in the United States.

Although birth rates among teenagers have declined over recent years, many more teenagers than before are having babies outside marriage. It has recently been reported (Furstenberg *et al.* 1989) that by the early 1980s almost two-thirds of white teenage mothers in the United States were unmarried when they fell pregnant. This

**Figure** 7.1 *Birth Rates for Australian Women aged 15–19 Years*

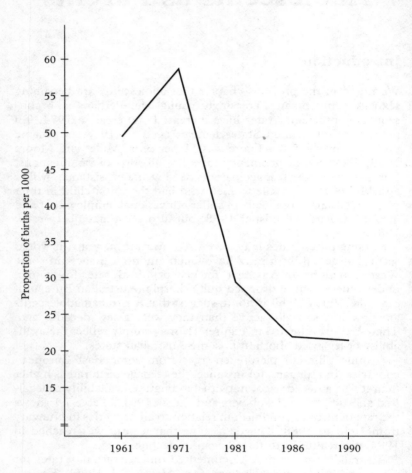

*Source:*    Australian Bureau of Statistics 1991a

compares with less than one-third in the early 1950s. By the early 1980s, 97 per cent of black teenagers in the United States were single when they became pregnant. Moreover, some reports suggest that 90 per cent of teenage mothers are keeping their babies, rather than giving them up for adoption (Newman and Newman 1986).

**Table 7.1** *Teenage Childbirth as a Proportion of General Deliveries of Hungarian Women*

| Year | % |
|------|------|
| 1946 | 2.17 |
| 1950 | 2.37 |
| 1966 | 3.31 |
| 1984 | 4.67 |
| 1985 | 4.61 |
| 1986 | 4.16 |
| 1987 | 3.99 |
| 1988 | 3.82 |

*Source:* Jakobovits and Zubek 1991

This chapter will examine the psychosocial characteristics associated with teenage pregnancy, as well as the resolution of pregnancy. It will also discuss birthing outcomes, the psychological adjustment of children and research into teenage fathers.

# The Risk of Early Pregnancy

Teenage mothers are having more babies compared with a generation ago. Moreover, the younger adolescents are when having their first child, the more likely they are to have another child while still a teenager (Meyerowitz and Malev 1973). Fifty-two per cent of white girls in the United States who become pregnant by the age of 14 years will be pregnant again by age 18. Among black adolescents, 52 per cent will be pregnant again by 17.

Various psychosocial factors have been found to be associated with teenage pregnancy. Recent reports (e.g. Meyerowitz and Malev 1973, Ralph *et al.* 1984, Walters *et al.* 1986), for example, cite several studies which have shown that teenage mothers are more likely to have lower self-esteem, be alienated from their own mothers and isolated from female friendships. Teenage mothers are quite likely to be underachievers at school, to have unmarried sisters with children, and to exhibit feelings of inadequacy and unworthiness. They are also likely to have a history of skipping school, delinquency and rebellion. According to some reports, teenage mothers are also likely to be dissatisfied with family relationships and their body image, while others appear to be externally controlled (or fatalistic) and to lack purpose in life. Farber (1991) cites evidence which suggests that teenage mothers are likely to come from lower socio-economic backgrounds and from single-mother families. They are also more likely to begin sexual activity at an earlier age.

Support for some of these views comes from a large retrospective study of more than 2000 women in the United Kingdom (Kiernan 1980). The author found that, compared with those who had their first child between the ages of 20 and 24, teenage mothers (aged 15 to 19) were more likely to have parents with relatively low levels of formal education, and to come from blue collar families. It was noted that parents were also less likely to be concerned about their teenagers' education. It was found that, once pregnant, adolescent mothers were less likely to undertake vocational training.

It is now accepted that pregnancy may also be linked to significant life-change events or stressors such as the death of a parent or another much-loved family member (Carlson *et al.* 1984). Following Mathis (1976), Carlson and colleagues argue that sexual activity may be one way of coping with significant stress during adolescence. Once pregnant, particular individual and demographic characteristics (e.g. race, age, social class) and social support network characteristics (e.g. family dynamics, peer support, church group, sexual partner, etc.) interact in determining the decision to continue or terminate the pregnancy.

Of some importance is the view that different racial, ethnic and socio-economic groups probably have different antecedents for pregnancy. Whereas *externality* has been shown to correlate with teenage pregnancy in most cases (e.g. Meyerowitz and Malev 1973), there is evidence of a link between *internal* locus of control and teenage pregnancy among black adolescents in the United States (Ralph *et al.* 1984). These writers suggest that black females, more than whites, may deliberately choose to become pregnant. If this is indeed the case, future research should seek to establish why.

Not all researchers support the view that ever-pregnant teenagers differ substantially in terms of their psychological processes from never-pregnant ones. For example, one research team recently surveyed over 1000 students in public schools in Georgia in the United States (Walters *et al.* 1986). They tested two random samples drawn from this student body, as well as matching groups of ever-pregnant and never-pregnant adolescents. The researchers found that personality factors such as external locus of control did not predict pregnancy. They concluded that, by and large, teenage pregnancy is 'coincidental', and suggested that inconsistent use of contraceptives and steady dating, combined with familial factors, best predicted pregnancy.

The researchers also suggested that, rather than attempting to develop models of risk, parents should assume that *all* teenagers are at risk from pregnancy. They therefore need to make informed and considered decisions about sexual behaviour. Thus it would seem that parents and authorities such as schools and church groups have an important educational role to play (Walters *et al.* 1986).

## Pregnancy Resolution

Very few teenagers deliberately choose to become pregnant. As Furstenberg and his colleagues (1989) so aptly put it: (p. 314)

> Indeed, if teens had to take the pill to *become* pregnant, relatively few would elect to do so.

Social scientists have long been interested in the decisions unmarried pregnant teenagers make regarding the resolution of their unintended pregnancies (Eisen and Zellman 1984). It has been reported that about 40 per cent of pregnant teenagers decide to have an abortion, 13 per cent will miscarry, while almost half will give birth. Of these, fewer than 10 per cent will give their child up for adoption. Of those who give birth, most will raise their child as single mothers, at least in the short term (Farber 1991).

Much research to date has been concerned with describing the differences between girls who choose various pregnancy outcomes. This literature can be divided into three general perspectives (Farber 1991). The first is more 'psychologically' oriented. The focus here is on the belief that some girls 'choose' motherhood and that their behaviour is akin to other so-called 'deviant' behaviours, like drug use. A second focus is on subcultural norms. In the United States, for example, the view is propagated that poor blacks form a subculture, this being used to explain their higher rates of illegitimacy. Finally, there is the view that some adolescents choose motherhood from economic considerations: that is, motherhood is one way by which welfare benefits can be obtained (Farber 1991).

To date, it is not clear to what extent each of these approaches can be validated. Pregnancy resolution is a complex process, determined, as we shall see, by a number of factors.

### The Decision to Keep the Baby

One researcher conducted in-depth interviews with black and white adolescents aged fifteen to twenty who decided to keep their babies (Farber 1991). For them, this decision was viewed as ethical and responsible: in other words, it was 'the right thing to do'. Other scholars in this area have identified six factors which adolescents rate as very important in their decision to keep their babies (Warren and Johnson1989). These are:

- the partner desired the baby
- a fear of the abortion procedure
- equating abortion with loss of a part of self
- getting married
- resistance to the family's wishes for abortion.

Adolescents' decisions about various aspects of pregnancy are very much in line with familial and personal values in such matters as abortion, adoption, sanctity of life and so on. It would also seem that, among more affluent adolescents, a struggle very often develops over the right decision. Among lower class teenagers, however, it appears as though it is generally accepted that pregnancy results in motherhood, while possible alternatives such as abortion and adoption are not discussed with family members in too much detail (Farber 1991).

One sixteen-year-old white lower class teenager described her decision to keep her baby in the following terms (Farber 1991: 713):

> My dad was telling me, you know, 'It's your decision to make. If you want to keep it, fine. If you want to abort it, I'm going to tell you right now – we don't like the idea of your having an abortion. And we don't like adoption either' . . . So they finally decided that I would keep the baby. Then we went over to [her boyfriend's] house, and his mother comes out and she said, 'I know what it's like. I wasn't married to Thomas's father. I was young and pregnant. Tell me how I can help you out. If you need anything, you've got people to help you out.'
> Then finally it hit me: 'Hey, there's nothing I can do about it.'

There appears to be no one single reason why adolescents decide to keep their babies. Very often, rather than calculating their *own* self-interest, they respond to psycho-emotional needs and the expectations and desires of their own family. They also consider moral and ethical issues. Values, beliefs and attitudes about pregnancy and its resolution appear to be intrinsically bound up with class and race. Thus more whites than blacks consider abortion (at least in the United States), while poorer teenagers are much more likely quickly to reject abortion as well as adoption (Farber 1991).

Some writers have observed that blacks in the United States are generally opposed to abortion and adoption. This has recently been confirmed after in-depth interviews with young black adolescents (Pete and DeSantis 1990): Both adolescents and their parents viewed abortion negatively and thought that it was the girl's responsibility to have the baby. There seems to be a dearth of research in this area among minority black adolescents in countries such as Australia, Canada, New Zealand and Britain. At this stage, it is not clear to what extent the trends observed in the United States apply to black teenagers in other developed countries.

Many pregnancy resolution decisions are made in the context of the family (Geber and Resnick 1988, Ortiz and Vazquez-Nuttall 1987, Pete and DeSantis 1990). Research to date suggests that some differences in family functioning exist between those girls who decide to keep their babies or place them for adoption on the one hand, and adolescent norms on the other. In one study, it was found that only one-third of girls who decided to keep their babies or place them out for adoption described their families as being 'balanced' (Geber and Resnick 1988). Thus many adolescents in these two groups perceived their families to be rigid, and as not being able to adapt to changed circumstances: that is, to an adolescent pregnancy in the home.

Evidence suggests that there are also some important cultural differences which need to be noted. In one study among Puerto Rican girls, for example, data showed that teenagers who decided to keep their babies received more support from their families and friends than did those who decided to terminate their pregnancy. They also received more support from their families than comparable samples of white or black girls (Ortiz and Vazquez-Nuttall 1987). The authors explain these differences in terms of Latin American culture and the value placed by its members on the family.

Very often, adolescent girls making these important decisions about whether to keep their babies or not, or to terminate their pregnancies, desire greater cohesion or 'enmeshment' with their families. As has been remarked, this is quite unusual, since most adolescents seek more involvement with peers and greater independence from their parents (Geber and Resnick 1988). This desire reflects, no doubt, the peculiar position in which pregnant adolescents find themselves and may be an important coping mechanism in a stressful situation. Of course, not all adolescent parents-to-be are likely to respond in this way. As the authors found, those who are alienated from their families are unsurprisingly much less likely to seek support from them.

## The Decision to Terminate the Pregnancy

In the United States, white adolescents are 13 per cent more likely than blacks to end pregnancy through abortion (Farber 1991), although this has been disputed (e.g. Henshaw and Van Vort 1989). There are also regional differences in rates of abortion within countries such as the United States (Miller and Moore 1990).

Several studies have revealed that those adolescents who decide to terminate their pregnancy tend not to have dropped out of high school and usually have higher educational aspirations than girls who decide to keep their babies (e.g. Eisen *et al.* 1983). In the United States, it is usually young white or older black adolescents who choose abortion (Farber 1991). Those who opt for abortion are also more likely to have mothers with higher educational levels who tend to supervise their adolescent daughters more closely (Farber 1991). In addition, girls who decide to have an abortion tend to be less religious and less likely to have friends who are teenage mothers. They are also more likely to receive support from their sexual partner, mother and close friends (Furstenberg *et al.* 1989, Miller and Moore 1990).

Demb (1991) conducted in-depth interviews with a small number of inner-city black adolescents within a week after they had had an abortion. Their ages ranged from thirteen to seventeen. Although each girl's circumstances was quite different, the author was able to detect the following underlying characteristics. Firstly, the decision to abort was not taken lightly. All girls experienced a certain amount of distress, even though some might try to hide their emotions. Indeed, some are so successful at this that adults very often think of them as 'unfeeling'. Secondly, some adolescents receive counselling about the options available to them, although it is not clear to what extent this varies for different racial and socio-economic groups.

It would appear, however, that for girls who decide to terminate their pregnancy, adoption is not considered to be a serious option. As Demb (1991: 101) observed:

> The girls tended to take the position that if they were to have a baby it would make no sense to give it away.

Many adolescents experience negative emotional reactions prior to the actual abortion. One research team (Warren and Johnson 1989) reviewed several reports which suggest that many adolescents experience anxiety, hostility, depression, guilt and shame. Following abortion, however, these negative emotions tend to decrease: indeed, some teenagers even experience relief. Interestingly, it has been noted that black teenagers in the United States report lower pre-abortion anxiety than do their white counterparts, although blacks find the *decision* to have an abortion much harder to make than do whites. Other studies have also shown that those females who have the support of their partner find it much easier to decide to terminate their pregnancy.

## Adoption

Not many teenage mothers place their children out for adoption (Farber 1991, Newman and Newman 1986). It is estimated that only about 3 per cent of pregnant adolescents who carry to term will place their baby for adoption (Sobol and Daly 1992). The figures among black teenagers in the United States are much lower, although it is not clear whether racial differences exist in other societies. Although white American teenagers have always pre-ferred adoption compared with blacks, it would seem as though this option is losing its appeal. The reason for this is not clear. It could be that teenagers who in the past would have favoured adoption are now able to have legalised abortions.

Demb (1991) observed that a majority of inner-city infants born to teenagers and who are placed for adoption, are usually placed by default rather than choice. Very often these infants are born to drug-addicted mothers or mothers who are not able to make ra-tional decisions about the welfare of their babies. In many cases, these mothers have also been deserted by their sexual partner.

As already noted, studies have found that those adolescents who do place their babies for adoption usually have the support of their families. According to one report, adolescents whose mothers fa-vour adoption are very much more likely to choose adoption (Herr 1989). It was also found that adolescents choosing adoption were less likely to know other teenagers who were single parents. This highlights the importance of the peer group as a socialising agent which transmits values and attitudes regarding sexuality (Miller and Moore 1990).

Other studies have noted that adolescents who place their babies for adoption tend to be older than those who keep their children. They also tend to come from financially better-off families and have higher academic motivation. They usually uphold traditional family values and live at home with both parents (Sobol and Daly, 1992).

A summary of the relevant research literature suggests that three factors influence a teenager's decision to place her baby for adop-tion (Sobol and Daly 1992): these are individual social, and organ-isational. Table 7.2 summarises each of them. Individual factors include the desire to complete school, the young mother's emo-

**Table 7.2** *Factors Influencing Decision to Place Baby for Adoption*

| To place | Not to place |
| --- | --- |
| **Individual Factors** | |
| Unprepared for parenthood | Not emotionally prepared to place child |
| Wanting to finish high school | Not prepared to after carrying child to term |
| Not emotionally ready | |
| No financial resources | |
| Not able to provide home environment | |
| | |
| **Social Factors** | |
| Mother likely to encourage placement | Black family values (don't abandon baby) |
| Peers likely to be encouraging | |
| Mother more influential than teenager's partner | |
| | |
| **Organisational Factors** | |
| | Not familiar with administrative procedures |
| | Counsellors don't provide all the information |
| | Teenagers concerned about confidentiality |
| | Availability of abortion |
| | Society accepting of unwed parenthood |
| | Availability of welfare |

*Source:*   Sobol and Daly 1992

tional preparedness and lack of financial resources. Social factors include peer influences as well as those of the pregnant adolescent's mother. Finally, there are several organisational factors, influencing the decision not to place, such as the availability of abortion and social welfare benefits.

According to one report, informal adoption following out-of-wedlock teenage pregnancy is quite common among black families in the United States. The authors state that this practice originated with slavery. Some writers regard informal adoption as a *mutual obligation system*, a way of coping with poverty and a way of demonstrating a commitment to the survival of the group (Sandven and Resnick 1990).

Sandven and Resnick interviewed fifty-four urban black adolescents who had recently made an adoption or parenting decision about their infants. They found that twenty teenagers chose informal adoption, although parent and child remained with the original family unit (the so-called 'shared' group). Nine mothers chose informal adoption by which the child received primary care from another person (the so-called 'gift' group). Twenty-five mothers decided to raise their child outside the original family unit (the 'exclusive' group).

The authors found that most teenagers did not want to become pregnant. In addition, they noted some differences between the three groups of mothers. For instance, the girls in the 'shared' group expressed positive feelings towards their mothers. Thus the mothers of these girls seemed to play an important role in helping them decide to keep their babies and to remain in the original family unit. These girls, therefore, had the added benefit of family support in raising their children. Although some of the girls in the 'exclusive' group appeared independent and motivated, others were disorganised and rebellious. The authors concluded that the girls probably had had family interactions which were 'problematic' (Sandven and Resnick 1990). Finally, the researchers found that the girls in the 'gift' group had a history of drug, alcohol and sexual abuse. They tended to be younger than the other mothers and had experienced problems at school.

Kalmuss (1992) challenges the view that the demand for formal adoption among black adolescents is low. It is suggested that available data do not support this perception and that research should be conducted to determine answers to a variety of questions, including:

- Knowledge and attitudes among blacks about formal adoption
- perceptions of support in the black community for adults who adopt unrelated infants
- the assumptions that black teenagers have about demand in the formal adoption system
- black teenagers' attitudes toward adoption.

## Satisfaction with the Decision

How satisfied are teenagers with their pregnancy resolution decision? Not many researchers have examined the attitudes and adjustment of adolescent mothers following pregnancy resolution. In one study, 299 white and Mexican-American adolescents aged 13–19 years were interviewed 6 months after the birth of their children or the termination of their pregnancies (Eisen and Zellman 1984). The authors were interested in the adolescents' reported satisfaction with their decision, and whether any demographic, economic or psychosocial factors were related to its level.

A high proportion (82 per cent) of teenage mothers in the sample said that they would make the same decision again. There were no age or ethnic group differences. The authors found that satisfaction was consistently high across the various resolution groups. For example, 80 per cent (N = 148) said that they would choose abortion again, 87 per cent (N = 57) were prepared to choose single motherhood again, while 80 per cent (N = 36) said that they would marry again. Those who were happy with the abortion decision were more likely to be older and to have a mother with a relatively high level of education. These adolescent mothers were also likely to have good school grades and to use contraceptives consistently *after* abortions.

Those adolescents who said that they would choose single motherhood again, were more likely not to have attended school during the six months after delivery. This finding underlines the difficulties faced by young single mothers who attempt to complete high school. They have to cope with being mothers, students and teenagers, as well as very often coping with child care facilities which are inadequate (Eisen and Zellman 1984). What is more, the mothers of these teenagers also usually endorse single motherhood.

One can conclude that, in terms of post-decision satisfaction, there is no best or worst decision (Eisen and Zellman 1984). Pregnant teenagers need professional counselling in which all their options are made clear to them. The circumstances of each adolescent are different, and they should be encouraged to make a decision that best reflects their own values and beliefs, as well as their personal aspirations. Their decision should not reflect parental pressures. It is clear that only by so doing is the mother likely to be satisfied with the decision she has taken (Eisen and Zellman 1984).

## Birthing Outcomes

Pregnant teenagers are at greater risk for birthing complications than other women. The death rates for babies born to mothers younger than fifteen years are higher than for babies born to mothers of fifteen to nineteen. Moreover, children born to mothers under the age of twenty are more likely to suffer from various birth defects and injuries (Sprinthall and Collins 1988).

The young mother is also quite likely to have a difficult pregnancy and birth. Teenagers tend to suffer excessive or poor weight gain, premature rupture of membranes and intra-uterine growth retardation, to name just a few problems. They are also likely to manifest higher toxemia and related complications, and to have prolonged labour (Sprinthall and Collins 1988). Risks among prostituting adolescents are even greater. A report in this regard detected various sexually transmitted diseases among the mothers in their sample. The authors noted that 22 per cent of mothers' infants were premature, while several were diagnosed with respiratory distress syndrome, drug effects, sepsis, intra-uterine foetal demise and positive toxicology screens (Deisher *et al.* 1991).

Several research reports into pregnancy among teenagers have noted birthing complications such as lower birth weights (Lee and Walters 1983) and increased risk of prematurity (Davis 1988). In a noteworthy large-scale study (Correy *et al.* 1984), of almost 50,000 births to women of various age groups in Australia, the association between a wide range of risk factors (such as birth weight) and outcome was examined. The results indicated that, when adolescent births were compared with those for women over eighteen, significant differences in outcome emerged for nearly all risk factors (see Table 7.3). Thus women younger than sixteen tended to have children with lower birth weight and lower apgar scores. They were also more likely to have had a forceps delivery and to suffer hypertension during pregnancy. Interestingly, those younger than sixteen and older than eighteen years were more likely to deliver by Caesarean section.

From Table 7.3 one is led to believe that negative birthing outcome for teenage mothers might be the result of their relatively younger age. Further statistical analysis of the data, however, has somewhat modified this view. It was found that, when teenagers were *matched* with older women in terms of marital status and socio-economic level, most of the significant differences observed in Table 7.3 disappeared. To illustrate this point, Table 7.4 compares the birth outcomes of adolescents and adults aged eighteen to thirty-four in socio-economic Category 5 (that is, unemployed and unskilled workers). Only two significant differences now emerge between the teenagers and the older group. The table shows that adolescents were *less* likely to undergo Caesarean section and forceps delivery than older women. There were no other significant differences between the age groups (Correy *et al.* 1984).

The findings presented above suggest that other factors besides age are important in determining birth outcome for teenagers. Not only are socio-economic and marital status important, but so too are ante-natal care, alcohol and cigarette use and diet (Correy *et al.* 1984, Davis 1988). For instance, evidence shows that some adolescents are less likely than other pregnant women to visit health care facilities on a regular basis. Rather, many of them seem to prefer symptom-specific care. Antenatal care and monitoring is especially

**Table 7.3** Comparison of Birth Outcomes to Adolescent Mothers and Mothers aged 18 Years and Older

| | < 16 years (n = 188) | < 17 years (n = 693) | < 18 years (n = 1719) | ≥ 18 years (n = 46591) |
|---|---|---|---|---|
| Mean birthweight (g)* | 3143.42 (SD ± 556.14) | 3202.15 (SD ± 528.80) | 3212.00 (SD ± 597.27) | 3345.19 (SD ± 575.47) |
| Birthweight < 2500g* | 21 (11.2%) | 65 (9.4%) | 151 (8.8%) | 2609 (5.6%) |
| Gestation period < 38 weeks | 26 (13.8%) | 88 (12.7%) | 221 (12.9%) | 3330 (7.2%) |
| Apgar score (at 1 minute) below 7* | 38 (20.2%) | 132 (19.0%) | 312 (18.2%) | 5459 (11.8%) |
| Congenital abnormalities | 7 (3.7%) | 19 (2.7%) | 48 (2.8%) | 913 (2.0%) |
| Perinatal mortality* | 5 (2.7%) | 22 (3.2%) | 48 (2.8%) | 720 (1.6%) |
| Hypertension in pregnancy (transient hypertension in labour excluded)* | 41 (21.8%) | 131 (18.9%) | 293 (17.0%) | 6406 (13.8%) |
| Antepartum haemorrhage (placenta praevia excluded) | 1 (0.5%) | 16 (2.3%) | 47 (2.7%) | 1007 (2.2%) |
| Caesarean section* | 13 (6.9%) | 38 (5.5%) | 92 (5.4%) | 3684 (7.9%) |
| Forceps delivery* | 58 (30.9%) | 178 (25.7%) | 432 (25.1%) | 9667 (21.5%) |

*Groups differ significantly

Source: Correy et al. 1984

**Table 7.4** *Comparison of Adolescent and Adult (18–34 yrs) birth outcomes in social class 5*

| | Adolescents | | | Adults |
| | <16 years (n = 156) | <17 years (n = 529) | < 18 years (n = 1159) | (18–34 years) (n = 4720) |
| --- | --- | --- | --- | --- |
| Mean birthweight (g) | 3140.28 (SD ± 560.94) | 3207.69 (SD ± 590.04) | 3211.67 (SD ± 580.02) | 3214.31 (SD ± 576.30) |
| Birthweight < 2500 g | 20 (13.1%) | 51 (9.6%) | 101 (8.7%) | 404 (8.5%) |
| Gestation period < 38 weeks | 22 (14.4%) | 66 (12.8%) | 140 (12.1%) | 494 (10.4%) |
| Apgar scores (at 1 minute) below 7 | 32 (20.9%) | 105 (19.8%) | 216 (18.6%) | 782 (16.6%) |
| Congenital abnormalities | 7 (4.6%) | 14 (2.6%) | 30 (2.6%) | 135 (2.9%) |
| Perinatal mortality | 4 (2.6%) | 18 (3.4%) | 30 (2.6%) | 123 (2.6%) |
| Hypertension in pregnancy (transient hypertension in labour excluded) | 29 (19.0%) | 104 (19.7%) | 214 (18.5%) | 1057 (22.4%) |
| Antepartum haemorrhage (placenta praevia excluded) | 0 (0.0%) | 9 (1.7%) | 29 (2.5%) | 138 (2.9%) |
| Caesarean section* | 9 (5.9%) | 29 (5.5%) | 66 (5.7%) | 482 (10.2%) |
| Forceps deliveries* | 44 (28.8%) | 139 (26.3%) | 303 (26.1%) | 1721 (36.5%) |

*Groups differ significantly

*Source:* Correy *et al.* 1984

important during the crucial first trimester of pregnancy (Davis 1988).

## Parental Practices

Do teenagers exhibit certain parental qualities not evident in other groups of parents? Although there is a relative dearth of research, there is some evidence pertaining to three areas (Brooks-Gunn and Furstenberg 1986). These are behaviour toward the child, knowledge of child development and attitudes to parenting.

Some writers have noted deficits in the interaction patterns of adolescent mothers (Christ *et al.* 1990, Culp *et al.* 1991), who appear less verbal and responsive than older mothers. In one study, researchers were interested in the responses of adolescent and non-adolescent mothers, matched for their level of education, during feeding and play times (Culp *et al.* 1991). Culp and his colleagues found that adolescent mothers showed less delight and were less facially and verbally responsive than were older mothers when feeding. During play times, adolescent mothers were found to be less patient, inventive and had a less positive attitude. The writers concluded that intervention strategies might be appropriate for adolescent mothers, and that they be taught to be more verbally and emotionally responsive.

Of some note is the fact that teenage mothers do exhibit emotional *warmth* to their offspring, and that they do not differ in this regard from older mothers. At the same time, however, adolescent mothers have been observed to provide less *stimulation* to their children as measured by the HOME inventory, although they tend to be no less responsive to their children's needs than older mothers. According to another review, adolescent mothers tend to have unrealistic expectations regarding child development. One study noted that a large proportion of mothers underestimated their child's cognitive, language and social functioning abilities. Even when controlling for the effects of socio-economic background, it would seem that teenage mothers have inappropriate expectations about developmental milestones (Brooks-Gunn and Furstenberg 1986).

With respect to attitudes toward child-rearing, some evidence points to the fact that younger mothers are more likely to be punitive towards their children. They also appear less able or willing to control such things as bedtime, and are not likely to know many of the child's friends.

# Psychological Adjustment of Children

Many of the children of teenagers, it has been noted, will live in poverty, in single-mother households (Dubow and Luster 1990). Psychological research has been concerned with the emotional, cognitive, and behavioural well-being of children born to teenage parents. Writers have noted certain behavioural and emotional deficits in these children. Some have reported particular psychosocial and cognitive deficits among them such as acting-out behaviour and problems with self-esteem (Oppel and Royston 1971), learning problems, hostility and impulsivity (Kinard and Reinherz 1984). Children of teenage mothers have also been found to perform poorly at school (Dubow and Luster 1990).

Some writers have suggested that teenage mothering has negative effects on children's academic performances and that differences between the children of adolescent and older mothers are noticeable in the pre-school years (Brooks-Gunn and Furstenberg 1986). Moreover, by the time these children reach high school, they are likely to have relatively lower academic aspirations than other adolescents, and to show signs of maladjustment. For instance, one study cited found that 49 per cent of adolescent mothers interviewed reported that their children had been suspended from school.

Not all children born to teenage parents exhibit behavioural or emotional deficits, of course. There is an enormous amount of variability among children born to teenage mothers. Indeed, many such children show adequate emotional adjustment and school performance. Several risk factors predict negative adjustment in these children, while several protective factors act as buffers against negative adjustment (Dubow and Luster 1990). These are listed in Table 7.5.

Empirical support has been found for these risk and protective factors. In a large follow-up study conducted in the United States, the importance of these to adjustment in the children of teenage mothers was examined (Dubow and Luster 1990). The authors studied 721 children aged 8–15 years who formed a subset of a much larger sample. They were included in the research because they were born to teenage mothers. Also included were many of the risk and protective factors listed in Table 6.4, as well as several measures of behavioural and academic performance.

Results showed that the children scored higher than the general population on the behavioural problem index, while also being weaker than average in terms of intellectual performance. As ex-

**Table 7.5** *Predictors of Positive and Negative Adjustment in Children of Teenage Mothers*

| Risk factors | Protective factors |
| --- | --- |
| Many siblings | Quality of home environment (i.e. cognitively and emotionally supportive) |
| Father-absent homes | High intellectual ability of child |
| Poverty | Positive self-concept |
| Maternal maladjustment | |
| Maternal education less than twelve years | |
| Low maternal age at child's birth | |
| Urban residence | |

*Source:* Dubow and Luster 1990

pected, however, several protective factors were found to buffer them against emotional maladjustment. The following were identified as being particularly important: an emotionally supportive home, the child's verbal intelligence and self esteem. Of these, self-esteem seems particularly important. As the authors noted, positive self-esteem in children is related to social competence, independence, inquisitiveness and assertiveness. Thus, they see programs which aim to enhance the self-esteem of children of teenage parents as being particularly beneficial.

With respect to the risk factors studied, the authors found that poverty and low self-esteem of the mother were related to behaviour problems, while urban residence and mother's low level of education were negatively related to ability in mathematics, reading and comprehension. It was also noted that factors such as poverty and the adjustment of the mother herself were important in predicting how sensitive she would be to the socio-emotional needs of her child. Dubow and Luster (1990: 402) noted that

> the children in this study who experienced multiple stressors were at greatest risk . . . the risk of developing problems increased linearly with the number of risk factors to which children were exposed.

These general conclusions have received support from a number of other sources. For example, elsewhere it has been noted that age of teenage parents alone is less important in explaining quality of parental behaviours, but that one needs to consider a wide range of *socio-ecological factors* (Lamb and Elster 1985). One such factor is socio-economic status of the single mother. It has been noted that mothers not dependent on welfare and who have completed high school, seem to place their children in a social and emotional advantage over those from less well-off families (Baldwin and Cain 1980).

Finally, it is important to note that research in this area has been characterised by various methodological problems (Kinard and Reinherz 1984). For instance, in many cases select groups of children attending various clinics and assessment centres have been studied (e.g. Christ *et al.* 1990). Thus many researchers have included in their samples only the offspring of teenagers presenting themselves for professional assistance. It is not clear to what extent such results are biased. In other cases, the maternal age of the mother when giving birth has been defined inconsistently, depending on whether the first-born is the focus of study, or not. On other occasions, age groups have also been inconsistently defined: that is, researchers disagree on the meaning of 'young' and 'older' adolescents. Finally, researchers have used different measures of the behaviour under consideration, while not all have considered the importance of risk and protective factors (Dubow and Luster 1990).

## Adolescent Mothers in Adulthood

There is a general belief that teenage mothers are at a decided disadvantage economically, educationally and occupationally. Not many studies have tested this claim longitudinally. A notable exception, however, is the study, spanning seventeen years, conducted by Furstenberg and colleagues (1987).

They concluded by saying that the view that teenage mothers are all caught up in a cycle of poverty and welfare dependency is an oversimplification. Although many such mothers do, in fact, less well that those who postponed motherhood, there are those who manage to complete school, find a job and thus escape the poverty cycle. For example, the authors noted that most of the schooling which occurred after the birth of the first child took place late in the longitudinal time span. Whereas only 8.8 per cent of the sample had some post-high school training, five years into the study, this figure had risen to 24.7 per cent after the age of seventeen.

Relationships with men tended to be less than satisfactory. It was found that 24 per cent of the sample were in their second or third marriages, and that only 16 per cent were still married to the father of the first child. Support was found for the general view that teenage mothers have several children, with half of the mothers having at least four. They tended to be born in the first few years of the study, that is, while most mothers were still relatively young. Only a small proportion of respondents (about one-fifth) used contraception on a regular basis.

Another commonly-held view is that teenage mothers are reliant on welfare assistance for long periods of time after the birth of the first child. According to the longitudinal study reviewed here, about two-thirds of the mothers were no longer dependent on subsidies in the latter segment of the research. In view of these and other findings, Furstenberg *et al.* (1987: 9) noted that there is

> tremendous variation in outcomes of early parenthood . . . many women have not all followed the predictable course of life-long dis-advantage, even if they are not doing as well as their peers who post-poned parenthood . . . The failure to take account of pre-existing differences may have led to an overestimation of the impact of pre-mature parenthood on the life course of women.

## Teenage Fathers

In reviews of teenage parenthood, fathers are very often ignored, with most attention being devoted to teenage mothers. This may be due to the fact that most medical and social science writers view the father as of secondary importance. Another reason may simply be that increasing numbers of infants are now being raised in teenage single-mother households. Yet another reason might be that there is some dispute as to just how many babies born to teenage mothers have fathers who are teenagers. There is evidence to suggest that almost one-half of babies born to teenage mothers have fathers older than twenty years (Robinson 1988a, 1988b). A further reason might be that adolescent fathers have tended to be neglected because of Western society's 'mother-centered bias' (Parke *et al.* 1980). As Parke and colleagues note (p. 88):

> This neglect of the father stems, in part, from our assumption concern-ing the primacy of the mother-infant relationship.

Evidence shows that black teenagers in the United States have a higher parenthood rate by age (nineteen years) than whites or Hispanics (Elster 1991). The comparable rates are: blacks 15 per cent, Hispanics 11 per cent and whites 6.5 per cent. These rates remain even after controlling for social class differences.

Teenage fathers appear to be no less informed about general aspects of sexuality than their non-father peers. Like their peers, they tend to use contraception inconsistently. However, they differ from non-fathers in that they are more likely to accept teenage pregnancy as something that is not out of the ordinary. They are also more likely to favour abortion and themselves to be the children of teenage parents (Robinson 1988b). With respect to marriage and child-rearing, evidence shows that teenage fathers, like teenage mothers, are quite likely to have inappropriate developmental expectations of their children (Parke *et al.* 1980), although fathers do not differ in this respect from non-fathers (Robinson 1988a).

Teenage fathers who do decide to live with their partner and infant face strains no different from those on teenage mothers. It has been suggested that teenage fathers experience the same emotional cycle of elation and despair faced by teenage mothers (Robinson 1988a). Teenage fathers have reported being sad, anxious, fearful, depressed, happy, overwhelmed and shocked. Many also face bleak prospects: unemployment or school difficulties. Indeed, Marsiglio (1986) found that adolescent fathers, compared with adolescents who were not parents, were much less likely to complete high school.

Although writers have noted signs of depression and stress among teenage fathers, they do not differ significantly on a number of personality traits from older fathers with teenage partners (Robinson 1988b). In addition, teenage fathers suffer the stress of largely being separated from their peer group as well as the added strains of assuming new roles and responsibilities (in some cases, marriage), for which they might not be prepared. Teenagers fathers are also likely to have a poor academic record prior to parenthood and to find a job before most other boys (Neville and Parke 1991).

Teenage fathers (and mothers) find the changed roles and new responsibilities most difficult to deal with. Robinson (1988a) explains their predicament in the following terms (p. 56):

> teenagers have an even more traumatic time because of the premature role transition. Prospective fathers, having to deal not only with the worries of pregnancy but also with the stresses of normal adolescent development as well as the unscheduled developmental tasks of adulthood, face a triple developmental crisis . . . They either forego further education or attempt a 'triple-track' pattern of undertaking education, work, and parenthood simultaneously, and in some cases they take on marriage as a fourth accelerated task.

Contrary to popular myth, many teenage fathers show an interest in their sexual partner and child (Danziger and Radin 1990, Robinson 1988b). Indeed, Danziger and Radin suggested that the willingness of teenage fathers to be involved in their children's lives has been underestimated. Many fathers attend antenatal clinics with their partner, continue to date after the birth of their child, and some maintain regular contact. In one study (cited in Robinson 1988b), two-thirds of the fathers contributed towards the support of both mother and child. This has been confirmed by another report which showed that many adolescent fathers want to remain involved with their children and that many show financial concern (Elster and Hendricks 1986).

Finally, not many of these teenage couples will marry. In fact, only about 10 per cent will, with many of these alliances ending in divorce. Many such marriages are characterised by conflict, resulting in a divorce rate for under-18s that is three times higher than that for couples who had their first child in their twenties (Robinson 1988b).

## Theoretical Considerations

Several developmental tasks during the teenage years were noted in the first chapter. Paramount among these are the development of

---

**Figure 7.2** *Profile*

Janet and Rod had been in the city for a few months now. Although they enjoyed the exciting 'feel' of the place, neither could find work and there never seemed to be enough money for 'having a good time'. So they decided to return to their home town. By this time, Janet was seven months pregnant and beginning to feel rather uncomfortable. To the surprise of most people back home, Rod was committed himself to staying with her and looking after 'his' child. They shared a bedroom in his parents' house and got on a waiting list for public accommodation. In this respect, their prospects seemed better than in the city.

Janet gave birth to their second child two years later. She and Rod got on well together; they seldom quarrelled; they were renting their own apartment (at subsidised rates) and they had many friends. However, Rod had still not found a steady job. Not having completed school, he only managed to find occasional casual employment as a cleaner, labourer or whatever came his way. This seemed to be the case for most of the people they knew. Rod's ambition was to become a plumber, but he couldn't get an apprenticeship. Most of the boys they took these days had completed high school. Rod's parents were of little support and encouragement, his own father having lost his job some months before when the local paper mill (the biggest employer in town) was forced to shed some of its workforce.

The apartment was beginning to feel too small for the four of them. Rod sometimes felt utterly hopeless.

a strong sense of self, as well as the development of a vocational identity. For some teenagers this is a slow, yet steady, process. It is suggested here that adolescent parenthood impedes these important developmental tasks. According to the literature cited, many teenage parents exhibit certain psychosocial problems. It is quite likely that pregnancy and parenthood lead to identity diffusion and unnecessarily delay the attainment of identity achievement.

## Summary

Although adolescent birth rates have declined in some Western nations, it is not clear to what extent this has happened in other countries, notably those in Eastern Europe. Future research should document these trends in non-Western nations as well as the attitudes and beliefs of these teenagers concerning aspects of parenting and child-rearing.

More and more adolescent mothers are keeping their babies. Together with abortion, this accounts for the vast majority of pregnancy resolution decisions. Adoption appears much less popular, notably among black teenagers in the United States. It is generally agreed that pregnant teenagers need professional counselling regarding pregnancy resolution, and that they should be encouraged to make a decision that best reflects their personal circumstances as well as their own values, beliefs and aspirations.

One must express concern at the risks that the children of teenage mothers face concerning their prospects for emotional adjustment and school outcome. The risk and protective factors are well documented. It is hoped that intervention programs can be instituted so as to enhance protective factors such as positive self-esteem while offsetting some of the risk factors. Such intervention programs could have important effects on child well-being.

In conclusion, Elster and Hendricks (1986) have also noted the importance of intervention programs for adolescent fathers. Although many young fathers want to be involved in decision-making regarding their child, they are often prevented from so doing by the mother's parents. For those who maintain close contact with mother and child, intervention strategies may be needed to make the young father aware of vocational and educational opportunities, and to help him build a strong and supportive social network.

## Additional Readings

Brooks-Gunn, J. and Furstenberg, F. (1986) 'The Children of
   Adolescent Mothers: Physical, Academic, and Psychological
   Outcomes,' *Developmental Review* 6: 224–51
Dubow, E. and Luster, T. (1990) 'Adjustment of Children Born to
   Teenage Mothers: The Contribution of Risk and Protective
   Factors,' *Journal of Marriage and the Family* 52: 393–404
Furstenberg, F., Brooks-Gunn, J. and Morgan, S. (1987) *'Adoles-
   cent Mothers in Later Life'*. Cambridge: Cambridge University
   Press
Furstenberg, F., Brooks-Gunn, J. and Chase-Lansdale, L. (1989)
   'Teenaged Pregnancy and Childbearing', *American Psychologist*
   44: 313–20

## Exercise

1. Consider some of the risks to psychological and emotional adjustment that may result from unwanted teenage parenthood. Contact your local community health centre and seek their cooperation in trying to locate young teenage mothers/fathers. If you can manage to interview these parents, examine the circumstances surrounding their parenthood. Was it planned, what support was received from both sets of parents, did they complete school, are they currently employed, what plans do they have for the future, and so forth? To what extent do your findings support those reported in the literature? What can you conclude about teenage parenthood?

# 8 Work and Money

## Introduction

An important developmental task during adolescence is identity achievement. Although this is a process that extends beyond the bounds of that period of the life span referred to as 'adolescence', it is during the teenage years that the individual should develop a sense of personal identity as opposed to role confusion and identity diffusion (see Chapter 2). It is conceivable that this important process is facilitated, particularly in late adolescence, by the development of a vocational identity. Selecting a vocation, or embarking on a course of study with a particular career in mind is an important part of a developing sense of self. Having a job that is perceived to be worthwhile and valued by society, and doing that job well, enhances personal self-esteem (Feather 1990).

There has been a remarkable change in the employment opportunities of youth over recent decades. It is no longer reasonable to assume that a teenager, upon leaving school, will automatically find employment to match his or her ability and interests. Presently, some nations, like Australia, New Zealand, Britain, Canada and the United States face relatively high levels of unemployment and low levels of economic growth. It is to be expected that the unemployment rate among youth in them is somewhat higher. Indeed, youth unemployment in Britain rose by 120 per cent between 1972 and 1977 (Banks and Ullah 1988). Moreover, some countries also face budgetary crises, with the result that governments are unable to spend vast sums of money on job creation and retraining schemes for youth. Coupled with these factors is the move to automation, making many factory jobs redundant (Furnham and Stacey 1991).

Employment prospects for youth have undergone other radical changes in recent years. In many respects, there are now more job options available to them. Occupations are less sex-stereotyped than they were a few decades ago. At school, girls are being encouraged to study mathematics and science. This has led more females to embark on careers that were once regarded as 'male'. More females are graduating as medical doctors, engineers and lawyers, while it is no longer uncommon to find male nurses and social workers. More females are now involved in local and national government. These changes in societal attitudes and expectations

169

have therefore opened up new employment and career opportunities for teenagers in the late twentieth century.

An important question that intrigues psychologists is how individuals come to hold certain attitudes and beliefs about work and related matters to do with money. It is to this topic that we now turn.

## Learning about Work and Money

### Developmental Changes

Individuals go through various stages of vocational identity formation (Ginzberg 1972, Holland 1976). Beginning in childhood, vocational preference passes from the *fantasy period* to the *tentative period* during pre-adolescence, and on to the *realistic period* with late adolescence. During the fantasy period vocational preference is characterised by the exciting aspects of a job. Thus appearing on the cover of a glossy magazine or walking on the moon may appeal to some. Many young boys find the idea of being a truck or racing car driver exciting. During pre-adolescence, however, the individual is discovering new interests, values and personal capacities, resulting in changed vocational preferences.

Individual beliefs and values are constantly being reformulated so that by the time the teenager is in late adolescence, much clearer ideas have been formed. Around this time, the late adolescent has specific and crystallised ideas about his or her interests and capabilities and will attempt to integrate these into a self-concept. In other words, ideas about a future vocation are very much a reflection of the adolescent's interests and personal values. Late adolescents looking for a job or embarking on post-school study usually select vocations or courses of study consistent with their self-esteem and world view (Holland 1976).

As with the development of a vocational identity, children go through developmental stages as they learn about money. Various studies with different groups of children have found that, when quite young (around 4–6 years), children have very little understanding of monetary affairs. By the time they enter adolescence (about 11 years), however, children come to understand that one needs money to buy goods. Soon after (about 12 years), young adolescents realise that financial dishonesty and cheating are possible (Stacey 1982).

## Acquiring Beliefs about Work and Money

The vocation a teenager will ultimately decide upon, as well as personal attitudes toward work and money, are shaped by many factors, including intelligence, personal values and beliefs and social class (Holland 1976, Little 1967). In addition, factors like attitudes, values and class are intricately bound up with one's experiences *within* the family. Not surprisingly, therefore, many writers are united in their view that the family is an important socialising force determining how adolescents learn about work and money. Like so many other attitudes and values, it is within the family context that adolescents acquire the work ethic and various other work-related beliefs. As Barling and his colleagues put it (1991: 725):

> There are now empirical data available to support the notion that family socialization plays a significant role in the formation of children and adolescents' occupational aspirations and expectations.

By and large, children (especially males) tend to adopt similar careers to their fathers, while occupationally successful parents tend to have children who also achieve occupational success (Barling *et al.* 1991). Children are influenced by their parents' perceptions of employment and they assign similar importance to job rewards as do their parents. This supports the view that the family is an important context in which socialisation occurs and in which children learn about the world.

This line of thought is echoed by others. In a review of work ethic beliefs, Furnham (1990) discusses the important role that parenting style and attitudes play in shaping the personality and work attitudes of their children. As discussed in Chapter 3, one's personality is, in part, a product of parenting style as well as the nature of communication between parent and child. Furnham proposes that a warm, caring and nurturing family environment is likely to result in children who are internally controlled: that is, those who believe that what happens to them is largely due to their own efforts. By contrast, inconsistent parental discipline is likely to result in children with an external locus of control who view the world as an unpredictable place.

Importantly from our perspective, research evidence demonstrates a link between personality and one's level of achievement, motivation and beliefs regarding the work ethic. For instance, it is known that those with an internal locus of control are likely to work harder at both intellectual and performance tasks. So-called internals are also likely to endorse work ethic beliefs to a greater degree than so-called externals. They are also likely to score higher than externals on measures of job satisfaction and motivation (Feather 1983, Furnham *et al.* 1992).

Several other studies have documented the important role that parents play in a child's early encounters with economic principles. It is clear from such studies that the influence of adults is varied and far-reaching. One study, for example, examined the perceptions of British adults to pocket money or allowances received by children (Furnham and Thomas 1984). It was found that mothers were more inclined to believe that children should work for their pocket money or allowance. They were also quite willing to negotiate with the children about appropriate 'rates of pay'. Some interesting class differences were also evident. The researchers found that more middle class than working class adults were in favour of giving children pocket money by eight years of age, while some working class adults disapproved of the idea completely. Almost all the middle class adults thought that children should receive pocket money weekly, while 16 per cent of the working class adults thought that children should receive money only when they needed it. Of further interest was the finding that working class adults thought boys should receive more pocket money than girls.

These results point to the important and different ways children learn about money within the family context. Some may learn that pocket money is a right which should be received automatically, while others may be taught that money is received for work done around the house. Either way, parents appear to be an important agent in this learning process, transmitting their beliefs and values to the child. As Furnham (1990: 117) noted:

> This research shows . . . how adults teach their children about money, the virtues of thrift and saving . . . There seems to be sufficient evidence that parents with PWE (Protestant work ethic) beliefs stress the importance of postponement of gratification and saving; the planning of the use of money; and that money has to be earned.

Perhaps not surprisingly, parents and children share similar views about economic beliefs and the work ethic. In a comparison of the attitudes of a set of parents and children, it was found that mothers and fathers tended to resemble one another on these matters to a large extent, although there were slight differences between mothers and fathers and their children. Fathers tended to resemble their children with respect to economic beliefs, need for achievement and locus of control (powerful others). Mothers, on the other hand, tended to resemble their children in terms of economic beliefs and external locus of control. Parents and children were thus matched closest on economic beliefs (Furnham 1987a).

Given the findings discussed above, it is not unreasonable to assume that family socialisation predicts adolescent attitudes towards a wide variety of work-related beliefs. In a Canadian study, for example, researchers were interested in whether one could predict adolescent attitudes towards unions on the basis of two family-related matters: adolescents' perceptions of the union activities of their parents and their perceptions of parental attitudes towards unions (Barling *et al.* 1991).

The results showed that adolescent perceptions of parental attitudes to unions was closely linked to their own union attitudes, although there was no significant link between adolescent perceptions of parental union *activity*, and their own attitudes. The authors concluded that parents are important in transmitting work-related beliefs to their children. As they found, the perceptions that adolescents have of their family *vis-à-vis* the world of work and employment are important in shaping their *own* views about such matters. The family is therefore a strong socialising agent transmitting a range of attitudes and beliefs, including economic, to the adolescent.

## Family Transitions and Adolescent Work Values

As we noted in Chapter 3, the break-up of the original family unit is no longer a rare event. Not surprisingly, therefore, some researchers have examined the effects of family disruption and single parenthood on the work goals and values of adolescents in such families.

Traditionally, researchers working in the area of divorce have adopted a *crisis* perspective (see also Chapter 3): that is, a basic premise underlying this research has been to view the family unit of mother, father, and children as 'normal', notwithstanding the fact that blended, step- and single-parent families now make up a large proportion of families in many Western countries. According to some like Barber and Eccles (1992), rather than focus on the crisis perspective, the *processes* of family functioning in new families should be enjoying research attention. Single-parent families can be warm and nurturant and teenagers would much rather live in harmonious single-parent families than in conflict-ridden traditional families. These authors suggest that we focus on the long-term rather than short-term effects of family disruption and conclude that we need (Barber and Eccles 1992: 113):

a reconsideration of the position that the nuclear family is the only ideal context for the socialization of children.

Adolescents in single-mother households can have their work goals and aspirations shaped in a variety of different ways. Although most single mothers *have* to work, evidence suggests that maternal employment *per se* is not detrimental to adolescent identity formation. Rather, a wide range of factors such as income, mother's attitude to work, family stress, age and sex of adolescent, etc. need to be considered. For example, there is now abundant evidence which shows a great similarity between the occupational plans and values of males and females in late adolescence, with many more females entering high-status occupations. Yet many males and females still make gender-typed occupational decisions (Barber and Eccles 1992). It would seem, however, that adolescent males and females in single-mother households are *less* likely to consider traditional occupations. According to the authors, studies have found that in many instances, girls in single-mother households are unlikely to find investing time and energy in the family sphere attractive. They prefer the investment of time in the occupational sphere. Those who do consider marital roles are much more likely to ensure that they are not financially dependent on their husbands.

Single mothers are often overcommitted in the workplace, and this has important effects on adolescent adjustment and work aspirations (Barber and Eccles 1992). Although the effects of such over-commitment may sometimes be negative, evidence shows it is possible that financial rewards may offset some of the negative aspects of being in full-time work. Of importance, too, is the role model that the mother presents as an employed woman. According to the review, women in non-traditional jobs are more likely to have daughters who aspire to similar ones. In addition, if the single mother has a positive attitude to her work and successfully integrates her occupational and family commitments, this is likely to have positive effects on her daughter's occupational identity formation. Thus in homes where family disruption has occurred, adolescent work values and aspirations are closely linked to maternal employment, and expectations, gender role values pertaining to work and the family and the adolescent's self-concept (Barber and Eccles 1992). Work values are therefore determined by a complex web of family influences.

# Attitudes to Work and Money Matters

Not only does the family help shape work-related attitudes, there are also cultural differences (e.g. Lynn *et al.* 1991, Vondracek *et al.* 1990). In one study, Lynn and his colleagues compared attitudes to work among British and Japanese students in late adolescence. They argued that there may be different cultural motivations for work effort, and that such differences may be linked to national differences in economic growth. In order to examine these questions, adolescents completed measures of work and family orientation, achievement motivation, savings, money beliefs and career preferences.

Noticeable differences were observed between the groups. In the first instance, males in both samples scored higher on the competitiveness and money beliefs measure than did females. Secondly, among the British sample, there was a significant link between achievement motivation, academic achievement, occupational preference and actual achievement. Among the Japanese students, however, high competitiveness motivation was significantly related to money beliefs. The authors suggested that this higher competitive spirit among Japanese youth may be a reflection of higher economic growth rates for that country, although it is difficult to determine a cause-and-effect relationship (Lynn *et al.* 1991).

In an extensive report of the general social attitudes of almost 2000 British adolescents, one research team examined attitudes to various aspects of work (Furnham and Gunter 1989). Of some interest was the finding that adolescents have a clear idea of what they regard as the most and least important aspects of a job. Overall, there was some agreement as to what constitutes *job satisfaction*. These criteria are listed in Table 8.1. The table shows the percentage of respondents in the survey who rated each criterion as *very important* for job satisfaction. Generally, the respondents were in favour of intrinsic factors (e.g. job security, satisfying work, good working conditions) rather than extrinsic characteristics of work (e.g. short hours, high starting salary).

The researchers also observed some important *age differences* among the respondents. Older adolescents (who were much more likely to be employed) were more in favour of the intrinsic features of work than were younger ones. For instance, only 23 per cent of 17-year-olds rated a 'high starting salary' as very important, compared with 44 per cent of those aged 10–14 years. By contrast, 64 per cent of 17-year-olds thought having pleasant people to work with was very important, compared with only 47 per cent of 10–14

**Table 8.1** *Adolescents' Perceptions of a Satisfying Job*

| Criterion | Respondents agreeing (%) |
|---|---|
| Job security | 72 |
| Satisfying work | 62 |
| Good working conditions | 61 |
| Pleasant work colleagues | 56 |
| Opportunities for career development | 53 |
| High starting salary | 39 |
| A lot of responsibility | 25 |
| Short working hours | 22 |

*Source:*    Furnham and Gunter 1989

year-olds. As adolescents mature cognitively and socially and have experience of being in the workforce, they learn to appreciate the intrinsic rather than extrinsic features of work.

Adolescents have clearly-formed ideas about some, but not all, aspects of the economy and the value of work. Evidence to date indicates that late adolescent males are more likely to endorse the free enterprise system than are females, while adolescents who have saved more seem more trusting of business that those who have not saved as much. There also appear to be striking differences in this regard between British and American adolescents, such that the Americans, more than the British, are in favour of hard work and competitiveness (Furnham 1987b).

There are also demonstrable *within* cultural differences. Adolescents of different political persuasion hold different views about economic matters, such as public expenditure. For example, differences have been observed between adolescent supporters of the British Labour and Conservative parties (Furnham 1987b). It was found that Labour voters were much more in favour of government involvement in social welfare than were Conservative ones. It would seem that adolescents also have a clear idea of the differences *between* political groups. In the cited British study, teenagers judged the British Labour Party to spend more on housing, health and welfare and education, while the Conservative Party was judged to spend more on trade and industry and defence.

These studies all demonstrate that, at a relatively young age, individuals are able to make judgements about the value of work and the conditions necessary to promote job satisfaction. They are also able to judge the public expenditure policies of political parties which, no doubt, reflects their personal ideology. It is also clear that such judgements reflect adolescents' own political allegiances and general social beliefs.

## Personality and Work

Is it possible that certain personality types are best suited for a particular job? Is there a personality-job fit? Some authors have proposed just such a relationship. Holland (1973), for example, listed six types:

- Realistic      Practical career requiring few social skills (e.g. farming)
- Intellectual   Career requires abstract thinking (e.g. scientist)
- Social         Career uses verbal and interpersonal relations (e.g. teaching)
- Conventional   Career has structured activities (e.g. bank teller)
- Enterprising   Career uses verbal persuasion and leadership (e.g. politics)
- Artistic       Career that is self-expressive (e.g. writing).

Not only is personality related to certain occupational types, but has also been found to be associated with various aspects of work motivation, productivity, satisfaction, and work-related problems such as absenteeism and stress. Since it is beyond the scope of this chapter to discuss these aspects in detail, interested readers should consult more in-depth sources, like Furnham (1992). It is perhaps useful to note the following examples.

One personality trait that has important implications for job-related attitudes is locus of control. Differences in attitude and behaviour have been observed between those who are internally and externally controlled. 'Internals' have been shown to be more flexible in their career planning. They also work much harder, and are more motivated than 'externals' to get better jobs. A recent British study (Bonnett and Furnham 1991) examined the personality correlates of entrepreneurism in adolescents aged sixteen to nineteen. As predicted, those who made the effort to get involved in an entrepreneurial venture scored higher than a control group on internal locus of control and belief in the Protestant work ethic (see Table 8.2). These results support the view that a link exists between effort (work ethic and internality) and outcome (entrepreneurial venture).

Personality factors such as extraversion and neuroticism are also related to job attitudes. Because of their lower levels of cortical arousal, extraverts are better able to cope with working in an open-plan office, while introverts, on the other hand, are more productive in single-office accommodation. There are also personality differences with respect to job satisfaction. Evidence indicates that

**Table 8.2** *Mean Scores on Internality and Work Ethic for Entrepreneurial Groups*

| Scale | Mean | SD | F | p |
|---|---|---|---|---|
| Protestant work ethic | | | | |
| Entrepreneurial group | 88.84 | 10.14 | 4.25 | 0.04 |
| Control group | 85.75 | 10.25 | | |
| | | | | |
| Internal locus | | | | |
| Entrepreneurial group | 35.91 | 5.84 | 6.15 | 0.01 |
| Control group | 33.75 | 6.04 | | |

*Source:*    Bonnet and Furnham 1991

extraverts are more likely to be satisfied with their job, while neurotics tend to complain about the amount of work, their co-workers and their pay (Furnham 1992).

## Adolescents at Work

### Job Search Strategies

In times of relatively high youth unemployment, it is quite reasonable to assume that late adolescents who are still at school may have a clear idea of the job options available to them, as well as what strategies might assist them in getting their first full-time job. For example, some might believe that a university education will enhance their chances of gaining long-term employment, while others might consider an apprenticeship more beneficial. Still more might believe that it is best to leave school early if a job becomes available.

A study of teenagers in the United States revealed that they perceived certain barriers and aids as crucial in searching for one's first job (Dayton 1981). By and large, the teenagers in the study were of the opinion that personal attributes such as personality factors and academic ability were more useful in gaining employment than were external factors, such as governmental training schemes. A similar study was conducted more recently in Britain (Furnham 1984). Over 200 students from different schools in London were surveyed.

This study yielded sex and social class differences in the importance ratings given by adolescents to some job search strategies. Males, for instance, placed more emphasis on their written applications, while females seemed to prefer a more personal approach, such as visiting companies, gaining experience and so on. Some strategies were preferred by middle class as opposed to working class youth. For example, middle class youth were more inclined to place a job advertisement in the newspaper, study information trends and so on. These sex and social class preferences are summarised in Table 8.3.

Furnham (1984) acknowledges that his study does have some limitations. He notes, for instance, that the sample size was small, while his classification of teenagers as either working or middle class was rather inexact. Moreover, it is not clear to what extent his findings can be generalised to teenagers outside Britain. Research with larger samples in a variety of cultures is called for.

Research has also been conducted into the job search strategies of unemployed youth who have left school. In one recent Australian study, these issues were examined from the perspective of *expectancy-valence theory* (Feather and O'Brien 1987). The authors argued that the actions we perform result in positive or negative outcomes, and that we are more motivated to perform actions we believe will have a favourable outcome. Thus, if an unemployed person *strongly desires* employment, he or she will engage in all sorts of job search strategies in order to secure it. More work-shy individuals, on the other hand, are less likely to be motivated to find work.

The authors found partial support for this view. Although they did not find job seeking behaviour to be positively related to

**Table 8.3** *Adolescents' Job Search Strategies*

Males
  • Assemble a placement file of jobs going
  • Seek help from your family
  • Do volunteer work related to chosen job

Females
  • Apply to government agency
  • Visit companies and employers to learn more
  • Do summer or after-school work for experience

Middle class youth
  • Telephone potential employers
  • Register with a private employment service
  • Assemble a placement file of jobs going
  • Select a specific job and look for it
  • Study information on job trends
  • Place an advertisement in the newspaper
  • Take job interview training
  • Take vocational training

*Source:*    Furnham 1984

feelings of optimism and personal control, they did find search strategies to be significantly related to dissatisfaction with unemployment and a desire to find work. A separate study found that the stronger the desire for work among youth, the greater the depressive affect among those who could not find employment (Feather and Davenport 1981). Thus it would seem that job search strategies are, in part, guided by one's personal motivations and expectations about finding a job, as well as one's beliefs about the value of work. Job search behaviours therefore take on a unique quality, depending on the individual's desire and motivation to find work.

## Saving and Spending Patterns

It is well known that the purchasing power of adolescents has increased dramatically over recent years. Magazines, rock music, concerts and clothes for teenagers are big business. Beyond this, however, little is known about the personal characteristics associated with adolescent spending and saving.

One research project involved a large-scale survey of over 1500

---

**Figure 8.1** *Profile*

Larry, aged seventeen, was in his final year of high school. He lived at home with his parents and five sisters. He was the eldest. Home was cramped; there seemed to be too many of them for the small house. He couldn't wait to finish school, find a 'real' job and live on his own.

Larry had a part-time job at the local bakery. He had been there some years now, and got on well with the owner, who thought him a hard-working boy. Although he thought the work was rather tedious, Larry had managed to save enough to buy a small run-down car. That mattered less than the independence his own 'wheels' gave him. There was no way he could stop working now. He needed his freedom and the cash to run the car, to pay for insurance and servicing. Having a car also made Larry popular. Consequently, he often took out girls, and that was expensive, too.

Larry was soon performing near the bottom of his class, not because he was not interested, but simply because he worked too many hours every week. His parents didn't appear too concerned, however. They had never finished high school themselves and were proud that Larry had already got further than they had. Larry knew he needed a good final mark from high school to maximise his opportunities. He knew of many kids who did not make it to university and who couldn't find employment. He felt caught between having to improve his school grades and the financial benefits of his part-time job.

high school students in part-time employment in the United States (Pritchard *et al.* 1989). The researchers were interested in the saving and spending habits of the adolescents, as well as the extent to which such behaviours were associated with individual and family factors. It was found that many adolescents spent their money on discretionary items, such as clothes or entertainment. Most of those who tended to be heavy savers were white females who usually worked hard at school and planned further study. Savers also tended to be internally controlled. Those who spent their money on necessities (e.g. school books) tended to be female black public school students. Perhaps surprisingly, they also tended to be externally controlled and do less well at school, while working longer hours each week for less money. Not surprisingly, those who spent their money on necessities usually came from families with fewer economic resources.

One must approach these findings with some caution. It is difficult to predict to what extent they can be generalised to teenage samples in other affluent cultures such as Japan, Singapore and Hong Kong. Nonetheless, the findings reported here do support earlier suggestions about the importance of the family as the context within which adolescents from different social class backgrounds learn about work and money matters. As Pritchard *et al.* (1989: 721) noted,

> money has unique meanings for families, which are conveyed to their children through socialization processes.

## Social Relations in the Workplace

Some writers have been interested in what working adolescents learn *about* work. In particular, some have examined what working adolescents learn about authority in the workplace, how work is organised and whether adolescents' work-related attitudes are a function of certain personal factors, such as social class. Some would suggest that work accelerates adolescents' development of social sensitivity (e.g. perspective-taking), social insightfulness (e.g. understanding interpersonal processes) and social communication (e.g. manipulating others to achieve a goal).

In a study of female teenagers working part-time in a large hamburger chain in the United States, it was found that girls from different social backgrounds differed in their attitudes towards management, and that they had different strategies for dealing with work-related problems (Haaken and Korschgen 1988). The main

**Table 8.4** *Perceptions of Social Relations in the Workplace among Female Teenagers*

**Interactions with managers**
- *Positive or idealised:* e.g. form positive attachments to manager[1]
- *Functionally congenial:* e.g. form good working relationship with manager[1]
- *Avoidant or critical:* e.g. trying to maintain distance, focusing on conflictual relations with managers[2]

**Coping with workplace problems**
- *Resistance:* individual or group defiance[2]
- *Communicate with management:* Communicating directly with management[1]
- *Endure:* Passive resignation in dealing with workplace conflict[2]

*Note:*  1 generally characteristic of middle class workers
        2 generally characteristic of working class workers

*Source:*  Haaken and Korschgen 1988

findings from this study are summarised in Table 8.4. It shows, for example, that when interacting with managers, female teenagers usually adopt a variety of possible strategies, and that these differ depending on their social background. Working class females tend to focus on maintaining their *distance* from management as well as on *conflictual relations* with it. In coping with workplace problems, it was found that middle class girls were much more likely to *communicate* with management about their problems. These findings suggest that working teenage girls from different social class backgrounds perceive management differently, as reflected in their relations with those in authority. Working class girls, it seems, perceive greater social distance between themselves and management than do middle class ones. Moreover, this greater social distance also has implications for conflict resolution.

In conclusion, one must bear in mind that the findings reported here were based on a small number of female adolescents working in a particular employment setting. It is therefore not clear to what extent they can be generalised to teenagers of both sexes in a variety of occupational settings, or to teenagers in other cultures. Further research is necessary to examine these effects.

## Work and Stress

There is some debate about the effects of teenage employment on adolescents' psychosocial development (Haaken and Korschgen 1988). One line of thought, for instance, argues that adolescents need experience of the adult world and that work in general accelerates the developmental process towards adulthood (e.g. Heyneman

1976). Other writers have voiced concerns about youth employment, pointing to low wages, stressful jobs and poor working
conditions (e.g. Steinberg 1982). Some have noted a link between
work stress and increased use of alcohol and cigarettes among
youth (Manzi 1986). Another line of thought is that working facilitates the development of teenagers' personal responsibility but not
their social responsibility. It has been suggested that working may
impede family, peer, and school commitments, and increase the
development of cynical work-related attitudes among youth
(Steinberg *et al.* 1982).

In Table 8.5 are summarised some of the perceived effects on
adolescents of part-time work. The proposed negative effects, it
should be stressed, are particularly salient for those teenagers who
work quite long hours every week (15–20 hours or more).

Most teenagers in part-time work are generally in lower-status
jobs, in which employees are allowed little autonomy and initiative
(Greenberger *et al.* 1981). As the link between low status work,
stress and adverse health outcomes among adults is well established (e.g. Dohrenwend and Dohrenwend 1974), some (e.g.
Greenberger *et al.* 1981) argue that a similar association exists
among teenage workers. There are two possible reasons for this. In
the first place, the work itself may be dull and boring, which could

**Table 8.5** *Hypothesised Effects on Adolescents of Part-time Work*

**Positive outcomes**
Enhance education
Facilitate socialisation
Ease entry into full-time employment
Learn about job finding
Learn about yourself
Learn about the world of work
Help prepare for adult roles
Learn about survival in the real world

**Negative outcomes**
Low wages
Stressful job
Poor working conditions
Possible alcohol and drug use
Impedes school commitment and performance
Impedes extracurricular activities
Little formal instruction by supervisors
Much time devoted to low-level types of jobs
Develop cynical attitudes towards work
No long-term impact on educational and vocational plans.

*Sources:*    Manzi 1986, Steinberg 1982, Steinberg *et al.* 1982

lead to frustration and increased general stress. Secondly, it is possible that part-time work may interfere with family and school commitments, may be a major constraint on an adolescent's freedom, and might possibly exacerbate the usual crises of development faced by most adolescents. Greenberger *et al.* (1981: 693) summarise their position as follows:

> we would expect that work that permits little autonomy, allows little initiative, provides no sense of purpose . . . would be especially stressful for adolescents . . . they may have special salience for individuals at a developmental stage in which crises over autonomy, identity, intimacy, and achievement are normative.

In general, Greenberger and his associates found support for this view. They surveyed over 200 teenagers working part-time. Briefly, there was some evidence of a link between work stress, school absence and substance use. Males seemed more affected by noisy jobs and meaningless tasks. Girls seemed more affected by low wages and impersonal working environments. Surprisingly, boys working under stressful conditions tended to report fewer signs of psychological or physical stress, while just the opposite appeared to be the case for girls.

Of course, it is possible that work-generated stress may manifest itself in a variety of different forms. It is possible, for instance, that teenage work might have a negative impact on the parent-adolescent relationship, thus inducing stress. There appears to be some support for this view (Manning 1990). It was noted that considerable disagreement exists between parents and adolescents regarding independence, parental supervision, control of teenage activities and spending habits.

Future research needs to address the question of just what intervention strategies can be employed to assist adolescents at school who *have* to work part-time cope with the pressures of employment. Future studies should also examine the long-term effects of heightened parental-adolescent disagreements in those familes where teenagers are employed. Further longitudinal studies are called for (Greenberger *et al.* 1981). Until then, we might be advised to follow the advice of Greenberger and his colleagues, who caution that (p. 702):

> Adolescents' well-being may, however, be jeopardized by too much work and by working under stressful conditions.

### Coping with work stress

Teenagers develop a variety of coping mechanisms to deal with work-induced stress. Some use problem-focused strategies, such as coming up with solutions to the problem. Others use emotion-focused ones, such as trying to maintain pride. Others, no doubt, use a combination of the two (Manzi 1986). Examples of some of these mechanisms, which were employed by a small sample of adolescents in part-time employment, are shown in Table 8.6.

# The Effects of Unemployment

The psychological effects of unemployment on the adjustment of youth is an area that has generated considerable research. Perhaps this is due to the fact that unemployment is firmly on the political agenda in many countries. It might also be due to the fact that increases in unemployment have fallen disproportionately on those in late adolescence (Banks and Ullah 1988). These authors note that as we move towards the twenty-first century, we are witnessing the eradication of many youth jobs and apprenticeships. Likewise, it has been reported that youth unemployment increased in many OECD countries between 1980 and 1985. In Britain, for instance, it rose from 13.9 to 21.7 per cent, while in Canada, youth unemployent rose from 13.2 to 16.5 per cent for the same period (Junankar 1987).

### Psychological Effects

How likely is it that the experience of unemployment will lead to poor psychological adjustment among youth? After all, very few

**Table 8.6** *Examples of Adolescents' Coping Strategies in the Workplace*

---

**Problem-focused**
Take things one step at a time
Concentrate on what you have to do (the next step)
Knowing what has to be done, and doubling your efforts
Talking to someone to find out more about the problem
Coming up with a couple of different solutions

**Emotion-focused**
Maintaining pride and keeping a stiff upper lip
Wishing you could change what happened
Wishing the situation could go away or somehow be over with
Do not let it get to you; don't think about it too much
Try to look on the bright side of things; try to find good in the situation.

---

*Source:* Manzi 1986

individuals in late adolescence have families to support or mort-gages to pay. Moreover, it is possible for some teenagers to receive emotional and financial support from their parents during periods of unemployment. It has been argued that finding one's first job is an important developmental task, and therefore highly valued in our society. It is therefore not unreasonable to expect negative psychological consequences following unemployment, even among teenagers (Feather 1990).

Several studies have examined the effects of unemployment on individual adjustment. Useful summaries of this literature can be found in Banks and Ullah (1988), Barling (1989), Feather (1990), Furnham (1985), O' Brien (1986) and Warr (1987). Winefield and Tiggemann (1990a) caution that not all published reports are methodologically sound. They note that some simply compare unemployed with non-unemployed youth, failing to examine psy-chological functioning *before* the onset of unemployment.

The results of longitudinal research over relatively short periods of up to twelve months suggest that not being able to find a job after school has a detrimental effect on perceptions of the family by the adolescent and parents (Patton and Noller 1991), as well as on the unemployed's self-esteem, work ethic, mood, locus of control, stress symptoms, depressive affect, life satisfaction, attributions for unemployment and self-competence (e.g. Feather 1990, O'Brien 1990, Patton and Noller 1984, Tiggemann and Winefield 1984). It has also been found that reductions in level of psychological health are due to the *experience* of unemployment (Patton and Noller 1984). It is as though not being able to find a job irrespective of length of unemployment indicates to youth that society regards them as less than worthy. This has flow-on effects such as the lowering of self-esteem. Other findings concur with these senti-ments, although it is observed that differences between the em-ployed and unemployed may be due to the employed becoming 'healthier' (Tiggemann and Winefield 1984).

Longitudinal studies conducted over longer periods endorse the view that the employed become better-adjusted, while the un-employed actually show little deterioration in mental health. In one study, for example, adolescents were surveyed in school and again after intervals of two and three years (Winefield and Tiggemann 1990a). Although those who had never been employed had lower self-esteem than the group who had never been unemployed, the unemployed's level of self-esteem had not actually deteriorated. Indeed, other groups (those who had never been unemployed and those who found employment *after* a period of unemployment), showed quite large increases in their levels of self-esteem. Thus the employed seem to become psychologically 'healthier'.

Not only are there changes in personality functioning among the employed, but changes have also been observed in their attitudes and perceptions. For example, those who are employed are less likely to blame unemployment on external factors such as economic recession. Those who become unemployed, however, are more likely to see such external factors as important causes of their own unemployment. Research findings suggest that becoming employed is likely to increase the likelihood that those in work will see the unemployed as lacking in important individual characteristics, such as personal motivation (Feather 1990). In summary, therefore, it would appear that the experience of being in employment, or not, is associated with shifts in personality functioning and attitude.

## Length of Unemployment

Length of unemployment influences youth in a number of ways. It is now clear, for instance, that as the frequency of unsuccessful job applications increases, so the unemployed person's expectation of finding a job decreases. There is also reduced motivation to find a job, as well as evidence of apathy and resignation as the period of unemployment increases. For some unemployed, prolonged unemployment may also see a shift in attributions. Whereas they might previously have considered external factors to be important causes of their being unemployed, they may later, after lengthy unemployment, endorse negative internal causes (e.g. 'I'm just not good enough to find a job'; Feather and Davenport 1981).

Following research with adult British samples, a curvilinear hypothesis was proposed with respect to mental health and duration of unemployment (Warr and Jackson 1987). That is, it is suggested that psychological distress increases for some months after job loss, before declining. Not all evidence supports this view, however. One longitudinal study (Winefield and Tiggemann 1990b) followed a group of unemployed adolescents (aged 16–20 years) in Australia into young adulthood (19–24 years) and examined their self-esteem, negative mood, depressive affect and locus of control. The groups did not differ on self-esteem at Time 2, although results showed that depressive affect, negative mood and external locus of control increased as length of unemployment did. These results are illustrated graphically in Figure 8.1. As the results differ from those

**Figure 8.1** *Effects of Length of Unemployment on Psychological Health*

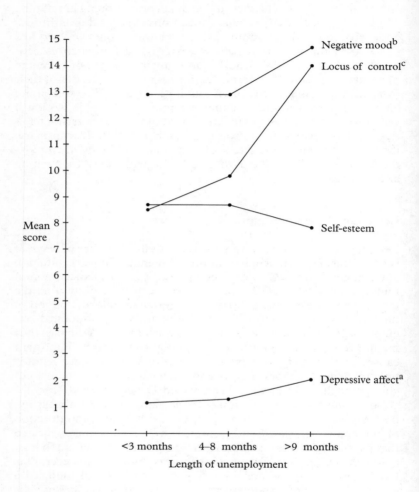

a = p < 0.01
b = p < 0.05
c = p < 0.001

*Source:*    Winefield and Tiggemann 1990b

obtained on adult samples, it could be that the psychological effects of unemployment are different for individuals in adolescence and adulthood.

The authors note that the curvilinear hypothesis may well be applicable to younger teenagers as well as much older adults. They suggest that these groups are better able to cope with long-term unemployment. Older adults, for example, may be under less pressure to find a job (e.g. early retirement is relatively common). They suggest that it is the nineteen or twenty-year-olds who are most likely to feel pressurised into finding employment, and hence most likely to manifest greater psychological distress as length of unemployment increases.

## Unemployment vs. Poor Quality Employment

Do all forms of employment promote mental health among adolescents? Is poor quality work a suitable substitute for unemployment? Several research studies have examined the effects of poor quality employment on psychological adjustment among youth. These suggest that jobs which do not utilise an adolescent's skills and talents and which do not provide variety and opportunity, will lead to a reduction in job satisfaction and increased stress (O'Brien, 1990; see also previous section on work stress).

Several longitudinal studies have been conducted to examine this issue (e.g. O'Brien and Feather 1990, Winefield, Tiggemann and Winefield 1991, Winefield, Tiggemann, Winefield and Goldney 1991). For instance, Winefield and his associates first interviewed respondents who were at school (Time 1) and then again seven and eight years later (Time 2). The respondents were divided into four separate groups, namely, satisfied employed, dissatisfied employed, unemployed and university students. Four psychological measures were administered at Time 1 and Time 2: self-esteem, depressive affect, locus of control and negative mood.

As no significant differences were observed between the groups on the psychological measures at Time 1, the authors concluded that differences observed at Time 2 were due to the effects of employment status. The authors detected some important trends at Time 2. In the first instance, self-esteem among all groups showed an increase over the period, while externality in locus of control showed some decline. Of some interest was the observation that the unemployed and dissatisfied employed groups performed less well than other groups on the remaining personality measures. Unemployed males exhibited higher negative mood and depressive affect than did males who were dissatisfied with their employment. Just the reverse was true for females, however. Thus one may conclude that being unemployed or in unsatisfactory employment has different effects on morale for males and females. This might be due to different pressures placed by society on men and women to find employment (Winefield *et al.* 1991).

Although the unemployed and dissatisfied employed show no deterioration in mental health, they are at a disadvantage compared to the employed group. As Winefield *et al.* (1991: 424) note, they

> do miss out on the psychological benefits enjoyed by young people who find satisfactory employment or undertake tertiary study.

## Theoretical Considerations

As noted, finding a worthwhile and satisfying job is one of the most important developmental tasks of adolescence. The outcome of vocational identity formation is shaped by several factors, intrinsic as well as extrinsic. Particular personality traits and personal values are related not only to job motivation and satisfaction, but also to career choice (e.g. Furnham 1992). In addition, there are several extrinsic factors which help shape vocational identity formation. These include the family, and work experiences such as stress and social relations. The formation of a vocational identity is therefore a complex process, and adolescents need as much help as possible in selecting the career that matches their personal beliefs and values.

## Summary

This chapter has reviewed the processes by which adolescents come to learn about the world of work and money. From the review, it is clear that these ideas are formed in the child's mind at a relatively young age. No doubt there are many important factors (such as ethnicity or social class) which are important in shaping an individual's beliefs about work and money. In this chapter, however, we have emphasised the family as an important socialising force, and noticed the extent to which parents' and adolescents' attitudes and beliefs correspond on matters relating to work attitudes and beliefs. It is quite clear that parents are important in helping their children acquire certain beliefs, attitudes and values connected with work and money.

More recent reviews of the literature (e.g. Barber and Eccles 1992) have hinted at important changes occurring in 'new' or 'non-traditional' families. In their review of single-mother households, for example, they note that in terms of vocational identity, single-mother families have a profound effect on the vocational choices of sons and daughters. Evidence suggests that occupational choices for these teenagers are less sex-stereotyped. These are noteworthy findings and need to be pursued in further research. Are the same trends found in children of single-father families, for instance?

The last segment of the chapter was devoted to adolescents at work and the important question of unemployment. Researchers have shed light on the job search strategies of youth and the psychological consequences of unemployment. Some have suggested that too much part-time work during adolescence may not be as beneficial as previously thought. Important longitudinal work has been done on the effects of unemployment as well as unsatisfactory employment, and their links to psychological distress.

Since relatively high levels of youth unemployment are likely in the forseeable future, the challenge facing mental health professionals is how to maintain pride and motivation in those who have little chance of finding full-time employment.

## Additional Reading

Barber, B. and Eccles, J. (1992) 'Long term Influence of Divorce and Single Parenting on Adolescent Family- and Work-related Values, Behaviors, and Aspirations', *Psychological Bulletin* 111: 108–26

Feather, N. (1990) *The Psychological Impact of Unemployment*. New York: Springer-Verlag

Furnham, A. (1992) *Personality at Work: The Role of Individual Differences in the Workplace*. London: Routledge

Holland, J. (1976) 'Vocational Preferences', in M. Dunnette (ed.), *Handbook of Industrial and Organizational Psychology*. Chicago: Rand McNally

## Exercise

1. Visit a business in your community which employs teenagers on a part-time casual basis. Interview some of them, noting details about their backgrounds; how many hours per week they work;

how old they are; what they tend to spend their money on; what their grades are like at school; and so on. Are there different spending patterns for different groups of youth? What reasons do they give for working part-time? What else are you able to deduce from your data? What does this suggest about the nature of part-time work among adolescents?

# 9 Orientation to Authority and Delinquency

## Introduction

The term 'juvenile delinquency' refers to illegal acts committed by young people (Eysenck and Gudjonsson 1989). When using the term delinquency we include a wide range of varying behaviours which also differ in their level of seriousness. Thus delinquency includes such acts as stealing money from milk bottles, gaining access to entertainment without paying, the fire-bombing of letter boxes, assault and rape. Also included are robbery, break-and-entry and larceny.

It is important to bear in mind that the age of legal responsibility for being delinquent varies from country to country. In England and Wales, for example, a juvenile is a person under the age of 17. At the same time, it is also held that children under the age of 10 years cannot be found guilty of an offence, and that rape cannot be committed by a boy who is under the age of 14. In the United States, on the other hand, 17 is regarded as the age of transition to adulthood in most states (Eysenck and Gudjonsson 1989). In the Australian state of Victoria, individuals under the age of 8 are legally presumed *not* to be capable of committing an offence.

Although it would appear from media reports that juvenile crime is on the increase, some writers would dispute this. We are reminded by West (1967), for example, that juvenile crime is commented upon by nearly every generation. To illustrate this point, he cites the following example, taken from a report published in England in 1818 (West 1967: 33):

> The lamentable depravity which, for the last few years, has shown itself so conspicuously amongst the young of both sexes, in the Metropolis and its environs, occasioned the formation of a Society for investigating the causes of the increase of Juvenile Delinquency.

This is not to suggest that the seriousness of delinquency has been overstated. On the contrary. As will be discussed below, delinquency causes serious hurt, emotional distress and enormous financial loss. It therefore warrants serious and careful analysis by psychologists and other professionals. Fortunately, however, it would seem that delinquent and anti-social acts are committed by a minority of adolescents. Evidence (Rigby *et al.* 1987) indicates that, by and large, many adolescents are reasonably accepting of institutional authority.

In this chapter we shall review some important theories of criminality and delinquency, as well as the social and personality factors related to delinquent behaviour. We begin by first examining general orientation to authority among adolescents.

## Orientation to Authority

From a very early age, young children have to learn to cope with individuals who are placed in positions of authority. As already discussed, children are socialised in the context of the *family* and have to develop relationships with parents who represent institutional authority. It is from parents that children hear the word '*No!*' for the first time. It is with parents that children first experience the thwarting of their desires and behaviour. How they respond and adapt to such constraints may have important implications for later adolescent behaviour *vis-à-vis* institutional authorities. Indeed, it was noted earlier (see Table 3.1) that differences in parenting style are related to adolescent behaviour outcomes, including problem behaviour, misconduct and drug use.

During adolescence the parent-child relationship changes in nature. Adolescents are much more questioning of authority than younger children, although this is regarded as a normal part of adolescent development and identity formation. It is expected that teenagers will, within established boundaries, experiment with different roles, behaviours and ideas (see Chapter 2). Teenagers are caught between their own desires and impulses on the one hand and the demands of friends and peer groups and the constraints of parents on the other. Each of these sets bounds or rules for acceptable behaviour, within which development must occur. For some individuals, however, the boundaries are too constraining. Some overstep the mark and go beyond what is normally regarded as acceptable behaviour.

Orientation to authority should be distinguished from concepts such as authoritarianism (Rigby and Rump 1979). Whereas orientation to authority refers to acceptance of it, authoritarianism in its original sense refers to superstition, projection of hostility, repressed emotionality, prejudice and intolerance of ambiguity. Research among Australian students has confirmed that these constructs are independent. Results of a factor analytic survey revealed that attitudes to authority figures (e.g. police, teachers, etc.) are quite distinct from various facets of authoritarianism (Rigby and Rump 1979).

It has also been demonstrated that there is a *generality* of attitude to authority. This suggests that adolescents who are accepting of the police are also likely to be accepting of other authority figures. Such individuals are also likely to hold relatively conservative social and political beliefs and to engage in pro-authority behaviours (Reicher and Emler 1985, Rigby and Rump 1979, Rigby *et al.* 1987).

Researchers (Reicher and Emler 1985) have identified various subdimensions of attitudes to authority. These are:

- alienation from the institutional system
- absolute priority of rules and authorities
- bias versus impartiality of authorities
- relationship to school rules and authority.

These dimensions are listed in Table 9.1, together with sample questionnaire items.

Other writers (e.g. Rigby and Rump 1979) are of the view that attitudes to authority can be generalised. However, rather than identifying dimensions of attitudes, they simply determine these to authorities such as the police, law, army and parents.

**Table 9.1** *Dimensions and Sample Items of Attitudes to Authority*

**Alienation from the institutional system**
1. You should not worry about doing things against school rules if you can get away with it
2. The police pick on me and give me a bad time

**Absolute priority of rules and authorities**
1. You should always do what a police officer tells you
2. You should never break the law

**Bias vs. impartiality of authorities**
1. A lot of teachers care more about an easy life than about what happens to their pupils
2. Teachers have got more time for you if you have got a posh accent

**Relationship to school rules and authority**
1. Teachers pick on me
2. Most school rules are stupid or petty.

*Source:* Reicher and Emler 1985

## Theories of Orientation to Authority

There are several theories each purporting to explain the development of orientation to institutional authority. In a recent review (Rigby 1990), the following perspectives were noted as important: psychoanalytic theory, identity formation theory, cognitive developmental theory and social factors. As many of the relevant issues pertaining to these broad theories were discussed in the first chapter, these perspectives will only be briefly summarised here.

*The psychoanalytical perspective*
According to this view, adolescence is marked by a dramatic rise in sexual and instinctual feelings. This results in inner conflict, causing the teenager to seek closer ties with the peer group and to break emotional and constraining links with the family. Thus the teenager seeks to strive for, and to attain, independence. In so doing, many adolescents question authority figures and the nature of authority itself. As Muuss (1988) explains:

> This process of emotional detachment results, at least for a time, in rejection, and hostility towards parents and other authority figures.

*Identity Formation Theory*
Marcia's identity statuses were reviewed in Chapter 2. Characteristic of the moratorium phase is the fact that adolescents are not committed to a set of beliefs, values, or ideology. Although the moratorium phase is regarded as essential for final identity achievement, some teenagers appear totally alienated from society. Relationships with peers and parents are viewed as meaningless (Rigby 1990), with the result that some enagage in delinquent and other forms of anti-social behaviour.

*Cognitive Developmental Theory*
Younger children are much more likely than adolescents to be accepting of parental and other authorities. Adolescents, capable of abstract reasoning, are more likely to question authority. Research evidence has shown that adolescents who disagree with their parents about various strategies for resolving problems are more likely than others to have reached relatively advanced levels of identity achievement (Peterson 1990).

*Social influences*
There are some important social determinants of orientation to authority (Rigby 1990). Included are the role of the peer group and

the decline of patriarchal authority. The influences of the peer group are well known, and were previously discussed (Chapter 4).

With respect to the decline of patriarchal authority, it is suggested that the socio-economic basis of the family has slowly shifted over the generations to the mother, while the role of the father has been trivialised. This has resulted in a breakdown of respect for authority figures. However, little empirical support for this position has been offered (Rigby 1990).

## Authority Attitudes and Behaviour

Can one expect attitudes to authority to be related to a particular behavioural disposition? Evidence suggests that there is support for such a view (Rigby 1986). According to the theory of reasoned action (Ajzen and Fishbein 1980), behaviour can be predicted from the individual's *intention* to commit it. Intention is the function of two factors, namely, positive or negative evaluation of actually performing the behaviour (so-called behavioural beliefs), and subjective norms, which reflect the individual's perceptions of social pressure. An adolescent, therefore, who is keen to be accepted by the peer group and who may regard gaining access to a movie theatre as quite thrilling or exciting, is likely to attempt this in the hope of impressing other members of the peer group.

There is a distinction between beliefs, attitudes, intentions and behaviours. Ajzen and Fishbein (1980) are of the opinion that, although intentions are the best predictors of behaviour, 'appropriate measures of attitudes' (p. 27) can also be usefully employed to do so. Thus general beliefs and attitudes about the object, as well as beliefs about performing the behaviour, can also be used to predict it, although they are less reliable than intentions.

It would appear that a link exists between attitudinal and behavioural orientation to authority. An investigation among a sample of Australian adolescents found support for the view that attitudes to various institutional authorities are related to indices of peer and self-reported behaviour. The strength of association tended to be higher for self-reported rather than peer-reported behaviour (correlations of 0.29 and 0.71 respectively).

# Orientation to Authority: Individual Differences

A considerable amount of research has examined the personality correlates of orientation to authority. Independent studies have all tended to agree that negative orientation to authority is associated with a particular constellation of personality and individual difference variables. Included are such traits as impulsiveness, religiosity, extraversion, achievement motivation, venturesomeness, Eysenckian psychoticism, risk-taking and external locus of control.

In one study, for example, it was demonstrated that an acceptance of authority is related to high levels of religiosity (Rigby and Densley 1985). It was found that Catholic adolescents who were accepting of authority were more likely to (a) believe in God, and (b) attend church regularly. In another study, it was noted that those who perceive themselves to be internally controlled were more supportive of institutional authorities. In explaining these findings, it was concluded that the possibility exists that internals (those who believe that what happens to them occurs through their own volition) feel sure enough of themselves *not* to feel threatened by institutional authorities (Heaven 1988).

In another study, the relationships between orientation to authority, beliefs in certain values and particular personality dimensions among Australian adolescents were examined (Heaven and Furnham, 1991). Following an earlier lead (Feather 1982), the researchers argued that values, although abstract in nature, are *normative*: that is, they act as frames of reference that guide behaviour and attitudes. Values are therefore a useful tool, which aid our understanding of human behaviour. The researchers expected that an endorsement of values would be significantly related to all aspects of orientation to authority. Specifically, they argued that conservative values would be related to a positive orientation. Secondly, they were interested in the relative influence of personality factors such as extraversion, neuroticism and psychoticism.

The main results of this study are presented in Table 9.2 and show the best predictors of pro-authority attitudes and pro-authority behaviour. It is evident that the contribution of personality (namely, psychoticism) to total variance explained was rather limited for both attitudinal and behavioural aspects of authority. With respect to attitudes, for instance, endorsement of values made a modest contribution of 8 per cent to variance explained, followed by pro-authority behaviour (16 per cent) and psychoticism (3 per cent). With respect to pro-authority behaviour, values explained 22 per cent of the variance, followed by attitudes (14 per cent) and psychoticism (6 per cent).

These results show the close links which exist between attitudes to authority and behavioural dispositions. Secondly, the results show that, although the contribution of personality (in this case psychoticism) to explaining orientation to authority is significant,

**Table 9.2** *Predictors of Orientation to Authority*

| Variables | $R^2$ | Beta | t |
|---|---|---|---|
| **Positive attitudes to authority** | | | |
| Values | | | |
| National strength and order | 0.02 | 0.16 | 2.16* |
| Traditional religiosity | 0.05 | 0.17 | 2.35* |
| Propriety in dress and manners | 0.07 | 0.17 | 1.80 |
| Religious commitment | 0.08 | −0.07 | −0.69 |
| Pro-authority behaviour | 0.24 | 0.46 | 6.18** |
| Psychoticism | 0.27 | −0.22 | −2.73** |
| **Pro-authority behaviour** | | | |
| Values | | | |
| National strength and order | 0.02 | 0.14 | 1.90 |
| Traditional religiosity | 0.15 | 0.37 | 5.29** |
| Personal growth and inner harmony | 0.15 | 0.00 | 0.02 |
| Positive orientation to others | 0.16 | 0.10 | 1.21 |
| Propriety in dress and manners | 0.22 | 0.32 | 3.86** |
| Religous commitment | 0.22 | −0.02 | −0.22 |
| Attitudes to authority | 0.36 | 0.39 | 6.18** |
| Psychoticism | 0.42 | −0.30 | −4.28** |

* $p < 0.05$.   ** $p < 0.01$.

*Source*:   Heaven and Furnham 1991

its overall contribution is rather small. It is therefore likely that other factors not measured here are important in explaining orientation to authority.

As negative attitudes to authority could be viewed as symbolic of general counter-conformity, it is reasonable to expect that adolescents who have them are likely to engage in a range of anti-authority behaviours, such as smoking. Support for this thesis was obtained from a study of 193 adolescents (Heaven 1989). It was observed that smoking in females was related to general negative attitudes to authority as well as negative attitudes to law. Among males, smoking was related to negative attitudes to the army (see Table 9.3).

How is one to explain these rather different results for the two sexes? It was suggested that, for females, 'law' is traditionally associated with male power, dominance and male authority. Feminist theory predicts that rebellious females will reject such manifestations of 'male power'. Likewise, if one assumes that 'army' is traditionally associated with things masculine, and with authority and discipline, one can expect that young males' rebelliousness will be directed toward this image (Heaven 1989).

**Table 9.3** *Kendall Correlations between Smoking Behaviour and Attitudes to Authority*

|  | Smoking behaviour | |
| Scales | Females | Males |
| --- | --- | --- |
| Attitudes to authority | 0.21* | 0.13 |
| Subscales: | | |
| Police | 0.12 | 0.11 |
| Army | 0.03 | 0.19* |
| Teachers | 0.06 | 0.13 |
| Law | 0.27** | −0.14 |

\* $p < 0.05$.   \*\* $p < 0.01$

*Source:*   Heaven 1989

# Orientation to Authority and Delinquency

According to some reports, adolescents who reject institutional authority are likely to commit acts of delinquency. Researchers have noted significant associations between negative attitudes to authority and self-report delinquency measures (Reicher and Emler 1985, Rigby, Mak and Slee 1989).

Some writers (e.g. Reicher and Emler 1985) have argued that the so-called personality *deficit model* of delinquency is incomplete. Rather, they suggest that delinquent acts reflect a *negative quality* in the relationship between the adolescent and wider society. As they suggest (Reicher and Emler 1985: 161):

> we propose that juvenile delinquency may be regarded as the reflection of a negative relationship between the young person and the system of social regulation . . . called 'legal-rational authority', or, more simply, between the young person and formal authority.

According to this view, therefore, the very nature of the relationship between adolescent and authority figures is damaged to such an extent that the teenager is likely to engage in a variety of antisocial behaviours. Reicher and Emler (1985) found support for such a relationship among a sample of British 13-year-olds. It is important to stress that the authors are not proposing a cause-effect relationship, but rather that orientation to authority and self-report delinquency are different manifestations of the same behaviour syndrome. As the authors (Reicher and Emler 1985) suggest, adolescents have different social identities: a delinquent identity comprises various attitudinal and behavioural components, each of which reflect it to some degree.

# Delinquency

The actual extent of juvenile delinquency is unclear, although many suspect that official figures under-represent the true situation. Official figures are also very sensitive to changes in method of reporting, definitions of crime and age of legal responsibility. Nonetheless, nearly all writers would agree that delinquency is a serious problem, with huge associated financial costs. School vandalism, for instance, costs many millions of dollars every year. Large sums of money are required all over the world for policing and the administration of juvenile justice systems. In the United States it costs $1 billion per year to maintain the juvenile justice system (Patterson *et al.* 1989).

### Incidence of Delinquency

When studying the incidence of juvenile offenses, one is immediately struck by conflicting figures and different methods of reporting data. According to one report, the percentage of those arrested in the United States who are under 18 appears to be declining steadily. In 1974 the rate was 27.2 per cent of all arrests. By 1987 the rate was 16.5 per cent (Dusek 1991). From these figures, however, it is not clear to what extent adolescents are changing their behaviour or becoming more adept at avoiding detection and subsequent arrest.

**Figure 9.1** *Proportion of Persons Aged 8–24 years Proceeded Against for Certain Crimes*

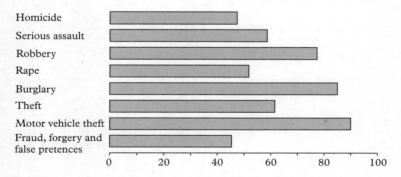

*Source:* Australian Bureau of Statistics 1985

Australian data reveal that adolescent groups constitute a large percentage of proceedings for certain offences. Based on data from Australia's second most populous state, Victoria, Figure 9.1 shows the proportion of those aged 8 to 24 years proceeded against for certain crimes during 1983. Individuals in this age category made up about 80 per cent or more of all proceedings for robbery, burglary and motor vehicle theft (Australian Bureau of Statistics 1985).

Table 9.4 shows the likelihood of different age groups being proceeded against for different crimes in Victoria in 1983. Different criminal activities are listed for age groups 8–16, 17–20, and 25 years and over. Individuals under the age of 20 years were more likely to be proceeded against for all the crimes listed.

## The Structure of Problem Behaviour

Delinquent behaviour is part of a syndrome of problem behaviour (Donovan and Jessor 1985, Donovan, Jessor and Costa 1988). That is, delinquent behaviour is usually associated with other problem behaviours such as alcohol use, illicit drug use and sexual promiscuity. Evidence for this view comes from a number of different longitudinal studies conducted in the United States. It is now believed that a single common factor accounts for various problem behaviours in both male and female adolescent groups. This common factor or underlying theme, which explains the syndrome of problem behaviour, is *unconventionality* in personality and social attributes (Donovan and Jessor 1985). It is also clear from the

**Table 9.4** *Persons Proceeded Against by Police in Victoria, Australia, 1983*

| Crime | Age groups | | |
|---|---|---|---|
| | 8–16 | 17–20 | >25 |
| Homicide | 0.5 | 7.5 | 1.9 |
| Serious assault | 20.4 | 108.5 | 19.3 |
| Robbery | 12.9 | 38.9 | 3.2 |
| Rape | 2.4 | 10.7 | 2.7 |
| Burglary | 440.2 | 440.5 | 33.0 |
| Theft | 819.0 | 891.7 | 232.3 |
| Motor vehicle theft | 156.4 | 321.6 | 10.1 |
| Fraud | 26.4 | 125.3 | 42.2 |

*Note:* Rate per 100,000 population in age group

*Source:*   Australian Bureau of Statistics 1985

available evidence that one can rank in order behaviours, from those most, to those least determined by unconventionality, as follows:

- Number of times drunk in past six months
- Frequency of marijuana use in past six months
- General deviant behaviour in past six months
- Sexual intercourse experience.

This ordering suggests that sexual experience is not regarded as being as unconventional as marijuana use or drunken behaviour.

Besides the possible influence of personality and social attributes on problem behaviour, Donovan and colleagues suggest that there may be other explanations for such a syndrome of problem behaviour. In the first instance, engaging in these behaviours may be one way of achieving a particular set of goals. Secondly, such behaviours are quite often learned together, and continue to be performed together. Thirdly, they often occur in social contexts where other adolescents are present, resulting in peer pressure on the individual. Questions of *social ecology*, or the context within which behaviours are performed are therefore important (Donovan and Jessor 1985).

## The Stability of Delinquent Behaviour

Are anti-social and delinquent children likely to manifest delinquent behaviours as adolescents? According to some studies, this is highly likely. One review (Loeber 1982) found evidence for this *stability hypothesis*, especially for those young males who were initially rated as extremely anti-social. For example, it was noted that of boys about 8–9 years of age who were judged to be above the 95th percentile in rated aggressiveness, 38.5 per cent were judged to be in the same percentile 10 years later.

Chronic delinquency is best predicted by three other factors. These are (Loeber 1982):

- Early age of onset of delinquency
- Engaging in delinquent behaviour in more than one setting, and
- Engaging in a variety of behaviours.

Although anti-social and delinquent behaviour tends to be stable over time, there do appear to be changes in the sorts of behaviours engaged in (Loeber 1982). Stealing in the home, truancy and the use of alcohol and drugs tend to increase between middle childhood and age sixteen. Fighting, disobedience, and lying, on the other hand, tend to decrease across the adolescent years.

# Perspectives on Delinquency

There are several theoretical frameworks which guide psychological research into delinquency. These are personality factors, heredity and environment, biological theory, and social factors. Each of these will be briefly described.

### Delinquency and Personality

Some writers have argued quite eloquently that delinquency is related to particular personality dispositions. In particular, much research evidence pertaining to the influence of the factors extraversion-introversion, emotional stability and emotional independence (psychoticism) on delinquency has been accumulated (e.g. Eysenck and Gudjonsson 1989, Furnham and Thompson 1991, Heaven 1993). These three dimensions can be regarded as major personality types, subsuming traits such as hostility, dominance, impulsiveness, venturesomeness, risk-taking and others (Eysenck and Eysenck 1985).

According to one view, delinquency results from high levels of neuroticism, extraversion and psychoticism. At the basis of this cause-effect relationship is the functioning of the ascending reticular activating system which controls levels of physiological arousal (Eysenck and Eysenck 1985). Those high on extraversion are said to be low in arousal. In order to raise their levels, these individuals engage in various thrill-enhancing and venturesome activities. It is also possible that the same applies to those who are high on psychoticism (Eysenck and Gudjonsson 1989). Eysenck and colleagues note that not all stimulus-seekers are likely to engage in delinquent behaviours; some divert their energies into more acceptable ones.

Although there is considerable evidence to support the role of these and other personality dimensions, some findings appear equivocal. For example, one recent British study found evidence that extraversion, but not neuroticism or psychoticism, was implicated in delinquency (Furnham and Thompson, 1991).

Whereas many studies can be criticised on the grounds that they look at the relationship between one or two factors and delinquency *in isolation*, a recent report attempted to discern the relationship between delinquency and several personality factors (Heaven 1993). Included was a range of personality traits as well as the personality types psychoticism and sociability (extraversion) (see Eysenck and Eysenck 1985 for a discussion of traits and types). Quite different results were obtained for adolescent males and females.

It was found that both psychoticism and sociability were significant predictors of delinquency for both sexes. However, whereas the personality traits were directly related to delinquency for males, they were not for females. Rather, psychoticism was found to *mediate* the effects of the traits for girls. Moreover, social class had a significant effect for females, but not for males: that is, girls from lower social strata were more likely to engage in delinquent acts than were boys. In addition, the effects of social desirability differed for the sexes, being more pronounced for females than males. Thus the nature of delinquency appears to be quite different for adolescent boys and girls. The paths of influence are shown in Figures 9.2 and 9.3, for males and females respectively.

Several noteworthy longitudinal studies have been conducted examining the relationship between various individual difference variables and delinquency (see Binder 1988, for a review). One of the earlier studies was conducted by the Gluecks, who followed up over 500 juvenile offenders. A sample of non-delinquent boys, matched for intelligence as well as ethnic and socio-economic background, formed the control group. Delinquent boys were more likely to be less conventional, more assertive and extraverted, and less goal-oriented. They were also more likely to display hostility and destructiveness, but to be low in anxiety and insecurity.

In Britain, a longitudinal study of over 400 boys from different primary schools was conducted (West and Farrington 1973). It concluded that, besides some important social factors, the personality disposition of the child is an important predictor of delinquency. They argued as follows (p. 189):

> it was the unpopular boys rather than the popular ones, those with high 'neuroticism' scores rather than those with low, those from broken homes rather than those from intact homes, those with nervous mothers rather than those with stable mothers, those born illegitimate rather than those born to married parents, who in each instance were the ones more likely to become delinquents.

## Biological Explanations of Delinquency

In the previous section, the importance of cortical arousal as a link

**Figure 9.2** *Paths of Influence for Males*

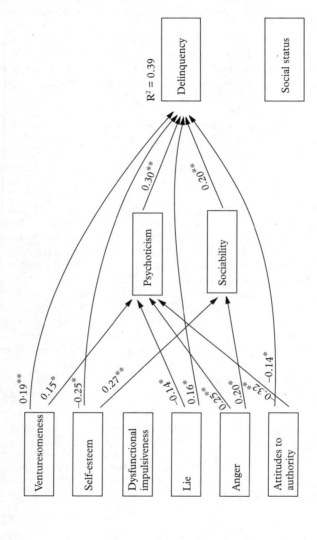

*P < 0.05; **P < 0.01.

*Source:*    Heaven 1993

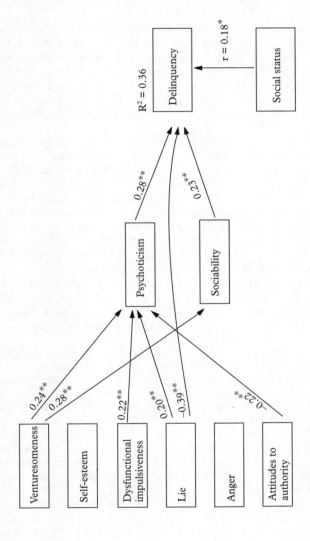

**Figure 9.3** *Paths of Influence for Females*

*P < 0.05; **P < 0.01.

*Source:*    Heaven 1993

between personality types such as extraversion and delinquency was mentioned. This section will review some of the main principles that are involved. More detailed accounts are available elsewhere (e.g. Eysenck and Eysenck 1985, Eysenck and Gudjonsson 1989, Strelau and Eysenck 1987).

Individual differences in extraversion-introversion can be traced to differences in the reticular system, such that extraverts are typically under-aroused. Experimental studies have demonstrated differences in these personality types on tasks such as continuous serial reaction, the orienting reaction, EEG recordings, and conditioning (Eysenck and Eysenck 1985). This theory has also been extended to the area of delinquency and criminality (Eysenck and Gudjonsson 1989).

This Eysenckian approach to understanding delinquency implicates arousal and conditioning, with the latter being facilitated by high arousal levels. In brief, delinquents who are usually *low* on arousal do not condition easily: that is, parents, teachers and others find it difficult (if not impossible) to teach such adolescents acceptable behaviour through reward and punishment, as discussed in the first chapter. Moreover, there is evidence to suggest that introverts and extraverts condition differently to different sorts of stimuli (Eysenck and Gudjonsson 1989): introverts respond better to negative stimuli such as pain or harmful punishment, while extraverts respond better to pleasant stimuli. Extraverts also have much higher pain thresholds than introverts, which is crucial to understanding the association between extraversion and delinquency. Eysenck and Gudjonsson (1989) explain as follows:

> There is no doubt that pain thresholds and pain tolerance are higher for extraverts than for the average person and lower for introverts . . . This would be directly relevant to criminal behavior, which often involves physical danger and pain . . . Hence, if the intensity of physical punishment is felt less strongly by extraverts, then clearly they should respond less to such types of conditioning.

Accordingly, extraverts who are typically low on arousal are much more likely to engage in risky, thrill-enhancing behaviours. Many such behaviours are typical of delinquents and criminals (Eysenck and Gudjonsson 1989).

Males are more likely to be involved in serious crime than are females with quite specific age and sex effects for violent and property offences. According to some (e.g. Ellis, cited in Eysenck and Gudjonsson 1989), androgens are finally responsible for differences in certain physiological processes which mediate the effects of the reticular formation system. Indeed, there are several studies which have documented the complex inter-relationships between testosterone levels, aggression and arousal.

Eysenck and Gudjonsson (1989) remind us that these ideas, very briefly summarised here, are based on work from different disciplines (e.g. biochemistry and psychology), and that they are linked together in complex ways not yet fully understood. Nonetheless, they conclude that biological processes incorporating arousal, androgenic influences, conditionability and pain tolerance have a significant impact on delinquent behaviour.

## Heredity and Environment

According to this perspective, some families have a greater propensity than others for delinquency and criminal behaviour (e.g. Eysenck and Gudjonsson 1989, West 1967). In order to test such predictions, researchers have resorted to twin and adoption studies. Identical twins share the same genetic material, while non-identical or fraternal twins are no more alike than other sibling pairs. Thus, it is generally assumed that any differences in behaviour between identical twins must be due to environmental influences.

In adoption studies, researchers have checked for similarities between adoptive parents and adopted children. The assumption here is that parents and children share environmental factors, and that similarities in behaviour must be due to the effects of the environment. When studying biological parents and their children who have been adopted out, similarities are thought to be due to genetic factors, since the parents and children in these instances share genetic material.

Space does not allow us to do full justice to what is a very complex debate, characterised by the fact that environmental and genetic influences can be broken down into various subcomponents. The following have been listed (Eysenck and Gudjonsson 1989: 92):

- Total genetic variance: This refers to all additive genetic variance – that is, all one's genes contributing to delinquency
- Non-additive genetic variance due to dominance at same gene loci
- Non-additive genetic variance due to interaction between different gene loci
- Assortative mating: Refers to an increment in total variance due to genetic resemblance between mates.

In a recent review of this literature (Eysenck and Gudjonsson 1989), several studies are listed in support of both the heredity and environmental views. For instance, several studies conducted from the 1930s to the 1960s show clearly that identical twins have much higher concordance rates for criminal behaviour than do fraternal twins. For all the studies cited in this regard, the average concordances are 66.7 and 30.4 per cent respectively. This is suggestive of a significant heredity effect. However, there is also an impressive *interaction* effect between heredity and environment.

In one study, for example, a research team contacted 662 adoptive sons. In cases where both the biological and adoptive fathers had a criminal record, 36 per cent of the sons acquired a criminal record. Where neither father had a criminal record, only 10 per cent of sons acquired one. Of those sons whose biological, but not adoptive, father had a criminal record, 22 per cent acquired one. Of those whose biological father was not a criminal, but the adoptive father was, only 12 per cent of sons eventually acquired a criminal record. These findings suggest a complex relationship between heredity and environment.

It would seem that being reared by a criminal father does not necessarily lead to a son acquiring a record, if the biological parents are not criminal. Secondly, a genetic predisposition to engage in criminal behaviour is accentuated in those sons who are raised in an environment with a criminal father (Hutchings and Mednick, cited in Eysenck and Gudjonsson 1989).

It is therefore quite clear, and appears to be generally accepted among psychologists, that both genetic and environmental factors are important in explaining intelligence and social behaviour, including delinquency. Neither factor is capable on its own of fully explaining delinquent and anti-social behaviour. One must conclude that both factors have the ability to *mediate* the effect of the other on behaviour. Thus there is a move toward a more balanced view regarding the significance of each factor (Plomin 1989).

In conclusion, one must bear in mind that genetic effects on behaviour are polygenic in nature. In other words, behaviour is not determined by single genes but rather reflects the effects of many. This fact in itself would undermine a simple reductionist view of delinquency (Plomin 1989).

## Social Factors and Delinquency

Several social factors have been identified as contributing to adolescents' delinquent behaviour (e.g. Farrington 1992, Hanson *et al.*

1984, Loeber and Dishion 1983, West and Farrington 1973). For example, some authors have listed school and family influences, peer influences, socio-economic deprivation, ethnic origin, parental criminality, child's poor academic performance and socialised aggressive disorder, to name just a few.

On the basis of an earlier longitudinal study (West and Farrington 1973), much information was generated about the importance of family life in the etiology of delinquency. Many, but not all, of these early findings have since been corroborated. For instance, whereas it was first believed that family size may be a significant correlate of delinquency, recent work has emphasised the importance of *family process* (Loeber and Dishion 1983). Specifically, criminal activity by one or more parents or siblings, increases the risk of delinquency. Criminal parents, these authors argue, are less likely to exercise necessary discipline, and are likely to lack the appropriate parenting skills. As Loeber and Dishion (1983: 82) explain:

> It can be assumed that some parents, including those diagnosed as antisocial, are less skilled in rearing children than others. Thus, in some households, parents maintain few rules, do not exercise discipline when needed, or do not supervise youngsters.

The importance of family life in the etiology of delinquency is generally agreed upon (see also Chapter 3). For instance, parental psychopathology has been strongly linked to maladjustment and delinquency (Chapter 3; see also West and Farrington 1973). Important factors that one must consider in this regard are parental neuroticism, parental instability and psychopathic traits in parents. Some authors have also commented on the importance of *social learning* within the context of the family (Neapolitan 1981). It has been shown that children learn aggressive behaviour (a form of delinquency) as a result of family experiences. In particular, there is evidence to suggest that sons who closely identify with a father who uses excessive physical force are more likely than other sons to engage in aggressive behaviour. It also seems that when aggressive sons are physically punished by their mother, they are likely to commit aggressive acts against others in an attempt to re-assert their masculinity.

Harsh and inconsistent discipline within the home as well as little parental involvement with the child have also enjoyed research attention as possible precursors of delinquency. According to one perspective, the *social-interactional*, parents of delinquent children very often unwittingly, although directly, train them to engage in anti-social behaviour. According to this view, parents tend to use positive reinforcement and punishment in a rather *ad hoc* fashion, thus reacting to deviant and pro-social behaviour inconsistently (Patterson *et al.* 1989). The final outcome is that children lack appropriate social skills, and are trained to be coercive and anti-social. This view is supported by numerous research studies cited by Patterson and colleagues.

In leading to adolescent delinquent behaviour, poor parental discipline also has other effects. Non-delinquent or 'normal' adolescents are likely to reject the delinquent, who is also likely to perform poorly in school. In order to bolster self-esteem and gain peer acceptance, the anti-social teenager seeks refuge in the deviant peer group, with its norms for unacceptable behaviour. This, of course, serves to reinforce the delinquent behaviour (Patterson *et al.* 1989).

There are certain contextual factors which impinge on family functioning and which are likely to make parental styles less effective (Patterson *et al.* 1989). Not only is there stability of delinquent behaviour within individuals, but also across generations. Anti-social parents tend to raise anti-social teenagers. Furthermore, several other within-family factors are likely to act as stressors, such as parental income, level of education, parental unemployment and divorce and separation.

Other studies have focused on the nature of parent-adolescent relationships (e.g. Hanson *et al.* 1984). These authors hold the view that homes with mothers showing little support and emotional warmth towards teenagers, and who have low levels of mother-son affection, are more likely to produce sons who are delinquent. A likely consequence of such parenting style is that adolescents seek an emotional anchor in the peer group, often therefore engaging in negative behaviours.

Some authors have also referred to the *importance* of the peer group to adolescents who engage in delinquent behaviour (Hanson *et al.* 1984, Farrington 1992). This refers to how much the adolescents *value* the peer group. For instance, Hanson and her colleagues identified a factor they called *socialised aggression* as measured by the Behaviour Problem Checklist. This factor indicates the extent to which the teenager belongs to a gang, has bad companions, skips school and stays out late at night. They found this factor to be a major correlate of adolescent crime, no doubt due to the fact that, by engaging in socialised aggression, adolescents elicit a certain amount of peer support.

## Theoretical Considerations

It is clear that several theories contribute to an understanding of orientation to authority and delinquency: social learning, biological and Erikson's psychoanalytic view.

In the first instance, there is evidence that children who engage in anti-social, aggressive and delinquent behaviours learn to do so by observing others. This may occur through the medium of television, or by watching and experiencing particular behaviour patterns in the home. According to this view, some children are socialised to be aggressive. They are taught by family members to respond to others in a coercive manner. Very often in such homes, violent and anti-social behaviour is a prerequisite for survival.

Perhaps this may explain why delinquent children are not identity achieved. Identity formation presupposes a warm, emotionally supportive and considerate family environment. In such homes the channels of communication are kept open. Delinquent children, by contrast, are identity diffused and therefore strongly attached to the deviant peer group.

Finally, it is probably true that biological and heredity factors mediate the effects of learning and identity formation as just mentioned. These mediating effects vary, of course, from individual to individual, reflecting different social experiences, individual differences, polygenic influences and concentrations of hormones.

## Summary

It is possible to distinguish between general orientation to authority and delinquency among adolescents. In the former, researchers have studied general attitudes and behavioural orientation. In the latter, most studies have focused on self-reported delinquency.

This chapter noted several major theoretical perspectives on juvenile delinquency. These range from genetic/biological approaches, to social learning. As noted in the previous section, each of these approaches appears intuitively sensible, and is supported by empirical findings. The challenge for future researchers is to illustrate the links that exist between these approaches, and the extent to which some factors mediate the effects of others in explaining delinquency.

Of concern to community leaders, parents and educators must be the fact that young people under the age of twenty make up a disproportionate number of arrests for serious offences such as vehicle theft, burglary, robbery and forcible rape. What is to be done? Is it sufficient to argue, for example, that hormonal influences are causative and that there is not much one can do about it? Clearly not. Although such biological factors are important, there are policy implications here which governments and community leaders must address. There can be no doubt that social factors such as high youth unemployment, the availability of drugs, and family disruption and violence must be considered and also acted upon.

## Additional Reading

Donovan, J. and Jessor, R. (1985) 'Structure of Problem Behavior in Adolescence and Young Adulthood', *Journal of Consulting and Clinical Psychology* 53: 890–904

Eysenck, H. and Gudjonsson, G. (1989) *The Causes and Cures of Criminality*. New York: Plenum

West, D. (1967) *The Young Offender*. Harmondsworth: Penguin

West, D. and Farrington, D. (1973) *Who Becomes Delinquent? Second Report of the Cambridge Study in Delinquent Development*. London: Heinemann

## Exercise

1. Most research to date on the correlates of delinquency has been cross-sectional in nature. Devise a longitudinal study of the psychosocial predictors of self-reported delinquency. Find a suitable measure of the dependent variable. Include the following independent measures: family-related attitudes and personality factors. Select several measures and explain the rationale for their inclusion. Provide details of a sampling frame and time lapse between Testing 1 and Testing 2.

# 10 Hopelessness, Depression and Suicide

## Introduction

At first glance, a chapter on depression and suicide among adolescents may seem a little out of place. After all, is adolescence not an 'exciting' stage of the life span, filled with new opportunity? Some readers may be surprised to learn, however, that suicide is one of the leading causes of death among teenagers, after accidents (Dusek 1991). Worldwide, data show that suicide is the fourth major cause of death for this age group (Petti and Larson 1987). It would also appear that the rate is steadily increasing.

Many authors who discuss the nature of suicide acknowledge its link with feelings of hopelessness and depression (e.g. Kashani, Reid and Rosenberg 1989). As some writers have explained, suicide is normally not something contemplated on the spur of the moment (Conger and Petersen 1984). Rather, it is usually the result of a long period of attempting to find solutions to trying problems, be they at school or of an interpersonal kind. To the teenager contemplating suicide, such an action appears the only viable solution to an increasingly hopeless and depressing situation. Very often, just one more bad event is enough to drive the teenager to suicide: a broken relationship, another bad grade at school, the death of a loved one, the separation of parents.

It is not surprising, then, that considerable research has been devoted to understanding the links between hopelessness, depression and suicide. In the present chapter, we shall note some of the important psychological correlates and antecedents of hopelessness and depression, and conclude by examining suicide. We begin with the nature of hopelessness.

## Hopelessness

Some authors regard hopelessness as central to understanding depression and, ultimately, suicide. Hopelessness can be defined (Kazdin *et al.* 1983: 504) as

. . . negative expectancies toward oneself and toward the future.

Minkoff and his colleagues (1973: 455) define hopelessness thus:

> The person . . . expects or believes that nothing will turn out right for him, nothing he does will succeed, his important goals are unattainable, and his worst problems will never be solved.

It is clear from these definitions that there appears to be a very strong cognitive element to hopelessness. It is quite likely that those who suffer from such feelings have a cognitive 'set' or a pre-exisiting *expectation* that things may not work out, that the future is likely to be disappointing and that failure is unavoidable. Close scrutiny of measures of hoplessness reveals that, in addition to the cognitive component, one's affect and motivation are also important in determining hopelessness (e.g. Beck *et al*. 1974). As will be discussed later, depression is also characterised by a negative cognitive set, an expectation that failure is imminent. In this respect, therefore, hopelessness is closely related to depression.

In Table 10.1 are presented items from a hopelessness scale for children which was devised by Kazdin and his colleagues (1983). It was modelled after a psychometrically sound scale used initially for adults (Beck *et al*. 1974). It is clear from the table that some items are worded positively, whilst others are negatively worded in order to control for the effects of response set. The higher the total score obtained on the measure, the greater the feeling of hopelessness.

**Table 10.1** *The Hopelessness Scale for Children*

**True**
1. I might as well give up, because I can't make things better for myself
2. I don't have good luck, and there's no reason to think I will when I grow up
3. All I can see ahead of me are bad things, not good things
4. I don't think I will get what I really want
5. Things just won't work out the way I want them to
6. I never get what I want, so it's dumb to want anything
7. I don't think I will have any real fun when I grow up
8. Tomorrow seems unclear and confusing to me
9. There's no use in really trying to get something I want, because I probably won't get it

**False**
1. I want to grow up because I think things will be better
2. When things are going badly, I know that they won't be bad all of the time
3. I can imagine what my life will be like when I'm ____ (10 years older)
4. I have enough time to finish the things I really want to do
5. Someday I will be good at doing the things I really care about
6. I will get more good things in life than most other kids
7. When I grow up I think I will be happier than I am now
8. I will have more good times than bad times.

*Source:* Kazdin *et al*. 1983

As has been suggested, there are close links between hopelessness and depression. There is some empirical support for this view. Research among adults, for example, has shown hopelessness, depression and suicide to be closely interrelated (e.g. Kovacs *et al.* 1975, Minkoff *et al.* 1973, Wetzel 1976). It has also been found that, when the effects of hopelessness are controlled for, the relationship between depression and suicide very often disappears. What this means is that hopelessness is a much stronger predictor of those who want to live than depression (Kovacs *et al.* 1975, Wetzel *et al.* 1980), although this view has been disputed by others (e.g. Asarnow *et al.* 1987).

Table 10.2 summarises the main findings of some studies which have examined the relationship between hopelessness, depression and suicide.

Similar results are obtained with very young adolescents and those in pubescence. One research team, for instance, conducted a study among a sample who had been admitted to an in-patient facility for disturbed children (Kazdin *et al.* 1983). As predicted, the authors found that feelings of hopelessness were related to depression and low self-esteem. Of special significance was the observation that scores on the measure of hopelessness were best able to differentiate between those children who repeatedly thought about or had attempted suicide and those who had not. These findings are noteworthy since they suggest some similarities between younger respondents and those in adulthood.

Teenagers with little hope about themselves or their future can also be differentiated from hopeful adolescents in a number of other ways. Hopeless adolescents tend to be more anxious, and to have more school problems than hopeful ones (Kashani *et al.* 1989). Hopeless teenagers also tend to be dysfunctional in areas related to friends and family.

In summary, available evidence suggests that a strong case can be made for the view that hopelessness is an important element of

**Table 10.2** *Relationships between Hopelessness, Depression and Suicidal Intent*

| | Correlation of suicidal intent with hopelessness and depression | | | |
| Study | Hopelessness | Depression | Controlling for depression | Controlling for hopelessness |
| --- | --- | --- | --- | --- |
| Wetzel *et al.* 1980 | 0.76* | 0.36* | 0.72* | −0.10 |
| Beck *et al.* 1975 | 0.38* | 0.30* | 0.24* | 0.06 |
| Kazdin *et al.* 1983 | 0.35* | 0.20* | 0.31* | 0.02 |

the syndrome of depression (Beck *et al.* 1975, Minkoff *et al.* 1973). Of course, this does not suggest a *causal* link with depression or suicide. Hopelessness is a negative cognitive set which influences our expectations for happiness, success and well-being. When a situation is regarded as 'desperate' or 'impossible', the risk of suicide increases. If we are to reduce risk for suicide, therapists should attempt to change these distorted cognitive expectations (Minkoff *et al.* 1973).

# Depression

First referred to as an affective disorder (Kovacs 1989, Rowe 1980), depression is now referred to as a mood disorder (Carson, Butcher and Coleman 1988). Depression involves changes in affect, ranging from positive (being elated ) to negative. In its most serious form, extreme negative mood swings can become dysfunctional to the point where the individual is incapable of normal day-to-day activity.

Much of our current knowledge of adolescent depression derives from what we know about the adult sort. This is not a methodologically sound strategy, of course, although researchers have more recently been at pains to include children and adolescents in their research programs.

Several authors (e.g. Angold 1988, Cantwell and Baker 1991) have remarked on the extent to which the term 'depression' varies in meaning. It is sometimes used to describe someone who is simply 'down in the dumps'. Sometimes, depression is used to refer to a pathological disorder.

According to the diagnostic classifications of the American Psychiatric Association (called DSM-111-R), there are a number of different types of mood disorder. The major disorders are known as major depression and bipolar disorder. There are also chronic disorders referred to as cyclothymic and dysthymic disorders (Davison and Neale 1990). These will be briefly outlined.

*Major depression*
This is characterised by one or more quite severe depressive episodes, with no manic (or elated) phases. In these cases, the individual loses contact with reality and hallucinations may be reported. Thus, this is a quite serious form of depression, in which normal day-to-day functioning is significantly impeded.

In addition to a depressed mood, major depression can also be characterised by the following symptoms (Cantwell and Baker 1991, Fleming, Offord and Boyle 1989):

- Overeating *or* poor appetite; not hungry
- Trouble sleeping *or* sleeps more than most others of the same age
- Has trouble enjoying self
- Feels worthless, inferior and/or guilty
- Cannot concentrate
- Deliberately harms self or attempts suicide or talks about killing self
- Underactive, slow moving, lacks energy *or* restless, hyperactive.

*Bipolar disorder*
This disorder involves both manic and depressive episodes. Once thought to be biologically determined, it is now thought to have a genetic component with a marker on chromosome 11 (Bootzin and Acocella 1988). Bipolar depression is less common than major depression, and also seems to affect those in the higher socio-economic bracket.

*Dysthymia*
In this form of depression, the person may be bothered by a 'depressed mood', but it is not particularly severe. Depression may be the result of a stressor such as the death of a loved one or the loss of a job. In such instances, the person may experience an intense negative mood swing which is usually only of a temporary nature. Classic dysthymics are typically introverted, morose and over-conscientious. They suffer from low self-esteem and also have disturbed eating and sleeping patterns. In addition, they also suffer from suicide ideation. As with major depression, dysthymia is more prevalent among women.

*Cyclothymic disorder*
The person suffers from frequent mood swings. It appears to be less severe than bipolar disorder.

## Depression Among Youth: Developmental Trends

It is now generally acknowledged that adolescents and those younger may suffer from what is usually referred to as depression (Bee 1989, Cantwell and Baker 1991, Schuster and Ashburn, 1992). Although very young children may feel 'sad' at the loss of a loved one, they are seldom able to accurately verbalise their sadness, grief or depression. However, by the time the child reaches adolescence, changes in cognitive development enable the teenager to verbalise and report their feelings more accurately.

The following developmental progression in depressive feelings has been noted (Rutter 1986):

- Middle of the first year of life: feelings of separation anxiety, or feelings of despair following admission to a hospital or institution
- Age 4–5 years: above feelings become less intense although they still experience 'sadness'
- Puberty: characterised by an increase in depressive feelings and a change in sex ratio (see later). Adolescent years marked by sharp increase in suicide rates.

There is some debate as to whether adolescents who are labelled as depressed display all the symptoms one would expect from an adult with the same disorder. Some authors (e.g. Bee 1989) have questioned whether adolescents experience the symptoms most often associated with depression. These include: loss of energy, feelings of worthlessness and lack of ability to concentrate. Not all research supports this view, however. In one study, the frequency of depressive symptoms in four populations of referred patients was compared (Carlson and Kashani 1988): pre-school children, pre-pubescent children, adolescents and adults. It was found that symptoms of psychotic depression (such as delusions) tend to increase with age, with adults more likely to experience them than adolescents. Some symptoms, such as a lowering of self-esteem and a depressed appearance, were more likely to decrease with increasing age. Other symptoms appear not to be age-specific. These include poor concentration, insomnia, suicide ideation and suicide attempts.

Further research evidence supports the view that depression follows certain developmental trends in children and adolescents. In one study, for example, the researchers were interested in describing the depressive symptoms in three different age groups (8, 12, and 17-year-olds). Only the data for the 12 and 17-year-olds are reported in Table 10.3 (Kashani, Rosenberg and Reid 1989).

Table 10.3 shows that several measures were used in the study and that each revealed certain age trends. According to the data, depression in older adolescents tends to be associated with such factors as being irritable, tired, agitated and not caring whether or not they get hurt. Among older adolescents depression is also

**Table 10.3** *Frequency of Depression-related Items in Two Groups of Adolescents*

| Depression-related items | 12-year-olds (N = 70) | | 17-year-olds (N = 70) | |
|---|---|---|---|---|
| | N | % | N | % |
| **Child assessment schedule** | | | | |
| More tired than before | 11 | 15.7 | 24 | 34.3 |
| Doesn't care whether hurts self | 11 | 15.7 | 26 | 37.1 |
| Agitation or hyperactivity when sad | 15 | 21.4 | 24 | 34.3 |
| Irritable a lot | 15 | 21.4 | 30 | 42.9 |
| | | | | |
| **Birleson scale** | | | | |
| Not looking forward to things as much as used to | 33 | 47.1 | 22 | 31.4 |
| Not liking to go out and play | 17 | 24.3 | 34 | 48.6 |
| Having stomach aches | 39 | 55.7 | 29 | 41.4 |
| Not having lots of energy | 29 | 41.4 | 47 | 67.1 |
| Not sticking up for self | 14 | 20.0 | 18 | 25.7 |
| Having horrible dreams | 19 | 27.1 | 17 | 24.3 |
| Feeling very bored | 65 | 92.9 | 59 | 84.3 |
| | | | | |
| **Hopelessness scale for children** | | | | |
| I won't get more of the good things out of life | 38 | 54.3 | 24 | 34.3 |
| Tomorrow is unclear and confusing | 9 | 12.9 | 24 | 34.3 |
| I won't get what I want | 7 | 10.0 | 2 | 2.9 |

*Source:*   Kashani *et al.* 1989

associated with isolation from the peer group, not having energy, not sticking up for oneself and thinking about tomorrow as confusing.

Depression among younger adolescents tends to be associated with not looking forward to things, having stomach aches, having horrible dreams, and feeling bored. Young adolescents who are depressed also tend to believe that they won't get more of the good things out of life than others. In addition, these adolescents believe that there is no use in trying to get what they want because they see little prospect of achieving their goals.

One study involved boys aged 14–15 years, some of whom were pubescent, while the rest were past puberty (Rutter 1986). Of interest was the observation that only a small proportion of pubescent boys showed any depressive symptoms. Among those past puberty, up to one-third reported depressive feelings. The author suggested that several factors may explain such developmental changes in depressive affect among youth. These are:

- Hormonal influences: For example, irritability during the pre-menstrual cycle
- Genetic factors: Refers to genotypical influences, but also the

possibility that depression in adolescence differs genetically from depression in pre-adolescence.
* Alterations in the frequency of stressors
* Vulnerability vs. protective factors: older adolescents who leave home are more at risk for depression
* Cognitive factors: Girls more likely than boys to attribute failure to their own lack of ability.

## Incidence of Adolescent Depression

When considering the prevalence rate of depression among adolescents, one should note at the outset that most studies reported in the literature are based upon samples drawn from highly industrialised societies. It is not clear to what extent adolescent depression occurs in other cultures (e.g. black South African youth) and what the corresponding incidence rates are.

The prevalence rate of depression among elementary school children, according to some reports, is estimated at about 5.2 per cent (Lefkowitz and Tesiny 1985). Other estimates suggest that 4.7 per cent of adolescents suffer from major depression, while about 3.3 per cent suffer from the dysthymic disorder (Kashani and colleagues 1987). It is estmated that about 8 per cent of adolescents suffer from some type of depression. It has also been reported that about 22 per cent of adolescents report depressive symptoms, although these appear to be of a sufficiently mild and temporary nature not to be dysfunctional (Kashani *et al.* 1987).

Finally, some authors have reported a threefold increase in depression from pre-adolescence to adolescence (Fleming *et al.* 1989), although this may simply reflect the fact that adolescents are better able to verbalise their feelings. It is also possible that the *manner of expression* changes as children get older, or that there are age differences in the susceptibility to stress (Rutter 1986).

## Sex Differences in Adolescent Depression

Several studies (e.g. Petersen, Sarigiani and Kennedy 1991) have noted sex differences in adolescent depression with more girls than boys reporting depressive episodes. This appears to be particularly the case during middle and late adolescence. Petersen and her colleagues (1991), for example, found noticeable sex differences between early and late adolescents in the United States. Their results are presented diagrammatically in Figure 10.1.

**Figure 10.1** *Reports of Depressive Episodes in Early and Middle Adolescence*

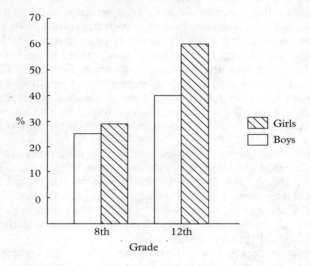

*Source:*    Peterson *et al.* 1991

In a large-scale Canadian study, the incidence of depression was noted to be higher for females for the less severe forms of depression, while no sex differences were noted in the incidence of more severe forms (Fleming and colleagues 1989). As the authors noted (p. 652):

> This . . . suggests that perhaps female adolescents are more likely than males to report depressive symptoms, but no more likely than males to have a clinical syndrome of depression.

There are several possible explanations for the observed sex differences in adolescent depression. The following have been given prominence by some writers. In the first place, it is likely that early-maturing girls may develop a negative body image which, in turn, may be related to depression. Such a predisposition may be exacerbated if early maturing girls experience stressful events at home or school (Petersen *et al.* 1991). Secondly, it has also been suggested that negative family events may serve as an antecedent for depression among girls, but not necessarily boys. Although this suggestion has not been adequately explained, it is held that some boys may develop particular coping mechanisms, while girls may not (Petersen *et al.* 1991). Clearly, such an hypothesis needs to be examined much more intensively.

Some authors have also commented on the relationships of self-esteem, mastery and social support with depression. For example, Avison and McAlpine (1992) on the basis of their research argued that, compared with boys, teenage girls' higher depression scores may be related to their generally lower self-esteem. They also observed that mastery and social support were significantly associated with lower depression only among females. According to the authors, a possible explanation may be that girls, due to lower self-esteem, are more sensitive to changes in parental support than are boys.

Some of the factors associated with general developmental change, as noted, may also explain sex differences in adolescent depression (Rutter 1986). Two important influences in this regard are hormonal factors and negative cognitive set. Hormonal changes are more likely to trigger depression in girls rather than boys, while it was noted that girls are more likely to attribute negative events to an internal stable disposition.

A relationship has also been observed between teenagers' perceptions of parents as caring, and low depression scores. Researchers have argued that warm, communicative and caring parents instil confidence, mastery and high self-esteem in their children. These are likely to reduce depression. A perception of parents as over-protective, however, appears to be linked to low levels of mastery and higher levels of depression (Avison and McAlpine 1992).

## Psychosocial Correlates of Depression

What are the psychosocial correlates of depression among teenagers? Those who have addressed such issues (e.g. Angold 1988, Cantwell and Baker 1991, Gore *et al.* 1992, Kovacs 1989, Siegel and Griffin 1984) suggest that a wide range of factors are related to depression in youth.

Depression in most of its various forms has been found to have negative consequences for social and cognitive aspects of development. There is now evidence, for example, that depression is linked to a slowing of some aspects of cognitive development. Depression has also been found to have negative effects on the acquisition of age-appropriate verbal skills. Perhaps not surprisingly, depression in adolescence has also been found to be related to academic underachievement (Kovacs 1989).

Some researchers have found that those who are depressed manifest particular social skills deficits. Available evidence indicates that peers who rate teenagers as depressed tend to judge them as being more isolated and less effective in social interactions. Studies also show that depressed teenagers tend not to be preferred as work or playmates. They tend to regard themselves poorly and have low expectations of success (see Kovacs 1989).

A review of the literature found that the age and sex of the teenager are important factors not to be overlooked when discussing depression. Evidence to date suggests that the correlates of depression among girls change from pre-adolescence to adolescence. Among pre-adolescent girls, depression appears to be associated with anxiety and feelings of being persecuted. For girls aged 12–16 years, on the other hand, the important predictors of depression are withdrawal, being sensitive, feelings of shyness and timidity, and liking to be alone (Cantwell and Baker 1991).

Some studies have compared adult depressives with adolescent depressives (see review by Cantwell and Baker 1991). These findings suggest that adolescents may experience less anorexia and weight loss, more psychomotor agitation and retardations, and more guilt and lower self-esteem. Very often, depressed adolescents are also characterised by anxiety and conduct disorders.

A review of the literature has suggested the following additional psychosocial risk factors for adolescent depression (Angold 1988):

- Increasing age: depression is more common among adolescents than pre-adolescents
- Social class: some suggest that adolescents from lower social classes may exhibit higher depression, although the findings tend to be equivocal; more research is needed
- Race – some reports of a 'depressive syndrome' among black adolescents, although findings are equivocal; more research is needed
- Family psychiatric history: there appears to be a strong link between parental depression and adolescent disturbance.

Important buffers *against* adolescent depression are peer and parental support, as well as individual coping responses. Some specific factors which have been identified are closeness with one or both parents, or with a good friend. There is empirical support for this view. For example, on the basis of one longitudinal study, it was found that parental and peer support moderate the negative effects of such factors as early adolescent changes. It was argued that parents and friends acts as a source of comfort and security in the changing world of the adolescent (Petersen *et al.* 1991).

*Negative self-perceptions*
As noted earlier in the chapter, a negative cognitive set may be important in explaining a predisposition for depression. This line of reasoning is based on research findings which have shown a close link between low self-esteem and other factors such as hopelessness and coping skills. Such findings, noted by Asarnow and colleagues (1987: 361), have lent credence to

> the notion of a cognitive triad in depression that is characterized by negative views of the self, the world, and the future.

Such negative cognitive biases in depression are generally regarded as quite important and have been examined in several studies of adults and adolescents. Specifically, studies have focused on factors such as locus of control, and the way in which causal attributions are made (McCauley *et al.* 1988, Siegel and Griffin 1984). Evidence indicates that teenagers who perceive that they have little control over their life events (so-called 'externals') are more likely to be depressed than so-called 'internals', who perceive themselves as in control of their life events. It has also been noted that depressed adolescents attribute the outcomes of negative events to internal, stable and global factors. Thus they are more likely to blame themselves for negative events.

Depressed teenagers tend to attribute positive events to *external*, stable and global dimensions: that is, to causes beyond their control. They seem to be characterised by a negative cognitive set which, in addition to being related to depression, also has links to low self-esteem, loneliness and poor health outcomes (Abramson, Seligman and Teasdale 1978). Finally, it has further been suggested that this depressive attributional style is only evident among those teenagers who are *low* in anxiety and conduct disorders (Craighead 1991).

*Stress, the family, and peers*
There is a widely-held view among researchers that stressful events are an important determining factor in adolescent depression. Some of these stress factors are biological changes (e.g. being smaller/taller for one's age), cognitive development, social changes (e.g. moving from one town to another), school transitions (e.g. changing schools), changes to the parent-child relationship (e.g. having parents who separate), changes in peer relationships (e.g. being left out of a group) and gender-role expectations (Gore *et al.* 1992).

Research among female adolescents has found that younger teenagers are more susceptible to the negative effects of stress than are older ones. Nonetheless, in both younger and older adolescents, negative stressors are associated with illness symptoms and depression (Siegel and Brown 1988). Positive events, not surprisingly, moderate the impact of negative stressors. Future research should examine the replicability of these findings among male adolescents.

Family socialisation processes are also important in determining the likelihood of depression in children and teenagers (Cole and Rehm 1986). Following the social learning model of Bandura (see Chapter 1), it is argued that adolescents adopt the reward and punishment models of parents. The authors note that depressed parents find it difficult to show affection for their children. Thus, parent-child communication is poor, with parents tending to reward their children less frequently. According to the model, depressed youngsters set high personal standards, are overly self-critical, and tend not to reward themselves. Such teenagers therefore find themselves in a vicious cycle attempting to achieve unrealistic goals. Not surprisingly, failure is not uncommon. When combined with a negative cognitive set this only serves to increase the likelihood of depressive feelings among adolescents.

Recent research has examined the extent to which family structure and the socio-economic condition of the household act as buffers against life stress and consequent depression during adolescence. In a study of over 1000 teenagers in the United States, support was found for the view that the family can buffer the adolescent against the negative effects of stress (Gore *et al.* 1992). The researchers found that teenagers with a low standard of living were more likely to react negatively to stress events. They also found that teenagers whose parents had low levels of formal education were less likely to cope adequately with personal stress.

Independent research tends to support these findings. For instance, among adolescent in-patients, high family and parental support tends to be related to low depression among teenagers, as is peer support. The authors noted that when family support was high, peer support was somewhat related to adolescent depression, but when parental support was low, peer support was *negatively* related to depression (Barrera and Garrison-Jones 1992). Thus it appears that high parental support conflicts with peer influences, which leads to depression. In the absence of parental support, the peer network acts as a buffer against depression by providing necessary emotional support.

# Suicide

As noted earlier, suicide is one of the leading causes of death among teenagers (Dusek 1991, McClure 1986). Although some writers regard suicide as simply a manifestation of destructive tendencies, others suggest that suicide and suicide ideation may be a desperate plea for help, an act of utter despair (Shulman and Margalit 1985). Although a single event such as the death of a loved one has the potential to lead to suicide, it may also be the symptom of underlying stress or an unhappy family situation. Suicide may result from years of psychological anguish and feelings of hopelessness. Thus, suicide ideation or attempted suicide is an undoubted signal to parents and teachers that the teenager is in need of immediate assistance.

## Theories of Suicide

Why do individuals commit suicide? Several psychological perspectives have been proposed which attempt to explain suicidal behaviour. Each of these will be briefly described below.

### The psycho-analytical approach

This approach assumes an unconscious intention as the main motivation for suicide (Leenaars 1990). It is argued that the suicidal person may experience a great sense of loss and rejection of a highly loved person or object. In such instances, suicide is seen as a way of coping with this loss. By killing themselves, they destroy the significant 'other' whose image is closely absorbed into the individual's psyche (Bootzin and Acocella 1988). Very often too, the suicidal person may experience guilt or self-criticism or harsh attitudes toward the self. For such individuals, suicide is one way of dealing with this low self-esteem. Finally, this approach also suggests that suicidal individuals are unable to organise and synthesise their experiences. This may be so acute that sometimes the suicidal person becomes dysfunctional.

### Cognitive-behavioural approach

According to this view, there is an important link between feelings of hopelessness, depression and suicide (Leenaars 1990). Hopelessness appears to be associated with a negative cognitive set, with the future seen as unrealistically bleak and unpromising. In such individuals, thought patterns are characterised by possible errors such as overgeneralisation, selective abstraction, inexact labelling and so forth. Not surprisingly, the negative cognitive set may lead to suicide. According to this approach, suicide is viewed as positively reinforcing in that it elicits attention and pity (Bootzin and Acocella 1988).

*Social learning approach*
The social learning approach posits that suicide is learned in very much the same way one learns other behaviours. It is argued, for example, that suicide can be shaped by childhood experiences of punishment. Thus, aggression is expressed inwards toward the self, rather than outwards (Leenaars 1990).

According to the social learning perspective, it is also possible that the suicidal person has not been adequately socialised into traditional culture. In other words, such individuals have not learned normal cultural values regarding life and death. Moreover, suicidal behaviour can be influenced (or reinforced) by subcultural norms as depicted on television, or as manifest by others known to the individual (so-called 'copy cat suicides') (Leenaars 1990).

*The multidimensional approach*
As this approach suggests, there are several possible causes of suicidal behaviour. Leenaars (1990: 163–64) suggests the following: The suicidal person

- May be experiencing unbearable psychological pain
- May wish to end all conscious experience
- May be in a state of heightened disturbance (e.g. feelings of rejection)
- May experience contradictory feelings and attitudes
- May experience overpowering emotions or logic (negative cognitive set).

*The neuroscience approach*
This perspective holds that mood disorders have a biological basis. Given the close relationship that is often observed between depression and suicide, some argue that suicide may be biologically based. It is argued that suicide, impulsiveness, and aggressive behaviour are associated with a decreased flow of serotonin from the brainstem to the frontal lobes of the cortex (Leenaars 1990).

## Incidence of Adolescent Suicide

Many countries have recorded a steady increase in youth suicide rates over recent years. Lester (1988) has summarised the changes in suicide rate for 15–24-year-olds in several countries from 1970–80. Table 10.4 shows that the largest increases have occurred in Norway, Spain, Switzerland, Thailand, New Zealand, Scotland and Israel. Some countries (e.g. Venezuela and Guatemala) have recorded sharp reductions in the adolescent suicide rate. Countries which have shown sharp rises in the suicide rate for males only are Australia, Canada, France, Greece, Israel, Italy, Thailand and the United States. Countries which have recorded sharp rises in the suicide rate among females only are Austria, Bulgaria, England and Wales and Singapore.

As noted, the Australian suicide rate for those aged 15–24 years is much higher for males than it is for females. Figure 10.2 illustrates this difference and also indicates the extent to which the

**Table 10.4** *Suicide Rates from 1970–80 in Various Countries for 15–24-year-olds*

| Country | 1970 | % change by 1980 |
|---|---|---|
| Australia | 8.6 | +30.2 |
| Austria | 16.5 | +9.1 |
| Bulgaria | 6.9 | +34.8 |
| Canada | 10.2 | +50.0 |
| Chile | 10.1 | −31.7 |
| Denmark | 8.5 | +42.4 |
| Finland | 14.7 | +60.5 |
| France | 7.0 | +52.9 |
| Germany (West) | 13.4 | −6.7 |
| Greece | 1.5 | +20.0 |
| Guatemala | 5.5 | −50.9 |
| Hong Kong | 7.7 | +1.3 |
| Hungary | 18.9 | +5.8 |
| Israel | 3.7 | +64.9 |
| Italy | 2.9 | +34.5 |
| Japan | 13.0 | −3.8 |
| Netherlands | 4.0 | +50.0 |
| New Zealand | 8.0 | +73.7 |
| Norway | 3.7 | +224.3 |
| Portugal | 4.5 | +2.2 |
| Singapore | 7.8 | +32.1 |
| Spain | 1.4 | +92.9 |
| Sweden | 13.3 | −13.5 |
| Switzerland | 13.0 | +80.0 |
| Thailand | 7.2 | +77.8 |
| UK (England and Wales) | 6.0 | +6.7 |
| UK (Scotland) | 5.8 | +65.5 |
| USA | 8.8 | +39.8 |
| Venezuela | 14.5 | −28.3 |

*Source:*    Lester 1988

**Figure 10.2** *Sex Differences in Suicide among Australian 15–24-year-olds*

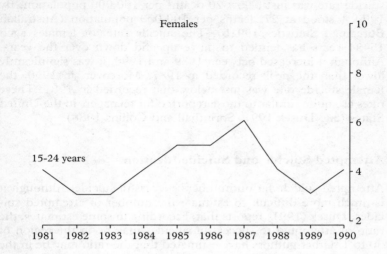

Females

15-24 years

1981 1982 1983 1984 1985 1986 1987 1988 1989 1990

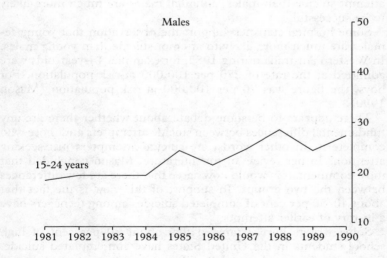

Males

15-24 years

1981 1982 1983 1984 1985 1986 1987 1988 1989 1990

*Source:*    Australian Bureau of Statistics 1991b

suicide rate has increased over recent years. In 1981, the male suicide rate was just below 20 deaths per 100,000 population. By 1990 it stood at 27 deaths per 100,000 population (Australian Bureau of Statistics 1991b). The suicide rate for females aged 15–24 years has tended to move up and down over the years. Although it increased between 1989 and 1990, it was significantly lower than the peak recorded in 1987. Moreover, in 1990, the female suicide rate was just below that recorded in 1981. These rates are quite similar to those reported for teenagers in the United States (e.g. Dusek 1991, Sprinthall and Collins 1988).

## Attempted Suicide and Suicide Ideation

Attempted suicide far outnumbers successful suicide. Although it is much more difficult to estimate the number of attempted suicides, Dusek (1991) reports that, according to some estimates, the ratio of attempted to successful suicides may be in the region of 50 to 1. Other authors have estimated that the ratio may be in the region of 100 to 1 (Mason 1990). Females are more likely to attempt suicide than males, although males are much more likely to be successful.

Some hospital statistics support the observation that young females are much more likely to attempt suicide than young males. In Western Australia during 1985, for example, 14-year-olds were admitted at the rate of 270 per 100,000 at-risk population. For boys, the figure was 70 per 100,000 at-risk population (Mason 1990).

There appears to be some debate about whether there are any fundamental differences between suicide attempters and those who complete it. In other words, are suicide attempters just seeking attention? In her review of this literature, Mason concluded that most commentators would now agree that there are few differences between the two groups. In support of this view is the fact that about 40–50 per cent of completed suicides among teenagers have a history of earlier attempts.

Some writers have estimated that about 30 per cent of high school students in the United States have contemplated suicide. Research evidence shows that different socio-environmental and psychological-behavioural measures predict suicide ideation for males and females. One study of over 400 high school students revealed that emotional and unemployment problems had direct effects upon suicide ideation for males. The absence of parental support had an indirect effect through emotional problems (Simons and Murphy 1985). For the females in the sample, emotional problems and delinquent behaviour had direct effects upon suicide ideation. Absence of parental support as well as employment problems were found to have indirect effects through emotional problems, low self-esteem, hopelessness and delinquent behaviour.

The authors concluded that parental support and employment problems are important antecedents of suicide ideation. These findings have important implications for family communication and interaction as well as government policy. They argued (p. 431)

> . . . programs and policies concerned with adolescent suicide should concentrate on strengthening the nurturing, supportive function of the family . . . [and] the employment problems faced by many teenagers.

## Method of Suicide

Males are much more likely than females to commit suicide by violent means, like using a firearm. Females are much more likely to kill themselves through poisoning (Conger and Petersen 1984, Mason 1990). In a review of all adolescent suicides in Finland for a one-year period, it was found that males were more likely to use firearms (45 per cent), hanging (27 per cent), and drugs (5 per cent). Females were more likely to commit suicide by drug use (33 per cent) and hanging (33 per cent), followed by firearms (11 per cent) (Marttunen, Aro and Lonnqvist 1992).

These differences in method may be just one reason why the suicide rate for males is higher: There is always a good chance that possible death through poisoning or drugs can be averted. Some authors do report, however, that the trend towards more violent suicide methods appears to be on the increase among young females (e.g. Mason 1990).

Changes in method of suicide for teenagers have been noted in England and Wales for two periods between 1970 and 1984 (see Table 10.5). Some of these data support the view that males are more likely to commit suicide by violent means. For instance, in the first time period (1970–74), the poisoning rate by solids or liquids was higher among females, although there was a decline between 1980–84. The table also shows that males were more likely than females to use firearms and explosives (McClure 1986).

**Table 10.5** *Changes in Method of Suicide in England and Wales between 1970–74 and 1980–84, for 15–19-year-olds*

| Cause of death | | 1970–74 Rate* | 1980–84 Rate* |
|---|---|---|---|
| Poisoning by solid or liquid | Male | 9.6 | 7.4 |
| | Female | 13.2 | 7.1 |
| Poisoning by gases in domestic use | Male | 1.5 | 0.2 |
| | Female | 0.0 | 0.0 |
| Poisoning by other gases and vapours | Male | 2.4 | 5.7 |
| | Female | 0.2 | 0.5 |
| Hanging, strangulation and suffocation | Male | 7.9 | 13.4 |
| | Female | 1.6 | 2.1 |
| Submersion (drowning) | Male | 0.5 | 0.4 |
| | Female | 0.6 | 0.2 |
| Firearms and explosives | Male | 1.9 | 5.4 |
| | Female | 0.4 | 0.0 |
| Cutting and piercing instruments | Male | 0.1 | 0.5 |
| | Female | 0.1 | 0.0 |
| Jumping from high place | Male | 1.5 | 2.7 |
| | Female | 1.0 | 1.8 |
| Other and unspecified means | Male | 3.0 | 5.0 |
| | Female | 0.7 | 1.6 |

*Average annual rate per million population

*Source:* McClure 1986

## Psychosocial Correlates of Suicidal Behaviour

Those who study suicide have noted several causes of adolescent suicide. These have been characterised as biological, psychological or sociological (Diekstra and Moritz 1987). Biological factors refer to bodily illness or certain disorders and physical handicaps. Some authors (e.g. Diekstra and Moritz 1987) have suggested that the psychological and sociological factors may be more important during adolescence. Some of these factors are (Mason 1990):

- Family discord/dysfunction
- Sexual, physical and emotional abuse
- Psychiatric problems in the family
- Loss (of a loved one or relationship)
- Depression and hopelessness

- School and peer group problems
- Unemployment
- Poverty/homelessness
- Alcohol/substance abuse
- Psychiatric disorders and physical disability
- Media coverage of suicide.

Are particular personality types more likely to commit suicide than others? Some researchers have described suicidal adolescents as perfectionist, impulsive and uncommunicative. Some suicidal adolescents have a history of psychiatric illness (Petti and Larson 1987).

Several authors have referred to the importance of life events and stressors. In one noteworthy study, De Wilde and colleagues (1992) compared adolescent suicide attempters with depressed and non-depressed adolescents in the Netherlands. At the time of the research, the teenagers averaged seventeen years, although they were examined *retrospectively* for life events before and after the age of twelve.

Life events before then that best predicted suicide attempts in adolescence were separation of parents and physical abuse. In addition, suicide attempters also tended to be negatively affected by general problematical life events. In other words, they were more affected by their cumulative effects. The life events *after* twelve that best predicted suicide in late adolescence were changes to the teenager's living conditions, parental separation/divorce and a change in caretaker or custodial parent. In addition, suicide attempters were much more likely than other adolescents to experience physical and/or sexual abuse. They were also adversely affected by the cumulative effects of negative life events. De Wilde and colleagues (1992: 49) concluded thus:

> Our study seems to confirm . . . that suicide attempters have a long-standing history of problems during childhood and adds to evidence that this is true not only when suicide attempters are compared with normal subjects but also when they are compared with depressed adolescents. This suggests that the risk of suicide during adolescence might be detected during childhood.

It is important to bear in mind that a stressful event is unlikely on its own to cause suicide. Life events are inter-related and, as such, may have cumulative effects. Moreover, other important factors such as individual personality traits and neurobiological factors are also important in explaining adolescent suicide (De Wilde *et al.* 1987).

## The Rural Adolescent

It has been suggested that rural adolescents face greater stressors than do urban ones (e.g. Forrest 1988). Those who live in small provincial towns or communities largely dependent on single economies such as farming, fishing or mining face unique problems. Many such communities are isolated and these teenagers face higher levels of unemployment and distance from resources and facilities urban teenagers take for granted. For instance, entertainment is very often limited, with many teenagers describing life as 'dull'. Moreover, there is added stress on farming families, due to current low commodity prices.

The suicide rate among rural adolescents has shown a significant increase in recent years (Bush 1990, Forrest 1988). It was noted earlier (see Figure 10.2) that the suicide rate among Australian males has risen sharply. Bush (1990) has suggested that this increase is due largely to the accelerating suicide rate in rural areas. In the Sydney metropolitan region, for example, the adolescent male suicide rate rose from 3.4 per 100,000 in 1966 to 3.8 per 100,000 in 1986. In the rural shires of New South Wales, however, the rate rose from below 3.5 in 1966 to 21.6 per 100,000 in 1986.

This dramatic rise in the male suicide rate in rural areas can perhaps best be understood in terms of social context. Bush (1990) suggests that men in rural areas face declining opportunities for employment. In addition, rural social networks tend to be close-knit and supportive, yet also conservative and prescriptive. Bush makes the point that what these young men need are new role models (e.g. there are alternatives to a life on the land), thus generating more diverse social networks.

## Theoretical Considerations

There are at least three theoretical perspectives worth considering when thinking about depression and suicide in adolescence. One is the biological. Evidence indicates that hormonal influences are critical in triggering depression and that the effect may be stronger for girls than boys. It is not entirely clear why this is the case. The fact remains that, beginning with puberty, depression rates for girls show a marked rise. As Rutter (1986) reminds us, during the premenstrual phase, many women suffer irritability and depression, while the latter has been found to be associated with the use of oral contraceptives. Parents and counsellors should therefore be cautious when recommending the use of such contraceptive methods.

Secondly, it is abundantly clear that the family network acts as an important buffer against depression and suicide. All adolescents will face challenges of one sort or another, some of which may seem insurmountable at the time. It is the role of the family to provide much-needed emotional support and adequate role models for their teenagers. Understanding and caring parents can greatly assist those who face difficulties, thus acting as a barrier against hopelessness, depression and suicide. There now appears to be some evidence that peer influences are also implicated in depression (Barerra and Garrison-Jones 1992). How parental and peer influences interact to moderate stress in relation to suicide ideation remains unclear.

Finally, one must also bear in mind the possibility, as psychologists have indicated, that suicide may result from an unconscious desire or motivation to compensate for a great loss. It is, of course, extremely difficult to test such a link. Certainly, there does seem to be a link between depression and feelings of loss. It is therefore highly likely that a link will also exist between suicide and feelings of loss and rejection.

## Summary

This chapter has reviewed the link between hopelessness, depression and suicide. Hopelessness, it was observed, is characterised by a negative cognitive set: namely, a belief that the future is bleak and unpromising, and that life is devoid of much value. Importantly, such an attitude is also characteristic of some mood disorders, whilst some depressives suffer from suicide ideation. There is thus an important thread which strongly links the three concepts.

The chapter also noted the alarming increase in youth suicides in many countries. It is not clear why these countries should show such dramatic increases. There appears to be no overall pattern which could be suggestive of particular causes of youth suicide cross-culturally. Future research should therefore attempt to uncover the different factors that account for the youth suicide rate across different cultures.

## Additional Reading

Angold, A. (1988) 'Childhood and Adolescent Depression 1: Epidemiological and Aetiological Aspects', *British Journal of Psychiatry* 152: 601–17

Fleming, J., Offord, D. and Boyle, M. (1989) 'Prevalence of Childhood and Adolescent Depression in the Community: Ontario Child Health Study', *British Journal of Psychiatry* 155: 647–54

Lester, D. (1990) *Current Concepts of Suicide*. Philadelphia: The Charles Press

Rutter, M., Izard, C. and Read, P. (1986) *Depression in Young People: Developmental and Clinical Perspectives*. New York: The Guilford Press

## Exercise

1. Are there marked city/rural and sex differences in suicide in your region? Try and obtain official statistics for your state or county and note the following:
   • city/rural suicide rates
   • sex differences in suicide rates
   • sex differences in method of suicide
   • age differences in suicide rate
   • note the trends in these for a 5 and 10-year period.
   What do these data suggest to you about adolescent suicide?

# Bibliography

Abramson, L., Seligman, M. and Teasdale, J. (1978) 'Learned Helplessness in Humans: Critique and Reformulation', *Journal of Abnormal Psychology* 87: 49–74

Adams, G., Abraham, K. and Markstrom, C. (1987) 'The Relations among Identity Development, Self-consciousness, and Self-focusing during Middle and Late Adolescence', *Developmental Psychology* 23: 292–97

Adelson, J. (1964) 'The Mystique of Adolescence', *Psychiatry* 27: 1–5

Ainley, J., Foreman, J. and Sheret, M. (1991) 'High School Factors that Influence Students to Remain at School', *Journal of Educational Research* 85: 69–80

Ajzen, I. and Fishbein, M. (1980) *Understanding Attitudes and Predicting Social Behavior*. Englewood Cliffs, NJ: Prentice-Hall

Amann-Gainotti, M. (1986) 'Sexual Socialization during Early Adolescence: The Menarche', *Adolescence* 21: 703–10

Amato, P. (1990) 'Dimensions of the Family Environment as Perceived by Children: A Multidimensional Scaling Analysis', *Journal of Marriage and the Family* 52: 613–20

— and Keith, B. (1991) 'Parental Divorce and the Well-being of Children: A Meta-analysis', *Psychological Bulletin* 110: 26–46

Angold, A. (1988) 'Childhood and Adolescent Depression 1: Epidemiological and Aetiological Aspects', *British Journal of Psychiatry* 152: 601–17

Archer, S. (1992) 'Gender Role Learning', in J. Coleman (ed.), *The School Years: Current Issues in the Socialization of Young People*, 2nd edn. London: Routledge

Asarnow, J., Carlson, G. and Guthrie, D. (1987) 'Coping Strategies, Self-perceptions, Hopelessness, and Perceived Family Environments in Depressed and Suicidal Children', *Journal of Consulting and Clinical Psychology* 55: 361–66

Asher, S. and Dodge, K. (1986) 'Identifying Children who are Rejected by their Peers', *Developmental Psychology* 22: 444–49

Australian Bureau of Statistics (1985) *Australia's Youth Population, 1984 — A Statistical Profile*, Catalogue No. 4111.0. Canberra: Government Printer

— (1991a) *Births, Australia 1990*, Catalogue No. 3301.0. Canberra: Government Printer

— (1991b) *Causes of Death: Australia 1990*, Catalogue No. 3303.0. Canberra: Government Printer

— (1992) *Schools, Australia 1991*, Preliminary, Catalogue No. 4220.0. Canberra: Government Printer

Ausubel, D., Montemayor, R. and Svajian, P. (1977) *Theory and Problems of Adolescent Development*. New York: Grune and Stratton

Avison, W. and McAlpine, D. (1992) 'Gender Differences in Symptoms of Depression among Adolescents', *Journal of Health and Social Behavior* 33: 77–96

Bahr, J. (1991) *Family Research: A Sixty-year Review, 1930–1990,* (Vol. 1). New York: Lexington Books

Baker, S., Thalberg, S. and Morrison, D. (1988) 'Parents' Behavioral Norms as Predictors of Adolescent Sexual Activity and Contraceptive Use', *Adolescence* 23: 265–82

Balassone, M. (1991) 'A Social Learning Model of Adolescent Contraceptive Behaviour', *Journal of Youth and Adolescence* 20: 593–616

Baldwin, W. and Cain, V. (1980) 'The Children of Teenage Parents', *Family Planning Perspectives* 12: 34–43

Banks, M. and Ullah, P. (1988) *Youth Unemployment in the 1980s: Its Psychological Effects.* London: Croom Helm

Barber, B. and Eccles, J. (1992) 'Long-term Influence of Divorce and Single Parenting on Adolescent Family- and Work-related Values, Behaviors, and Aspirations', *Psychological Bulletin* 111: 108–26

Barling, J. (1989) *Employment, Stress and Family Functioning.* Chichester: Wiley

—, Kelloway, E.K. and Bremermann, E.H. (1991) 'Preemployment Predictors of Union Attitudes: The Role of Family Socialization and Work Beliefs', *Journal of Applied Psychology* 76: 725–31

Barling, N. and Moore, S. (1990) 'Adolescents' Attitudes towards AIDS Precautions and Intention to Use Condoms', *Psychological Reports* 67: 883–90

Barnes, G., Farrell, M. and Windle, M. (1990) 'Parent-adolescent Interactions in the Development of Alcohol Abuse and Other Deviant Behaviors', in B. Barber and B. Rollins (eds), *Parent-adolescent Relationships.* Lanham, Maryland: University Press of America

Barnes, H. and Olson, D. (1985) 'Parent-adolescent Communication and the Circumplex Model', *Child Development* 56: 438–47

Barrera, M. and Garrison-Jones, C. (1992) 'Family and Peer Social Support as Specific Correlates of Adolescent Depressive Symptoms', *Journal of Abnormal Child Psychology* 20: 1–16

Beck, A., Kovacs, M. and Weissman, A. (1975) 'Hopelessness and Suicidal Behavior: An Overview', *Journal of the American Medical Association* 234: 1146–49

—, Weissman, A., Lester, D. and Trexler, L. (1974) 'The Measurement of Pessimism: The Hopelessness Scale', *Journal of Consulting & Clinical Psychology* 42: 861–65

Bee, H. (1989) *The Developing Child,* 5th edn. New York: Harper and Row

Berk, L. (1989) *Child Development.* Boston: Allyn and Bacon

Berndt, T. (1979) 'Developmental Changes in Conformity to Peers and Parents', *Developmental Psychology* 15: 606–16

— and Miller, K. (1990) 'Expectancies, Values, and Achievement in Junior High School', *Journal of Educational Psychology* 82: 319–26

Binder, A. (1988) 'Juvenile Delinquency', *Annual Review of Psychology* 39: 253–82

Bisnaire, L., Firestone, P. and Rynard, D. (1990) 'Factors Associated with Academic Achievement in Children following Parental Separation', *American Journal of Orthopsychiatry* 60: 67–76

Blakers, C. (1990) *Youth and Society: The Two Transitions*. Melbourne: ACER Research Monograph No. 38

Blaske, D., Borduin, C., Henggeler, S. and Mann, B. (1989) 'Individual, Family, and Peer Characteristics of Adolescent Sex Offenders and Assaultive Offenders', *Developmental Psychology* 25: 846–55

Blyth, D., Simmons, R. and Carlton-Ford, S. (1983) 'The Adjustment of Early Adolescents to School Transitions', *Journal of Early Adolescence* 3: 105–20

Boivin, M., Thomassin, L. and Alain, M. (1989) 'Peer Rejection and Self-perception among Early Elementary School Children: Aggressive-rejectees vs. Withdrawn-rejectees', in B. Schneider, G. Attili, J. Nadel and R. Weissberg (eds), *Social Competence in Developmental Perspective*. Boston: Kluwer

Bonnet, C. and Furnham, A. (1991) 'Who Wants to be an Entrepreneur? A Study of Adolescents interested in a Young Enterprise Scheme', *Journal of Economic Psychology* 12: 465–78

Bootzin, R. and Acocella, J. (1988) *Abnormal Psychology: Current Perspectives*, 5th edn. New York: Random House

Boyle, D. (1969) *A Student's Guide to Piaget*. Oxford: Pergamon Press

Brooks-Gunn, J. and Furstenberg, F. (1986) 'The Children of Adolescent Mothers: Physical, Academic and Psychological Outcomes', *Developmental Review* 6: 224–51

— (1989) 'Adolescent Sexual Behavior', *American Psychologist* 44: 249–57

Brooks-Gunn, J. and Lewis, M. (1984) 'The Development of Early Visual Self-recognition', *Developmental Review* 4: 215–39

Brown, B., Clasen, D. and Eicher, S. (1986) 'Perceptions of Peer Pressure, Peer Conformity Dispositions, and Self-reported Behavior among Adolescents', *Developmental Psychology* 22: 521–30

Buchanan, C., Eccles, J. and Becker, J. (1992) 'Are Adolescents the Victims of Raging Hormones: Evidence for Activational Effects of Hormones on Moods and Behavior at Adolescence', *Psychological Bulletin* 111: 62–107

—, Maccoby, E. and Dornbusch, S. (1991) 'Caught between Parents: Adolescents' Experience in Divorced Homes', *Child Development* 62: 1008–29

Buhrmester, D. (1990) 'Intimacy of Friendship, Interpersonal Competence, and Adjustment during Preadolescence and Adolescence', *Child Development* 61: 1101–11

Bumpass, L. (1984) 'Children in Marital Disruption: A Replication and Update', *Demography* 21: 71–82

Burlingame, W. (1970) 'The Youth Culture', in E. Evans (ed.), *Adolescents: Readings in Behavior and Development*. Hinsdale, Ill.: Dryden Press

Burns, R. (1979) *The Self-concept in Theory, Measurement, Development and Behaviour*. Longman: London

Bush, R. (1990) 'Rural Youth Suicide', *Rural Welfare Research Bulletin* 6: 25–27 (Wagga Wagga, Australia: Charles Sturt University)

Byrne, A. and Byrne, D. (1990) 'Adolescent Personality, School Type and Educational Outcomes: An Examination of Sex Differences', in P. Heaven and V. Callan (eds), *Adolescence: An Australian Perspective*. Sydney: Harcourt Brace Jovanovich

Callan, V. and Noller, P. (1987) *Marriage and the Family*. Sydney: Methuen

Campbell, E., Adams, G. and Dobson, W. (1984) 'Familial Correlates of Identity Formation in Late Adolescence: A Study of the Predictive Utility of Connectedness and Individuality in Family Matters', *Journal of Youth and Adolescence* 13: 509–25

Cantwell, D. and Baker, L. (1991) 'Manifestations of Depressive Affect in Adolescence', *Journal of Youth and Adolescence* 20: 121–33

Carlson, G. and Kashani, J. (1988) 'Phenomenology of Major Depression from Childhood through Adulthood: Analysis of Three Studies', *American Journal of Psychiatry* 145: 1222–25

Carlson, M., Kaiser, K., Yeaworth, R. and Carlson, R. (1984) 'An Exploratory Study of Life-change Events, Social Support and Pregnancy Decisions in Adolescents', *Adolescence* 19: 765–80

Carson, R., Butcher, J. and Coleman, J. (1988) *Abnormal Psychology and Modern Life*, 8th edn. Glenview, Ill.: Scott, Foresman and Co.

Chapman, J. and Lawes, M. (1984) 'Consistency of Causal Attributions for Expected and Actual Examination Outcome: A Study of the Expectancy Confirmation and Egotism Models', *British Journal of Educational Psychology* 54: 177–88

Cherian, V. (1991) Parental Aspiration and Academic Achievement of Xhosa Children', *Psychological Reports* 68: 547–53

Christ, M., Lahey, B., Frick, P., Russo, M., McBurnett, K., Loeber, R., Stouthamer-Loeber, M and Green, S. (1990) 'Serious Conduct Problems in the Children of Adolescent Mothers: Disentangling Confounded Correlations', *Journal of Consulting and Clinical Psychology* 58: 840–44

Cole, D. and Rehm, L. (1986) 'Family Interaction Patterns and Childhood Depression', *Journal of Abnormal Child Psychology* 14: 297–314

Cole, M. and Cole, S. (1989) *The Development of Children*. Scientific American Books

Coleman, J. (1992) 'Current Views of the Adolescent Process', in J. Coleman (ed.), *The School Years: Current Issues in the Socialization of Young People*, 2nd edn. London: Routledge

— and Hendry, L. (1990) *The Nature of Adolescence*, 2nd edn. London: Routledge

Coleman, M. and Ganong, L. (1990) 'Remarriage and Stepfamily Research in the 1980s: Increased Interest in an Old Family Form', *Journal of Marriage and the Family* 52: 925–40

Collins, W. (1990) 'Parent-child Relationships in the Transition to Adolescence: Continuity and Change in Interaction, Affect, and Cognition', in R. Montemayor, G. Adams and T. Gullotta (eds), *From Childhood to Adolescence: A Transition Period?* Newbury Park, California: Sage

Conger, J. and Petersen, A. (1984) *Adolescence and Youth: Psychological Development in a Changing World*, 3rd edn. New York: Harper and Row

Connel, R., Ashenden, D., Kessler, S. and Dowsett, G. (1982) *Making the Difference: Schools, Families and Social Divisions*. Sydney: Allen and Unwin

Correy, J., Kwok, P., Newman, N. and Curran, J. (1984) 'Adolescent Pregnancy in Tasmania', *Medical Journal of Australia* 141: 150–54

Costanzo, P. and Shaw, M. (1966) 'Conformity as a Function of Age Level', *Child Development* 37: 967–75

Craighead, W. (1991) 'Cognitive Factors and Classification Issues in Adolescent Depression', *Journal of Youth and Adolescence* 20: 311–26

Crain, W. (1985) *Theories of Development: Concepts and Applications*. Englewood Cliffs, NJ: Prentice-Hall

Crawford, J., Turtle, A. and Kippax, S. (1990) 'Student-favoured Strategies for AIDS Avoidance', *Australian Journal of Psychology* 42: 123–37

Culp, R., Culp, A., Osofsky, J. and Osofsky, H. (1991) 'Adolescent and Older Mothers' Interaction Patterns with their Six-month-old Infants', *Adolescence* 14: 195–200

Damon, W. and Hart, D. (1982) 'The Development of Self-Understanding from Infancy through Adolescence', *Child Development*, 53: 841–64

Dancy, B. and Handal, P. (1984) 'Perceived Family Climate, Psychological Adjustment and Peer Relationships of Black Adolescents: A Function of Parental Marital Status or Perceived Family Conflict?' *Journal of Community Psychology* 12: 222–29

Danziger, S. and Radin, N. (1990) 'Absent does not equal Uninvolved: Predictors of Fathering in Teen Mother Families', *Journal of Marriage and the Family* 52: 636–42

Darom, E. and Rich, Y. (1988) 'Sex Differences in Attitudes Toward School: Student Self-reports and Teacher Perceptions', *British Journal of Educational Psychology* 58: 350–55

Davis, G. and Leitenberg, H. (1987) 'Adolescent Sex Offenders', *Psychological Bulletin* 101: 417–27

Davis, R. (1988) 'Adolescent Pregnancy and Infant Mortality: Isolating the Effects of Race', *Adolescence* 23: 899–908

Davison, G. and Neale, J. (1990) *Abnormal Psychology*, 5th edn. New York: John Wiley and Sons

Dayton, C. (1981) 'The Young Person's Job Search: Insights from a Study', *Journal of Counselling Psychology* 28: 321–33

Deisher, R., Litchfield, C. and Hope, K. (1991) 'Birth Outcomes of Prostituting Adolescents', *Journal of Adolescent Health* 12: 528–33

Demb, J. (1991) 'Abortion in Inner-city Adolescents: What the Girls Say', *Family Systems Medicine* 9: 93–102

Demo, D. (1992) 'Parent-child Relations: Assessing Recent Changes', *Journal of Marriage and the Family* 54: 104–17

De Wilde, E., Kienhorst, I., Diekstra, R. and Wolters, W. (1992) 'The Relationship between Adolescent Suicidal Behavior and Life Events in Childhood and Adolescence', *American Journal of Psychiatry* 149: 45–51

Diekstra, R. and Moritz, B. (1987). 'Suicidal Behaviour among Adolescents: An Overview', in R. Diekstra and K. Hawton (eds), *Suicide in Adolescence*. Dordrecht: Martinus Nijhoff Publishers

Dishion, T., Patterson, G., Stoolmiller, M. and Skinner, M. (1991) 'Family, School, and Behavioral Antecedents to Early Adolescent Involvement with Antisocial Peers', *Developmental Psychology* 27: 172–80

Dohrenwend, B. and Dohrenwend, B. (eds) (1974) *Stressful Life Events*. New York: Wiley

Donovan, J. and Jessor, R. (1985) 'Structure of Problem Behavior in Adolescence and Young Adulthood', *Journal of Consulting and Clinical Psychology* 53: 890–904

— Jessor, R. and Costa, F. (1988) 'Syndrome of Problem Behavior in Adolescence: A Replication', *Journal of Consulting and Clinical Psychology* 56: 762–65

Dornbusch, S., Carlsmith, J., Bushwall, S., Ritter, P. *et al.* (1985) 'Single Parents, Extended Households, and the Control of Adolescents', *Child Development* 56: 326–41

—, Ritter, P., Liederman, P., Roberts, D. and Fraleigh, M. (1987) 'The Relation of Parenting Style to Adolescent School Performance', *Child Development*, 58: 1244–57

Douvan, E. and Adelson, J. (1966) *The Adolescent Experience*. New York: John Wiley

Dowling, J. (1980) 'Adjustment from Primary to Secondary School: A One Year Follow-up', *British Journal of Educational Psychology* 50: 26–32

Downey, G. and Coyne, J. (1990) 'Children of Depressed Parents: An Integrative Review', *Psychological Bulletin* 108: 50–76

Downs, W. and Rose, S. (1991) 'The Relationship of Adolescent Peer Groups to the Incidence of Psychological Problems', *Adolescence* 26: 473–492

Dubow, E. and Luster, T. (1990) 'Adjustment of Children Born to Teenage Mothers: The Contribution of Risk and Protective Factors', *Journal of Marriage and the Family* 52: 393–404

Dunphy, D. (1963) 'The Social Structure of Urban Adolescent Peer Groups', *Sociometry* 26: 230–76

— (1990) 'Peer Group Socialisation', in R. Muuss (ed.), *Adolescent Behavior and Society: A Book of Readings*. New York: McGraw-Hill

Dusek, J. (1991) *Adolescent Development and Behavior*, 2nd edn. Englewood Cliffs, NJ: Prentice-Hall

Eisen, M. and Zellman, G. (1984) 'Factors Predicting Pregnancy Resolution Decision Satisfaction of Unmarried Adolescents', *Journal of Genetic Psychology* 145: 231–39

Eisen, M., Zellman, G., Leibowitz, A., Chow, W. and Evans, J. (1983) 'Factors Discriminating Pregnancy Resolution Decisions of Unmarried Adolescents', *Genetic Psychology Monographs* 108: 69–95

Elkind, D. (1967) 'Egocentrism in Adolescence', *Child Development* 38: 1025–34

Elster, A. (1991) 'Teenage Fathers', in R. Lerner, A. Petersen and J. Brooks-Gunn (eds), *Encyclopedia of Adolescence*, Vol. 1. New York: Garland Publishing

— and Hendricks, L. (1986) 'Stresses and Coping Strategies of Adolescent Fathers' in A. Elster and M. Lamb (eds), *Adolescent Fatherhood*. Hillsdale, NJ: Lawrence Erlbaum

Entwistle, N. (1972) 'Personality and Academic Attainment', *British Journal of Educational Psychology* 42: 137–51

Erickson, P. and Rapkin, A. (1991) 'Unwanted Sexual Experiences among Middle and High School Youth', *Journal of Adolescent Health* 12: 319–25

Erikson, E. (1968) *Identity: Youth and Crisis*. New York: W.W. Norton and Company

Eysenck, H. (1985) *The Decline and Fall of the Freudian Empire*. Harmondsworth: Viking

— and Eysenck, M. (1985) *Personality and Individual Differences: A Natural Science Approach*. New York: Plenum

— and Gudjonsson, G. (1989) *The Causes and Cures of Criminality*. New York: Plenum

Farber, N. (1991) 'The Process of Pregnancy Resolution among Adolescent Mothers', *Adolescence* 26: 697–716

Farrington, D. (1992) 'Juvenile Delinquency', in J. Coleman (ed.), *The School Years: Current Issues in the Socialization of Young People*, 2nd edn. London: Routledge

Fasick, F. (1984) 'Parents, Peers, Youth Culture and Autonomy in Adolescence', *Adolescence* 19: 143–57

Feather, N. (1982) 'Human Values and the Prediction of Action: An Expectancy-valence Analysis', in N. Feather (ed.), *Expectations and Actions: Expectancy-value Models in Psychology*. Hillsdale, NJ: Lawrence Erlbaum

— (1983) 'Some Correlates of Attributional Style: Depressive Symptoms, Self-esteem, and Protestant Ethic Values', *Personality and Social Psychology Bulletin* 9: 125–35

— (1990) *The Psychological Impact of Unemployment*. New York: Springer-Verlag

— and Davenport, P. (1981). 'Unemployment and Depressive Affect: A Motivational and Attributional Analysis', *Journal of Personality and Social Psychology* 41: 422–36

— and O'Brien, G. (1987) 'Looking for Employment: An Expectancy-valence Analysis of Job-seeking Behaviour among Young People', *British Journal of Psychology* 78: 251–72

Fehrenbach, P. and Monastersky, C. (1988) 'Characteristics of Female Adolescent Sexual Offenders', *American Journal of Orthopsychiatry* 58: 148–51

— Smith, W., Monastersky, C. and Deisher, R. (1986) 'Adolescent Sexual Offenders: Offender and Offense Characteristics', *American Journal of Orthopsychiatry* 56: 225–33

Fine, M., Moreland, J. and Schwebel, A. (1983) 'Long term Effects of Divorce on Parent-child Relationships', *Developmental Psychology* 19: 703–13

Fleming, J., Offord, D. and Boyle, M. (1989) 'Prevalence of Childhood and Adolescent Depression in the Community: Ontario Child Health Study', *British Journal of Psychiatry* 155: 647–54

Foon, A. (1988) 'The Relationship between School Type and Adolescent Self-esteem, Attribution Styles, and Affiliation Needs: Implications for Educational Outcome', *British Journal of Educational Psychology* 58: 44–54

Forehand, R., McCombs, A., Long, N., Brody, G. and Fauber, R. (1988) 'Early Adolescent Adjustment to Recent Parental Divorce: The Role of Interparental Conflict and Adolescent Sex as Mediating Variables', *Journal of Consulting and Clinical Psychology* 56: 624–27

Forrest, S. (1988) 'Suicide and the Rural Adolescent', *Adolescence* 23: 341–47

Foster-Clark, F. and Blyth, D. (1991) 'Peer Relations and Influences', in R. Lerner, A. Petersen and J. Brooks-Gunn (eds), *Encyclopedia of Adolescence*, (Vol. 2). New York: Garland Publishing

Frost, A. and Pakiz, B. (1990) 'The Effects of Marital Disruption on Adolescents: Time as a Dynamic', *American Journal of Orthopsychiatry* 60: 544–55

Fry, P. and Coe, K. (1980) 'Achievement Performance of Internally and Externally Oriented Black and White High School Students under Conditions of Competition and Co-operation Expectancies', *British Journal of Educational Psychology* 50: 162–67

Furnham, A. (1984) 'Getting a Job: School-leavers' Perceptions of Employment Prospects', *British Journal of Educational Psychology* 54: 293–305

—— (1985) 'Youth Unemployment: A Review of the Literature', *Journal of Adolescence* 8: 109–24

—— (1987a) 'The Determinants and Structure of Adolescents' Beliefs about the Economy', *Journal of Adolescence* 10: 353–71

—— (1987b) 'Predicting Protestant Work Ethic Beliefs', *European Journal of Personality* 1: 93–106

—— (1990) *The Protestant Work Ethic: The Psychology of Work-related Beliefs and Behaviours*. London: Routledge

—— (1992) *Personality at Work: The Role of Individual Differences in the Workplace*. London: Routledge

—— and Gunter, B. (1989) *The Anatomy of Adolescence: Young People's Social Attitudes in Britain*. London: Routledge

—— Sadka, V. and Brewin, C. (1992) 'The Development of an Occupational Attributional Style Questionnaire', *Journal of Organizational Behaviour* 13: 27–39

—— and Stacey, B. (1991) *Young People's Understanding of Society*. London: Routledge

—— and Thomas, P. (1984) 'Adults' Perceptions of the Economic Socialization of Children', *Journal of Adolescence* 7: 217–31

—— and Thompson, J. (1991) 'Personality and Self-reported Delinquency', *Personality and Individual Differences* 12: 585–93

Furstenberg, F., Brooks-Gunn, J. and Chase-Lansdale, L. (1989) 'Teenaged Pregnancy and Childbearing', *American Psychologist* 44: 313–20

—, Brooks-Gunn, J. and Morgan, S. (1987) *Adolescent Mothers in Later Life*. Cambridge: Cambridge University Press

Gallois, C. and Callan, V. (1990) 'Sexuality in Adolescence', in P. Heaven and V. Callan (eds), *Adolescence: An Australian Perspective*. Sydney: Harcourt Brace Jovanovich

Garnets, L. and Kimmel, D. (1991) 'Lesbian and Gay Male Dimensions in the Psychological Study of Human Diversity', in J. Goodchilds (ed.), *Psychological Perspectives on Human Diversity in America: Master Lectures*. Washington, DC: American Psychological Association

Gavin, L. and Furman, W. (1989) 'Age Differences in Adolescents' Perceptions of their Peer Groups', *Developmental Psychology* 25: 827–34

Geber, G. and Resnick, M. (1988) 'Family Functioning of Adolescents who Parent and Place for Adoption', *Adolescence* 23: 417–28

Gecas, V. and Seff, M. (1990) 'Families and Adolescents: A Review of the 1980s', *Journal of Marriage and the Family* 52: 941–58

Ginzberg, E. (1972) 'Toward a Theory of Occupational Choice: A Restatement', *Vocational Guidance Quarterly* 20:169–76

Glasser, M. (1977) 'Homosexuality in Adolescence', *British Journal of Medical Psychology* 50: 217–25

Goldsmith, J. (1982) 'The Postdivorce Family System', in F. Walsh (ed.), *Normal Family Processes*. New York: The Guilford Press

Goldstein, M. (1988) 'The Family and Psychopathology', *Annual Review of Psychology* 39: 283–99

Gore, S., Aseltine, R. and Colton, M. (1992) 'Social Structure, Life Stress and Depressive Symptoms in a High School-aged Population', *Journal of Health and Social Behavior* 33: 97–113

Gordon, D. (1990) 'Formal Operational Thinking: The Role of Cognitive-developmental Processes in Adolescent Decision-making about Pregnancy and Contraception', *American Journal of Orthopsychiatry* 60: 346–56

Graetz, B. (1990) 'Private Schools and Educational Attainment: Cohort and Generational Effects', *Australian Journal of Education* 34: 174–91

Gray, P. (1991) *Psychology*. New York: Worth

Greenberger, E., Steinberg, L. and Vaux, A. (1981) 'Adolescents Who Work: Health and Behavioral Consequences of Job Stress', *Developmental Psychology* 17: 691–703

Grinder, R. (1990) 'The Promise of Critical Literacy for Irrelevant Adolescents', in R. Muuss (ed.), *Adolescent Behavior and Society: A Book of Readings*, 4th edn. New York: McGraw-Hill

Grindstaff, C. (1988) 'Adolescent Marriage and Childbearing: The Long-term Economic Outcome, Canada in the 1980s', *Adolescence* 23: 45–58

Haaken, J. and Korschgen, J. (1988). 'Adolescents and Conceptions of Social Relations in the Workplace', *Adolescence* 23: 1–14

Hall C. and Lindzey, G. (1978) *Theories of Personality*, 3rd edn. New York: John Wiley and Sons

Hamburg, D. (1990) 'Preparing for Life: The Critical Transition of Adolescence', in R. Muuss (ed.), *Adolescent Behavior and Society: A Book of Readings*. New York: McGraw-Hill

Hanson, C., Henggeler, S., Haefele, W. and Rodick, J. (1984) 'Demographic, Individual, and Family Relationship Correlates of Serious and Repeated Crime among Adolescents and their Siblings', *Journal of Consulting and Clinical Psychology* 52: 528–38

Harper, J. and Ryder, J. (1986) 'Parental Bonding, Self-esteem and Peer Acceptance in Father-absent Male Adolescents', *Australian Journal of Sex, Marriage and Family* 7: 17–26

Harris, J. and Liebert, R. (1987) *The Child*, 2nd edn. Englewood Cliffs, NJ: Prentice-Hall

Hart, G., MacHarper, T., Moore, D. and Roder, D. (1985) 'Aboriginal Pregnancies and Births in South Australia 1981–1982', *Medical Journal of Australia* 143, (special supplement): S54–S56

Harter, S. (1983) 'Developmental Perspectives on the Self-system', in P. Mussen (ed.), *Handbook of Child Psychology (Vol. 4): Socialization, Personality, and Social Development*. New York: John Wiley

— (1990) 'Processes Underlying Adolescent Self-concept Formation'. In R. Montemayor, G. Adams and T. Gullotta (eds.), *From Childhood to Adolescence: A Transitional Period?* Newbury Park, California: Sage

Hartup, W. (1983) 'Peer Relations', in P. Mussen (ed.), *Handbook of Child Psychology* (Vol. 4). New York: Wiley

— (1989) 'Social Relationships and their Developmental Significance', *American Psychologist* 44: 120–26

Havighurst, R. (1972) *Developmental Tasks and Education*, 3rd edn. New York: David McKay

Hayden, M. and Carpenter, P. (1990) 'From School to Higher Education in Australia', *Higher Education* 20: 175–96

Hays, R. (1985) 'A Longitudinal Study of Friendship Development', *Journal of Personality and Social Psychology* 48: 909–24

— (1988) 'Friendship', in S. Duck (ed.), *Handbook of Personal Relationships: Theory, Research and Interventions*. Chichester: John Wiley and Sons

Heaven, P. (1988) 'Locus of Control and Attitudes to Authority among Adolescents', *Personality and Individual Differences* 9: 181–83

— (1989) 'Adolescent Smoking, Toughmindedness, and Attitudes to Authority', *Australian Psychologist* 24: 27–35

— (1990) 'Attitudinal and Personality Correlates of Achievement Motivation among High School Students', *Personality and Individual Differences* 11: 705–10

— (1993) 'Personality Predictors of Self-reported Delinquency', *Personality and Individual Differences* 14: 67–76

— Connors, J. and Kellehear, A. (1992) 'Health Locus of Control Beliefs and Attitudes toward People with AIDS', *Australian Psychologist* 27: 172–75

— and Furnham, A. (1991) 'Orientation to Authority Among Adolescents: Relationships with Personality and Human Values', *Personality and Individual Differences* 12: 977–82

Henshaw, S. and Van Vort, J. (1989) 'Teenage Abortion, Birth, and Pregnancy Statistics: An Update', *Family Planning Perspectives* 21: 85–88

Herr, K. (1989) 'Adoption vs. Parenting Decisions among Pregnant Adolescents', *Adolescence* 24: 795–99

Hetherington, E., Stanley-Hagan, M. and Anderson, E. (1989) 'Marital Transitions: A Child's Perspective', *American Psychologist* 44: 303–12

Heyneman, S. (1976) 'Continuing Issues in Adolescence: A Summary of Current Transitions to Adulthood Debates', *Journal of Youth and Adolescence* 5: 309–23

Holland, J. (1973) *Making Vocational Choices: A Theory of Careers.* New York: Prentice-Hall

Holland, J. (1976) 'Vocational Preferences', in M. Dunnette (ed.), *Handbook of Industrial and Organizational Psychology.* Chicago: Rand McNally

Hollander, E. (1967) *Principles and Methods of Social Psychology.* New York: Oxford University Press

Hooker, K. (1991) 'Developmental Tasks', in R. Lerner, A. Petersen and J. Brooks-Gunn (eds), *Encyclopedia of Adolescence* (Vol. 1). New York: Garland Publishing

Hovestadt, A., Anderson, W., Piercy, F., Cochran, S. and Fine, M. (1985) 'A Family of Origin Scale', *Journal of Marital and Family Therapy* 11: 287–97

Huang, I. (1991) 'Family Stress and Coping', in S. Bahr (ed.), *Family Research: A Sixty-year Review, 1930–1990 (Vol. 1).* New York: Lexington Books

Hughes, F. and Noppe, L. (1985) *Human Development across the Life Span.* St Paul: West Publishing Company

Huston, A. (1983) 'Sex-typing', in P. Mussen (ed.), *Handbook of Child Psychology (Vol. 4): Socialization, Personality, and Social Development.* New York: Wiley

Irion, J., Coon, R. and Blanchard-Fields, F. (1988) 'The Influence of Divorce on Coping in Adolescence', *Journal of Youth and Adolescence* 17: 135–45

Jaccard, J. and Dittus, P. (1991) *Parent-teen Communication: Toward the Prevention of Unintended Pregnancies.* New York: Springer-Verlag

Jakobovits, A. and Zubek, L. (1991) 'The Adolescent Childbirth Rate in Hungary', *Journal of Adolescent Health* 12: 427–29

Jindal, S. and Panda, S. (1982) 'A Correlation Study of Achievement Motivation, Anxiety, Neuroticism and Extraversion of School Going Adolescents', *Journal of Psychological Researches* 26: 110–14

Jones, J. (1990) 'Outcomes of Girls' Schooling: Unravelling Some Social Differences', *Australian Journal of Education* 34: 153–67

Junankar, P. (1987) 'The Labour Market for Young People', in P. Junankar, (ed.), *From School to Unemployment? The Labour Market for Young People.* London: Macmillan

Kalmuss, D. (1992) 'Adoption and Black Teenagers: The Validity of a Pregnancy Resolution Strategy', *Journal of Marriage and the Family* 54: 485–95

Kandel, D. (1990) 'On Processes of Peer Influences in Adolescent Drug Use: A Developmental Perspective', in R. Muuss (ed.), *Adolescent Behavior and Society: A Book of Readings.* New York: McGraw-Hill

Kashani, J., Carlson, G., Beck, N., Hoeper, E., Corcoran, C., McAllister, J., Fallahi, C., Rosenberg, T., Reid, J. (1987) 'Depression, Depressive Symptoms, and Depressed Mood among a Community Sample of Adolescents', *American Journal of Psychiatry* 144: 931–34

Kashani, J., Reid, J. and Rosenberg, T. (1989) 'Levels of Hopelessness in Children and Adolescents: A Developmental Perspective', *Journal of Consulting and Clinical Psychology* 57: 496–99

Kashani, J., Rosenberg, T. and Reid, J. (1989) 'Developmental Perspectives in Child and Adolescent Depressive Symptoms in a Community Sample', *American Journal of Psychiatry* 146: 871–75

Kazdin, A., French, N., Unis, A., Esveldt-Dawson, K. and Sherick, R. (1983) 'Hopelessness, Depression, and Suicidal Intent among Psychiatrically Disturbed Inpatient Children', *Journal of Consulting and Clinical Psychology* 51: 504–10

Kiernan, K. (1980) 'Teenage Motherhood — Associated Factors and Consequences: The Experiences of a British Birth Cohort', *Journal of Biosocial Science* 12: 393–405

Kinard, E. and Reinherz, H. (1984) 'Behavioral and Emotional Functioning in Children of Adolescent Mothers', *American Journal of Orthopsychiatry* 54: 578–94

Kleinman, S., Handal, P., Enos, D., Searight, H. and Ross, M. (1989) 'Relationship between Perceived Family Climate and Adolescent Adjustment', *Journal of Clinical Child Psychology* 18: 351–59

Kovacs, M. (1989) 'Affective Disorders in Children and Adolescents', *American Psychologist* 44: 209–15

— Beck, A. and Weissman, A. (1975) 'Hopelessness: An Indicator of Suicidal Risk', *Suicide* 5: 98–103

Kurdek, L. (1988–89) 'Siblings' Reactions to Parental Divorce', *Journal of Divorce* 12 (2–3): 203–19

Lackovic-Grgin, K. and Dekovic, M. (1990) 'The Contribution of Significant Others to Adolescents' Self-esteem', *Adolescence* 25: 839–46

Lamb, M. and Elster, A. (1985) 'Adolescent Mother-infant-father Relationships', *Developmental Psychology* 21: 768–73

Lamborn, S., Mounts, N., Steinberg, L. and Dornbusch, S. (1991) 'Patterns of Competence and Adjustment among Adolescents from Authoritative, Authoritarian, Indulgent, and Neglectful Families', *Child Development* 62: 1049–65

Langlois, J. and Downs, A. (1980) 'Mothers, Fathers, and Peers as Socialization Agents of Sex-typed Play Behaviors in Young Children', *Child Development* 51: 1237–47

Larson, R. and Richards, M. (1991) 'Daily Companionship in Late Childhood and Early Adolescence: Changing Developmental Contexts', *Child Development* 62: 284–300

Lee, P. and Walters, W. (1983) 'Adolescent Primigravidae and their Obstetric Performance', *Australian and New Zealand Journal of Obstetrics and Gynaecology* 23: 3–7

Leenaars, A. (1990) 'Psychological Perspectives on Suicide', in D. Lester (ed.), *Current Concepts of Suicide*. Philadelphia: The Charles Press

Lefkowitz, M. and Tesiny, E. (1985) 'Depression in Children: Prevalence and Correlates', *Journal of Consulting and Clinical Psychology* 53: 647–56

Lester, D. (1988) 'Youth Suicide: A Cross-cultural Perspective', *Adolescence* 23: 953–58

Liebert, R. and Spiegler, M. (1990) *Personality: Strategies and Issues*. Pacific Grove, California: Brooks/Cole

Little, J. (1967) 'The Occupations of Non-college Youth', *American Educational Research Journal* 4: 147–53

Loeber, R. (1982) 'The Stability of Antisocial and Delinquent Child Behavior: A Review', *Child Development* 53: 1431–46

Loeber, R. and Dishion, T. (1983) 'Early Predictors of Male Delinquency: A Review', *Psychological Bulletin* 94: 68–99

Long, B. (1986) 'Parental Discord vs. Family Structure: Effects of Divorce on the Self-esteem of Daughters', *Journal of Youth and Adolescence* 15: 19–27

Long, N., Slater, E., Forehand, R. and Fauber, R. (1988) 'Continued High or Reduced Interparental Conflict Following Divorce: Relation to Young Adolescent Adjustment', *Journal of Consulting and Clinical Psychology* 56: 467–69

Lynn, R., Yamauchi, H. and Tachibana, Y. (1991) 'Attitudes Related to Work of Adolescents in the United Kingdom and Japan', *Psychological Reports* 68: 403–10

Maccoby, E. and Jacklin, C. (1974) *The Psychology of Sex Differences*. Stanford: Stanford University Press

Maccoby, E. and Martin, J. (1983) 'Socialization in the Context of the Family: Parent-child Interaction', in P. Mussen (ed.), *Handbook of Child Psychology (Vol. 4): Socialization, Personality, and Social Development*. New York: Wiley

Manaster, G. (1989) 'Adolescent Development: A Psychological Interpretation. Itasca, Ill.: Peacock

Manley, C., Searight, H., Skitka, L., Russo, J. and Schudy, K. (1990) 'The Reliability of the Family-of-origin Scale for Adolescents', *Family Therapy* 17: 273–80

Mannarino, A. (1978). 'Friendship Patterns and Self-concept Development in Pre-adolescent Males', *Journal of Genetic Psychology* 133: 105–10

Manning, W. (1990) 'Parenting Employed Teenagers', *Youth and Society* 22: 184–200

Manzi, P. (1986) 'Cognitive Appraisal, Stress, and Coping in Teenage Employment', *Vocational Guidance Quarterly*, March: 160–70

Marcia, J. (1966) 'Development and Validation of Ego-identity Status', *Journal of Personality and Social Psychology* 3: 551–58

Marcia, J. (1980) 'Identity in Adolescence', in J. Adelson (ed.), *Handbook of Adolescent Psychology*. New York: Wiley

Marsh, H. (1989) 'Effects of Attending Single-sex and Coeducational High Schools on Achievement, Attitudes, Behaviors, and Sex Differences', *Journal of Educational Psychology* 81: 70–85

—, Owens, L., Myers, M. and Smith, I. (1989) 'The Transition from Single-sex to Co-educational High Schools: Teacher Perceptions, Academic Achievement, and Self-concept', *British Journal of Educational Psychology* 59: 155–73

—, Relich, J. and Smith, I. (1983) 'Self-concept: The Construct Validity of Interpretations based upon the SDQ', *Journal of Personality and Social Psychology* 45: 173–87

Marsiglio, W. (1986) 'Teenage Fatherhood: High School Completion and Educational attainment', in A. Elster and M. Lamb (eds), *Adolescent Fatherhood*. Hillsdale, NJ: Lawrence Erlbaum

Marttunen, M., Aro, H. and Lonnqvist, J. (1992) 'Adolescent Suicide: Endpoint of Long-term Difficulties', *Journal of the American Academy of Child and Adolescent Psychiatry* 31: 649–54

Mason, G. (1990) *Youth Suicide in Australia: Prevention Strategies*. Canberra: Government Printer (Department of Employment, Education and Training)

Massad, C. (1981) 'Sex Role Identity and Adjustment during Adolescence', *Child Development* 52: 1290–98

Masselam, V., Marcus, R. and Stunkard, C. (1990) 'Parent-adolescent Communication, Family Functioning, and School Performance', *Adolescence* 25: 725–37

Masten, A. (1991) 'Developmental Psychopathology and the Adolescent', in R. Lerner, A. Petersen and J. Brooks-Gunn (eds), *Encyclopedia of Adolescence (Vol. 1)*. New York: Garland Publishing.

Mathis, J. (1976) 'Adolescent Sexuality and Social Change', *American Journal of Psychotherapy* 30: 433–40

Maticka-Tyndale, E. (1991) 'Modification of Sexual Activities in the Era of AIDS: A Trend Analysis of Adolescent Sexual Activities', *Youth and Society* 23: 31–49

McCauley, E., Mitchell, J., Burke, P. and Moss, S. (1988) 'Cognitive Attributes of Depression in Children and Adolescents', *Journal of Consulting and Clinical Psychology* 56: 903–8

McClure, G. (1986) 'Recent Changes in Suicide among Adolescents in England and Wales', *Journal of Adolescence* 9: 135–43

McCombs, A. and Forehand, R. (1989) 'Adolescent School Performance following Parental Divorce: Are there Family Factors that can Enhance Success?' *Adolescence* 24: 871–80

McKinney, J. and Vogel, J. (1987) 'Developmental Theories', in V. Van Hasselt and M. Hersen (eds), *Handbook of Adolescent Psychology*. New York: Pergamon Press

McLoughlin, D. and Whitfield, R. (1984) 'Adolescents and their Experience of Parental Divorce', *Journal of Adolescence* 7: 155–70

McMullen, R. (1987) 'Youth Prostitution: A Balance of Power', *Journal of Adolescence* 10: 35–43

Mednick, B., Baker, R., Reznick, C. and Hocevar, D. (1990). 'Long-term Effects of Divorce on Adolescent Academic Achievement', *Journal of Divorce* 13: 69–88

Meyerowitz, J. and Malev, J. (1973) 'Pubesent Attitudinal Correlates

Antecedent of Adolescent Illegitimate Pregnancy', *Journal of Youth and Adolescence* 2: 251–58

Miller, B. and Moore, K. (1990) 'Adolescent Sexual Behavior, Pregnancy, and Parenting: Research through the 1980s', *Journal of Marriage and the Family* 52: 1025–44

Miller, P. (1989) *Theories of Developmental Psychology* (2nd edn). New York: W.H. Freeman and Co

Minkoff, K., Bergman, E., Beck, A. and Beck, R. (1973) 'Hopelessness, Depression, and Attempted Suicide', *American Journal of Psychiatry* 130: 455–59

Montalvo, B. (1982) 'Interpersonal Arrangements in Disrupted Families', in F. Walsh (ed.), *Normal Family Processes*. New York: The Guilford Press

Montemayor, R. and Eisen, M. (1977) 'The Development of Self-conceptions from Childhood to Adolescence', *Developmental Psychology* 13: 314–19

Moore, S. and Rosenthal, D. (1991a) 'Adolescent Invulnerability and Perceptions of AIDS Risk', *Journal of Adolescent Research* 6: 164–80.

— (1991b) 'Condoms and Coitus: Adolescents' Attitudes to AIDS and Safe Sex Behaviour', *Journal of Adolescence* 14: 211–27

Moos, R. and Moos, B. (1986). *Family Environment Scale Manual*, 2nd edn. Palo Alto, CA: Consulting Psychologists Press

Morrison, D. (1985) 'Adolescent Contraceptive Behavior: A Review', *Psychological Bulletin* 98: 538–68

Mueller, K. and Powers, W. (1990) 'Parent-child Sexual Discussion: Perceived Communicator Style and Subsequent Behavior', *Adolescence* 25: 469–82

Muuss, R. (1988) *Theories of Adolescence*, 5th edn. New York: Random House

Neale, J. (1983) 'Children's Understanding of Their Parents' Divorces', *New Directions for Child Development* 19: 3–14

Neapolitan, J. (1981) 'Parental Influences on Aggressive Behavior: A Social Learning Approach', *Adolescence* 16: 831–40

Neville, B. and Parke, R. (1991) 'Adolescent Fathers', in R. Lerner, A. Petersen, and J. Brooks-Gunn (eds), *Encyclopedia of Adolescence* (Vol. 1). New York: Garland Publishing

Newcomer, S. and Udry, J. (1987) 'Parental Marital Status Effects on Adolescent Sexual Behavior', *Journal of Marriage and the Family* 49: 235–40

Newman, B. and Newman, P. (1986) *Adolescent Development*. Columbus: Merrill Publishing Co

— (1987). *Development through Life: A Psychological Approach*, 4th edn. Chicago: The Dorsey Press.

— (1988) 'Differences between Childhood and Adulthood: The Identity Watershed', *Adolescence* 23: 551–57

Noller, P. and Callan, V. (1990) 'Adolescents' Perceptions of the Nature of their Communication with Parents', *Journal of Youth and Adolescence* 19: 349–62

— (1991) *The Adolescent in the Family*. London: Routledge
— and Patton, W. (1990) 'Maintaining Family Relationships at Adolescence', in P. Heaven and V. Callan (eds), *Adolescence: An Australian Perspective*. Sydney: Harcourt Brace Jovanovich
O'Brien, G. (1986) *The Psychology of Work and Unemployment*. Chichester: Wiley
— (1990) 'Youth Unemployment and Employment', in P. Heaven and V. Callan (eds), *Adolescence: An Australian Perspective*. Sydney: Harcourt Brace Jovanovich
— and Feather, N. (1990) 'The Relative Effects of Unemployment and Quality of Employment on the Affect, Work Values and Personal Control of Adolescents', *Journal of Occupational Psychology* 63: 151–65
O'Brien, S. and Bierman, K. (1988) 'Conceptions and Perceived Influence of Peer Groups: Interviews with Preadolescents and Adolescents', *Child Development* 59: 1360–65
Ochiltree, G. (1990) *Children in Stepfamilies*. New York: Prentice-Hall
Offer, D. and Church, R. (1991) 'Adolescent Turmoil', in R. Lerner, A. Petersen and J. Brooks-Gunn (eds), *Encyclopedia of Adolescence* (Vol. 2). New York: Garland Publishing
O'Malley, P. and Bachman, J. (1983) 'Self-esteem: Change and Stability between Ages 13 and 23', *Developmental Psychology* 19: 257–68
Oppel, W. and Royston, A. (1971) 'Teen-age Births: Some Social, Psychological and Physical Sequelae', *American Journal of Public Health* 61: 751–56
Orlofsky, J. and O'Heron, C. (1987) 'Stereotypic and Nonstereotypic Sex Role Trait and Behavior Orientations: Implications for Personal Adjustment', *Journal of Personality and Social Psychology* 52: 1034–42
Ortiz, C. and Vazquez-Nuttall, E. (1987) 'Adolescent Pregnancy: Effects of Family Support, Education, and Religion on the Decision to Carry or Terminate among Puerto Rican Teenagers', *Adolescence* 22: 897–917
Paikoff, R. and Brooks-Gunn, J. (1990) 'Physiological Processes: What Role Do They Play during the Transition to Adolescence?', in R. Montemayor, G. Adams and T. Gullotta (eds), *From Childhood to Adolescence: A Transitional Period?* Newbury Park, California: Sage Publications
— (1991) 'Do Parent-child Relationships Change during Puberty?' *Psychological Bulletin* 110: 47–66
Papini, D., Sebby, R. and Clark, S. (1989) 'Affective Quality of Family Relations and Adolescent Identity Exploration', *Adolescence* 24: 457–66
Parish, T. (1987) 'Family and Environment', in V. Van Hasselt and M. Hersen (eds), *Handbook of Adolescent Psychology*. New York: Pergamon
Parke, R. and Asher, S. (1983). 'Social and Personality Development', *Annual Review of Psychology* 34: 465–509
— Power, T. and Fisher, T. (1980) 'The Adolescent Father's Impact on the Mother and Child', *Journal of Social Issues* 36: 88–106
— and Slaby, R. (1983) 'The Development of Aggression', in P. Mussen (ed.), *Handbook of Child Psychology* (Vol. 4). New York: Wiley

Parker, J. and Asher, S. (1987) 'Peer Relations and Later Personal Adjustment: Are Low-accepted Children at Risk?' *Psychological Bulletin* 102: 357–89

Parkhurst, J. and Asher, S. (1992) 'Peer Rejection in Middle School: Subgroup Differences in Behavior, Loneliness, and Interpersonal Concerns', *Developmental Psychology* 28: 231–41

Paspalanov, I. (1984) 'The Relation of nAch to Extraversion, Emotional Instability and Level of Anxiety in People of Different Social Status and Success', *Personality and Individual Differences* 5: 383–88

Patterson, G., DeBarsyshe, B. and Ramsey, E. (1989) 'A Developmental Perspective on Antisocial Behavior', *American Psychologist* 44: 329–35

Patton, W. and Noller, P. (1984) 'Unemployment and Youth: A Longitudinal Study', *Australian Journal of Psychology* 36: 399–413

— (1991) 'The Family and the Unemployed Adolescent', *Journal of Adolescence* 14: 343–61

Payne, M. and Furnham, A. (1990) 'Barbadian Adolescents' Views of the 'Ideal' Family', *Psychological Reports* 67: 611–18

Pendergrast, R., DuRant, R. and Gaillard, G. (1992) 'Attitudinal and Behavioral Correlates of Condom Use in Urban Adolescent Males', *Journal of Adolescent Health* 13: 133–39

Perry, D., Kusel, S. and Perry, L. (1988) 'Victims of Peer Aggression', *Developmental Psychology* 24: 807–14

Pete, J. and DeSantis, L. (1990) 'Sexual Decision-making in Young Black Adolescent Females', *Adolescence* 25: 145–54

Petersen, A. (1988) 'Adolescent Development', *Annual Review of Psychology* 39: 583–607

— Sarigiani, P. and Kennedy, R. (1991) 'Adolescent Depression: Why More Girls?, *Journal of Youth and Adolescence* 20: 247–71

Peterson, C. (1990) 'Disagreement, Negotiation and Conflict Resolution in Families with Adolescents', in P. Heaven and V. Callan (eds), *Adolescence: An Australian Perspective*. Sydney: Harcourt Brace Jovanovich

Petti, T. and Larson, C. (1987) 'Depression and Suicide', in V. Van Hasselt and M. Hersen (eds), *Handbook of Adolescent Psychology*. New York: Pergamon

Phares, E. (1991) *Introduction to Personality*, 3rd edn. New York: Harper Collins.

Pittman, R. (1991) 'Social Factors, Enrolment in Vocational/Technical courses, and High School Dropout Rates', *Journal of Educational Research* 84: 288–95

Pleck, J., Sonenstein, F. and Ku, L. (1991) 'Adolescent Males' Condom Use: Relationships between Perceived Costs-benefits and Consistency', *Journal of Marriage and the Family* 53: 733–45

Plomin, R. (1989) 'Environment and Genes: Determinants of Behavior', *American Psychologist* 44: 105–11

Poole, M. (1983) *Youth: Expectations and Transitions*. Melbourne: Routledge and Kegan Paul

— (1990) 'Attitudes to School, Careers and the Future', in P. Heaven and V. Callan (eds), *Adolescence: An Australian Perspective*. Sydney: Harcourt Brace Jovanovich

Power, C. (1984) 'Factors Influencing Retentivity and Satisfaction with Secondary Schooling', *Australian Journal of Education* 28: 115–25

Pritchard, M., Myers, B. and Cassidy, D. (1989) 'Factors Associated with Adolescent Saving and Spending Patterns', *Adolescence* 24: 711–23

Rabin, D. and Chrousos, G. (1991a) 'Gonadal Androgens', in R. Lerner, A. Petersen, and J. Brooks-Gunn (eds), *Encyclopedia of Adolescence* (Vol. 1). New York: Garland Publishing

— (1991b) 'Adrenal Androgens', in R. Lerner, A. Petersen, and J. Brooks-Gunn (eds), *Encyclopedia of Adolescence* (Vol. 1). New York: Garland Publishing

Ralph, N., Lochman, J. and Thomas, T. (1984) 'Psychosocial Characteristics of Pregnant and Nulliparous Adolescents', *Adolescence* 19: 283–94

Reicher, S. and Emler, N. (1985) 'Delinquent Behaviour and Attitudes to Formal Authority', *British Journal of Social Psychology* 24: 161–68

Remafedi, G. (1987) 'Homosexual Youth: A Challenge to Contemporary Society', *Journal of the American Medical Association* 258: 222–25

— (1991) 'Homosexuality, Adolescent', in R. Lerner, A. Petersen and J. Brooks-Gunn (eds), *Encyclopedia of Adolescence* (Vol. 1). New York: Garland Publishing

Richey, M. and Richey, H. (1980) 'The Significance of Best-friend Relationships in Adolescence', *Psychology in the Schools* 17: 536–40

Rigby, K. (1986) 'Orientation toward Authority: Attitudes and Behaviour', *Australian Journal of Psychology* 38: 153–60

— (1990) 'Youth and their Attitudes towards Institutional Authorities', in P. Heaven and V. Callan (eds), *Adolescence: An Australian Perspective.* Sydney: Harcourt Brace Jovanovich

— and Densley, T. (1985) 'Religiosity and Attitude Toward Institutional Authority among Adolescents', *Journal of Social Psychology* 125: 723–28

— Mak, A. and Slee, P. (1989) 'Impulsiveness, Orientation to Authority, and Gender as Factors in Self-reported Delinquency among Australian Adolescents', *Personality and Individual Differences* 10: 689–92

— and Rump, E. (1979) 'The Generality of Attitude to Authority', *Human Relations* 32: 469–87

— Schofield, P. and Slee, P. (1987) 'The Similarity of Attitudes towards Personal and Impersonal Types of Authority among Adolescent Schoolchildren', *Journal of Adolescence* 10: 241–53

— and Slee, P. (1991) 'Bullying among Australian School Children: Reported Behavior and Attitudes toward Victims', *Journal of Social Psychology* 131: 615–27

Robertson, J. and Simons, R. (1989) 'Family Factors, Self-esteem, and Adolescent Depression', *Journal of Marriage and the Family* 51: 125–38

Robinson, B. (1988a) *Teenage Fathers.* Lexington, Massachusetts: Lexington Books

— (1988b) 'Teenage Pregnacy from the Father's Perspective', *American Journal of Orthopsychiatry* 58: 46–51

Roscoe, B. and Kruger, T. (1990) 'AIDS: Late Adolescents' Sexual Knowledge and its Influence on Sexual Behavior', *Adolescence* 25: 39–48

— and Peterson, K. (1984) 'Older Adolescents: A Self-report of Engagement in Developmental Tasks', *Adolescence* 19: 391–96

Rosenberg, M. and Kaplan, H. (eds) (1982) *Social Psychology of the Self-concept.* Illinois: Harlam Davidson

Rosenthal, D., Hall, C. and Moore, S. (1992) 'AIDS, Adolescents, and Sexual Risk Taking: A Test of the Health Belief Model', *Australian Psychologist* 27: 166–71

— Moore, S. (1991) 'Risky Business: Adolescents and HIV/AIDS', *Youth Studies* 10: 20–25

Ross, M. and Fletcher, G. (1985) 'Attribution and Social Perception', in G. Lindzey and E. Aronson (eds), *Handbook of Social Psychology* (Vol. 2). New York: Random House

Rowe, C. (1980) *Outline of Psychiatry.* Dubuque, Iowa: W.C. Brown

Rowe, K. (1988) 'Single-sex and Mixed-sex Classes: The Effects of Class Type on Student Achievement, Confidence and Participation in Mathematics', *Australian Journal of Education* 32: 180–201

Rutter, M. (1986) 'The Developmental Psychopathology of Depression: Issues and Perspectives', in M. Rutter, C. Izard, and P. Read (eds), *Depression in Young People: Developmental and Clinical Perspectives.* New York: The Guilford Press

Ryan, G. (1991) 'The Juvenile Sex Offender's Family', in G. Ryan and S. Lane (eds), *Juvenile Sexual Offending: Causes, Consequences, and Correction.* Lexington: Lexington Books

Sanders, B. and Giolas, M. (1991 'Dissociation and Childhood Trauma in Psychologically Disturbed Adolescents', *American Journal of Psychiatry* 148: 50–53

Sandven, K and Resnick, M. (1990) 'Informal Adoption among Black Adolescent Mothers', *American Journal of Orthopsychiatry* 60: 210–24

Santrock, J. (1990) *Adolescence*, 4th edn. Dubuque, IA.: W.C. Brown Publishers

Savin-Williams, R. (1991) 'Gay and Lesbian Youth', in R. Lerner, A. Petersen and J. Brooks-Gunn (eds), *Encyclopedia of Adolescence* (Vol. 1). New York: Garland Publishing

— and Demo, D. (1984) 'Developmental Change and Stability in Adolescent Self-concept', *Developmental Psychology* 20: 1100–10

— and Small, S. (1986) 'The Timing of Puberty and its Relationship to Adolescent and Parent Perceptions of Family Interactions', *Developmental Psychology* 22: 342–47

Schaefer, E. (1959) 'A Circumplex Model for Maternal Behavior', *Journal of Abnormal and Social Psychology* 59: 226–35

Schaffer, B. and DeBlassie, R. (1984) 'Adolescent Prostitution', *Adolescence* 19: 689–96

Scheinfeld, D. (1983) 'Family Relationships and School Achievement among Boys of Lower-income Urban Black Families', *American Journal of Orthopsychiatry* 53: 127–43

Schneewind, K. (1990) 'The Analysis of Family and Parent-child Relations in a Systems-oriented Perspective', in B. Barber and B. Rollins (eds), *Parent-adolescent Relationships.* Lanham, Maryland: University Press of America

Schuster, C. and Ashburn, S. (1992) *The Process of Human Development: A Holistic Life-span Approach*, 3rd edn. Philadelphia: J.B. Lippincott Co

Scott, W. and Scott, R. (1987) 'Individual Pathology and Family Pathology', *Australian Journal of Psychology* 39: 183–205

Sebald, H. (1989) 'Adolescents' Peer Orientation: Changes in the Support System during the Past Three Decades', *Adolescence* 24: 937–46

Seddon, G. (1977) 'The Effects of Chronological Age on the Relationship of Academic Achievement with Extraversion and Neuroticism: A Follow-up Study', *British Journal of Educational Psychology* 47: 187–92

Seeman, M. and Seeman, J. (1962) 'Alienation and Learning in a Hospital Setting', *American Sociological Review* 27: 772–83

Sharabany, R., Gershoni, R. and Hofman, J. (1981) 'Girlfriend, Boyfriend: Age and Sex Differences in Intimate Friendship', *Developmental Psychology* 17: 800–8

Shavelson, R., Hubner, J. and Stanton, G. (1976) 'Self-concept: Validation of Construct Interpretations, *Review of Educational Research* 46: 407–41

Shulman, S. and Margalit, M. (1985) 'Suicide Behavior at School: A Systemic Perspective', *Journal of Adolescence* 8: 263–69

Siegel, J. and Brown, J. (1988) 'A Prospective Study of Stressful Circumstances, Illness Symptoms, and Depressed Mood among Adolescents', *Developmental Psychology* 24: 715–21

Siegel, L. and Griffin, N. (1984) 'Correlates of Depressive Symptoms in Adolescents', *Journal of Youth and Adolescence* 13: 475–87

Simon, J. and Feather, N. (1973) 'Causal Attributions for Success and Failure at University Examinations', *Journal of Personality and Social Psychology* 64: 46–56

Simons, R. and Murphy, P. (1985) 'Sex Differences in the Causes of Adolescent Suicide Ideation', *Journal of Youth and Adolescence* 14: 423–34

Slater, E. and Haber, J. (1984) 'Adolescent Adjustment following Divorce as a Function of Familial Conflict', *Journal of Consulting and Clinical Psychology* 52: 920–21

Small, S. (1988) 'Parental Self-esteem and its Relationship to Childrearing Practices, Parent-adolescent Interactions, and Adolescent Behavior', *Journal of Marriage and the Family* 50: 1063–72

Smith, E., Udry, J. and Morris, N. (1985) 'Pubertal Development and Friends: A Biosocial Explanation of Adolescent Sexual Behavior', *Journal of Health and Social Behavior* 26: 183–92

Sobol, M. and Daly, K. (1992) 'The Adoption Alternative for Pregnant Adolescents: Decision Making, Consequences, and Policy Implications', *Journal of Social Issues* 48: 143–61

Sprinthall, N. and Collins, W. (1988) *Adolescent Psychology: A Developmental Review*. New York: Random House

Stacey, B. (1982). 'Economic Socialization in the Pre-adult Years', *British Journal of Social Psychology* 21: 159–73

Steele, B. and Ryan, G. (1991) 'Deviancy: Development Gone Wrong', in G. Ryan and S. Lane (eds), *Juvenile Sexual Offending: Causes, Consequences, and Correction*. Lexington: Lexington Books

Stefanko, M. (1984) 'Trends in Adolescent Research: A Review of Articles Published in Adolescence: 1976–1981', *Adolescence* 19: 1–14

Steinberg, L. (1982) 'Jumping off the Work Experience Bandwagon', *Journal of Youth and Adolescence* 11: 183–205

— (1986) 'Latchkey Children and Susceptibility to Peer Pressure: An Ecological Analysis', *Developmental Psychology* 22: 433–39

— (1987) 'Single Parents, Stepparents, and the Susceptibility of Adolescents to Antisocial Peer Pressure', *Child Development* 58: 269–75

—, Elmen, J. and Mounts, N. (1989) 'Authoritative Parenting, Psychosocial maturity, and Academic Success Among Adolescents', *Child Development* 60: 1424–36

— Greenberger, E., Garduque, L., Ruggiero, M. and Vaux, A. (1982) 'Effects of Working on Adolescent Development', *Developmental Psychology* 18: 385–95

Strelau, S. and Eysenck, H. (1987) *Personality Dimensions and Arousal*. London: Plenum

Strunin, L. (1991) 'Adolescents' Perceptions of Risk for HIV Infection: Implications for Future Research', *Social Science and Medicine* 32: 221–28

Susman, E. (1991) 'Stress and the Adolescent', in R. Lerner, A. Petersen and J. Brooks-Gunn (eds), *Encyclopedia of Adolescence* (Vol. 2). New York: Garland Publishing

— Dorn, L. (1991) 'Hormones and Behavior in Adolescence', in R. Lerner, A. Petersen and J. Brooks-Gunn (eds) *Encyclopedia of Adolescence* (Vol. 1). New York: Garland Publishing

Talwar, R. and Lerner, J. (1991) 'Theories of Adolescent Behavior', in R. Lerner, A. Petersen and J. Brooks-Gunn (eds), *Encyclopedia of Adolescence* (Vol. 2). New York: Garland Publishing

Tanner, J. (1991) 'Adolescent Growth Spurt, 1', in R. Lerner, A. Petersen and J. Brooks-Gunn (eds), *Encyclopedia of Adolescence* (Vol. 1). New York: Garland Publishing

— and Davies, P. (1985) 'Clinical Longitudinal Standards for Height and Height Velocity for North American Children', *Journal of Pediatrics* 107: 317–29

Tedesco, L. and Gaier, E. (1988) 'Friendship Bonds in Adolescence', *Adolescence* 23: 127–36

Tiggemann, M. and Winefield, A. (1984) 'The Effects of Unemployment on the Mood, Self-esteem, Locus of Control, and Depressive Affect of School-leavers', *Journal of Occupational Psychology* 57: 33–42

Tucker, S. (1989) 'Adolescent Perceptions of Communication about Sexually Related Topics', *Adolescence* 24: 269–78

Turtle, A., Ford, B., Habgood, R., Grant, M., Bekiaris, J., Constantinou, C., Macek, M. and Polyzoidis, H. (1989) 'AIDS Related Beliefs and Behaviours of Australian University Students', *Medical Journal of Australia* 150: 371–76

Udry, J. (1988) 'Biological Predispositions and Social Control in Adolescent Sexual Behavior', *American Sociological Review* 53: 709–22

— and Billy, J. (1987) 'Initiation of Coitus in Early Adolescence', *American Sociological Review* 52: 841–55

Udry, J., Billy, J., Morris, N. Groff, T. and Raj, M (1985) 'Serum Andro-genic Hormones Motivate Sexual Behavior in Adolescent Human Males', *Fertility and Sterility* 43: 90–94

Violato, C. and Wiley, A. (1990) 'Images of Adolescence in English Literature: The Middle Ages to the Modern Period', *Adolescence* 25: 253–64

Visher, J. and Visher, E. (1982) 'Stepfamilies and Step-parenting', in F. Walsh (ed.), *Normal Family Processes*. New York: The Guilford Press

Vondracek, F., Shimizu, K., Schulenberg, J., Hostetler, M. and Sakayanagi, T. (1990) 'A Comparison between American and Japanese Students' Work Values', *Journal of Vocational Behavior* 36: 274–86

Wall, W. (1977) *Constructive Education for Adolescents*. London: Harrap

Wallerstein, J. (1984) 'Children of Divorce: Preliminary Report of a Ten Year Follow-up of Young Children', *American Journal of Orthopsychiatry* 54: 444–58

Walsh, F. (1982) 'Conceptualizations of Normal Family Functioning', in F. Walsh (ed.), *Normal Family Processes*. New York: The Guilford Press

Walters, L., Walters, J. and McHenry, P. (1986) 'Differentiation of Girls at Risk of Early Pregnancy from the General Population of Adoles-cents', *Journal of Genetic Psychology* 148: 19–29

Warr, P. (1987) *Work, Unemployment and Mental Health*. Oxford: Clarendon
— and Jackson, P. (1987) 'Adapting to the Unemployed Role: A Longitu-dinal Investigation', *Social Science and Medicine* 25: 1219–24

Warren, K. and Johnson, R. (1989) 'Family Environment, Affect, Am-bivalence and Decisions about Unplanned Adolescent Pregnancy', *Adolescence* 24: 505–22

Waterman, A. (1982) 'Identity Development from Adolescence to Adult-hood: An Extension of Theory and a Review of Research', *Developmen-tal Psychology* 18: 341–58

Wearing, B. (1984) 'The Impact of Changing Patterns of Family Living on Identity Formation in Late Adolescence', *Australian Journal of Sex, Marriage and Family* 5: 16–24

Weiner, B. (1979) 'A Theory of Motivation for Some Classroom Experi-ences', *Journal of Educational Psychology* 71: 3–25

Wentzel, K. (1991) 'Relations between Social Competence and Academic Achievement in Early Adolescence', *Child Development* 62: 1066–78

West, D. (1967) *The Young Offender*. Harmondsworth: Penguin Books
— and Farrington, D. (1973) *Who Becomes Delinquent? Second Report of the Cambridge Study in Delinquent Development*. London: Heinemann

Westman, J. (1983) 'The Impact of Divorce on Teenagers', *Clinical Pediatrics* 22: 692–97

Wetzel, R., Margulies, T., Davis, R. and Karam, E. (1980) 'Hopelessness, Depression and Suicide Intent', *Journal of Clinical Psychiatry* 41: 159–60
— (1976) 'Hopelessness, Depression, and Suicide Intent', *Archives of General Psychiatry* 33: 1069–73

Whitley, B. (1983) 'Sex Role Orientation and Self-esteem: A Critical Meta-analytic Review', *Journal of Personality and Social Psychology* 44: 765–78

Wielandt, H. and Boldsen, J. (1989) 'Age of First Intercourse', *Journal of Biosocial Science* 21: 169–77

Williams, S., Kimble, D., Covell, N., Weiss, L. *et al.* (1992) 'College Students Use Implicit Personality Theory instead of Safer Sex', *Journal of Applied Social Psychology* 22: 921–33

Williamson, J., Karp, D., Dalphin, J. and Gray, P. (1982) 'The Research Craft: An Introduction to Social Research Methods, 2nd edn. Boston: Little, Brown and Co

Wilson, S. and Medora, N. (1990) 'Gender Comparisons of College Students' Attitudes toward Sexual Behavior', *Adolescence* 25: 615–27

Winefield, A. and Tiggemann, M. (1990a) 'Employment Status and Psychological Well-being. A Longitudinal Study', *Journal of Applied Psychology* 75: 455–59

— (1990b) 'Length of Unemployment and Psychological Distress: Longitudinal and Cross-sectional Data', *Social Science and Medicine* 31: 461–65

—, — and Winefield, H. (1991) 'The Psychological Impact of Unemployment and Unsatisfactory Employment in Young Men and Women: Longitudinal and Cross-sectional Data', *British Journal of Psychology* 82: 473–86

—, —, — and Goldney, R. (1991) 'A Longitudinal Study of the Psychological Effects of Unemployment and Unsatisfactory Employment on Young Adults', *Journal of Applied Psychology* 76: 424–31

Winefield, H. and Winefield, A. (1992) 'Psychological Development in Adolescence and Youth: Education, Employment, and Vocational Identity', in P. Heaven (ed.), *Life Span Development*. Sydney: Harcourt Brace Jovanovich

—, —, Tiggemann, M. and Goldney, R. (1988) 'Psychological and Demographic Predictors of Entry to Tertiary Education in Young Australian Females and Males', *British Journal of Developmental Psychology* 6: 183–90

Wood, J., Chapin, K. and Hannah, M. (1988) 'Family Environment and its Relationship to Underachievement', *Adolescence* 23: 283–90

Zarbatany, L. Hartmann, D. and Rankin, D. (1990) 'The Psychological Functions of Preadolescent Peer Activities', *Child Development* 61: 1067–80

Zelnik, M. and Kantner, J. (1980) 'Sexual Activity, Contraceptive Use and Pregnancy among Metropolitan-area Teenagers: 1971–1979', *Family Planning Perspectives* 12: 230–37

Zimiles, H. and Lee, V. (1991) 'Adolescent Family Structure and Educational Progress', *Developmental Psychology* 27: 314–20

# Index